HOW DO YOU FIGHT A HORSE-SIZED DUCK?

Also by William Poundstone

HOW DO YOU FIGHT A HORSE-SIZED DUCK?

SECRETS TO SUCCEEDING AT INTERVIEW MIND GAMES AND GETTING THE JOB YOU WANT

WILLIAM POUNDSTONE

Little, Brown Spark
New York Boston London

For Bernard Feld

Little, Brown Spark
Hachette Book Group
1290 Avenue of the Americas, New York, NY 10104
littlebrownspark.com

First Edition: June 2021

Little, Brown Spark is an imprint of Little, Brown and Company, a division of Hachette Book Group, Inc. The Little, Brown Spark name and logo are trademarks of Hachette Book Group, Inc.

The publisher is not responsible for websites (or their content) that are not owned by the publisher.

The Hachette Speakers Bureau provides a wide range of authors for speaking events. To find out more, go to hachettespeakersbureau.com or call (866) 376-6591.

The photograph of a puzzled man on p. 105 is by Andrea Piacquadio (piacquadio.com).

ISBNs: 978-0-316-49454-0 (hardcover); 978-0-316-36626-7 (international)
LCCN 2020943153

Printing 1, 2021

LSC-C

Printed in the United States of America

Contents

Contents

HOW DO YOU FIGHT A HORSE-SIZED DUCK?

Foreword: The Cherry Tree Incident

Thomas Alva Edison established a light bulb factory at the bottom of a hill in Menlo Park, New Jersey. There, 75 employees toiled long into the night making incandescent bulbs. Edison, an insomniac who worked 20-hour days, hired an organist to supply music. A catered lunch was served at midnight. On one lunch break, Edison happened to mention the cherry tree on the hill above the factory. To his astonishment none of his employees knew of the cherry tree. Edison launched an investigation. He determined that 27 employees had walked by the cherry tree every day for six months and had failed to notice it.

The incident confirmed one of Edison's pet theories, that most people don't pay attention to the world around them. Edison felt his employees *should* notice things. This conviction eventually led him to compile a questionnaire to be given to those applying for a job with his companies. Edison found that most applicants, even those who came with college degrees and sterling references, were unable to answer his 48 "exceedingly simple" questions. They were not hired.

"Yet every large concern is employing many of these incompetents," Edison said in a 1921 interview, "causing loss to the companies—and, therefore, to the public—of untold millions. If concerns would only get up a little questionnaire and have candidates for positions take this test, at the least the worst of the incompetents could be prevented from being put into positions where their gross inability results in incalculable loss."

Much of the public must have taken Edison's peevish pronouncement as something approaching gospel. The famous inventor was seen as the patron saint of hard work and scientific know-how. A 1922 opinion poll rated Edison as, simply, the greatest living American.

Edison's comments about the questionnaire went viral, to the extent that was possible in the print age. A flurry of commentary, speculation, and outrage played out in newspapers and magazines over the coming months. The *New York Times* managed to run 23 articles and editorials on Edison's questionnaire in the month of May 1921 alone. This included one authentic scoop: a rejected applicant came forth to recount as many Edison questions as he could remember. Soon another Edison reject chimed in. *Times* reporters researched the answers and printed them in the paper of record.

The Edison questionnaire, it turned out, was a mixture of trivia and mental calculation.

What countries bound France?
Who wrote *Les Misérables*?
Name three powerful poisons.
What is the weight of air in a room 20 by 30 by 10?
What state has the largest amethyst mines?

The *Boston Herald* tested Massachusetts politicians with the Edison quiz. Its headline reported: "These Men Are Ignoramuses, According to Edison."

Journalists pressed the other great genius of the age, Albert

Einstein, for his opinion. The *New York Times* gleefully reported that Einstein stumbled on a *physics* question and had "thereby become one of us."

The physicist's downfall was "What is the speed of sound?" Einstein replied that "he could not say off-hand....He did not carry such information in his mind but it was readily available in textbooks."

Edison complained that the widespread exposure of his questionnaire had made it harder to recruit competent employees. He vowed to "make up new lists of questions," warning that "these will be copyrighted, and anyone using them as an Edison questionnaire will face a lawsuit."

By June 1922 Edison had devised a new set of 150 questions. This second list was likewise quickly exposed. It included more trivia ("What is grape-nuts made of?") and also more open-ended problems:

> You have only $10 in the world and are playing poker with a man you have never seen before. On the first deal he holds a pat hand. You have three eights before the draw. There is 50 cents in the pot. He bets a quarter. What are you going to do, and why?

Some employers took Edison's advice and began using similar questions. But the questionnaire drew at least as much indignation. Columbia University psychologist Edward Thorndike was among those damning it: "I am sure Mr. Edison would prefer a man who was loyal to his family, his school, and his church, honorable in character, honest about money, willing and able to put in an eight-hour day without shirking, to a man who could perform an elaborate set of stunts, verbal or otherwise, but lacked these qualities."

*   *   *

Psychologist Paul M. Dennis has argued that the Edison questionnaire played a large, under-recognized role in changing the conversation on hiring. In Edison's time as now, job interviews were subjective assessments of how well someone would fit in. However imperfect or even misguided, the Edison questionnaire offered a new paradigm. It was an attempt to ask questions whose answers might predict job performance. This aspiration has been enduringly influential. It jump-started a century of research attempting to determine whether interviews could forecast workplace performance and to identify the questions and techniques that were most predictive. It has also led to changes in hiring practices and new types of employee assessment, some as provocative—and controversial—as Edison's.

Recessions, pandemics, social media, and artificial intelligence are changing hiring at a chaotic pace. One constant of recent decades is that both employees and employers are more selective than ever. Graduates find themselves struggling with debt and an economy that no longer guarantees a good wage to the educated. There is the sense that landing a good-paying job is a lifeline, crucial in ways it wasn't for previous generations. Job seekers are also concerned about the social and ethical dimensions of work. They expect to see their own values reflected in an employer. Consequently applicants spend hours online researching potential employers. This has led to a profusion of job-search apps and "best places to work" lists. Annual features by LinkedIn, *Fortune,* and *Forbes* rate salaries, perks, and zeitgeist. Inevitably the publicity focuses attention on a relative handful of well-regarded employers. In good times and bad, the most desirable employers get a dozen or more qualified applicants for every open position. In 2017 Tesla received nearly 500,000 applicants for 2,500 open positions. That's 200 to 1—ten times more selective than Harvard.

For certain job seekers the height of aspiration is FAANG.

That's FAANG as in Facebook, Amazon, Apple, Netflix, and Google. The vampirish spelling is no coincidence. Like the Ivy League, FAANG companies are regarded with varying mixtures of envy and suspicion. Beyond that is a much more diverse circle of companies that regularly rank high in lists of best places to work. These include youth-oriented start-ups and long-established firms: Adobe, Bain & Company, Blinkist, Boston Consulting, Cisco, Deloitte, Docusign, Dropbox, Goldman Sachs, Hilton, HubSpot, Kimpton Hotels, Lululemon, Nvidia, Oracle, Salesforce, Southwest Airlines, Trader Joe's, Whole Foods, and Workday.

With so many talented job seekers flocking to high-profile firms, lesser-known employers are finding new ways to recruit. "If you're trying to hire competitively against companies like Google and Apple, you really need to find innovative ways to succeed," said Kieran Snyder, CEO of Textio, a Seattle-based firm that uses digital tools to craft job ads. Twenty-first-century hiring has been compared to matchmaking. Job seekers and companies have access to more information about each other than ever before. If either party doesn't feel completely right about a potential match, they swipe left.

"I was a 38-year-old single mom who didn't fit the twentysomething, male-entrepreneur mold," said Frida Polli, cofounder of Pymetrics. "I knew that career switchers like myself—including those from the military—were in the same boat." Polli was a Harvard and MIT neuroscientist with a business idea: to use statistical techniques to make hiring fairer and more efficient. Her elevator pitch ran, "Moneyball for HR."

She believed that employers placed too much weight on major-league credentials—a degree from Harvard or Stanford, experience with Deloitte or Google. A better system might be able to identify talent that was being overlooked.

Polli also recognized that the initial stages of hiring are the weakest link. Most of the winnowing takes place before the interview. She cites research indicating that recruiters average about six seconds per résumé, with about three-quarters of job applicants eliminated after that quick glance. Those who do sift résumés for a living may believe they've got the process down to a science. But true expertise is achieved by learning from mistakes. A recruiter who rejects a capable candidate never learns of it. Nor are recruiters generally aware of unconscious gender and ethnic biases in their decisions.

Many large employers have automated the vetting of résumés. Software scans résumés for keywords and word constructions relevant to a position. Those with enough hits are flagged for recruiter attention. But ultimately the résumé is not the person. Some mediocre people have impressive résumés (and vice versa). At best a résumé can tell what someone *has* done, not what they can do. As a midlife career switcher, Polli felt this acutely.

Polli's company, Pymetrics, markets psychometric games for hiring. These are puzzle-like challenges that job applicants play on their phones or computers. In effect the games replace automated screening of résumés or an initial phone interview. Pymetrics' clients span industries, from Burger King to Tesla. Whatever the employer, the games attempt to measure attributes predictive of success for a specific company and position. Here's one example:

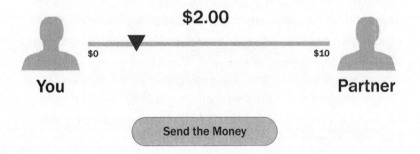

? You've been matched with a random partner and have received $10 for participating in this game. You now have the option of sending some of that money (anywhere from $0 to the full $10) to the partner. The money you send will be tripled and given to the partner. The partner will then be given the chance of returning some, all, or none of the money to you (anywhere from $0 to $30). That's the partner's decision. You get to keep whatever money you get back. How much of the $10 would you like to send?

Conceptually this is like that team-building exercise where you allow yourself to fall backward—hoping to be caught by someone you don't know all that well. You drag a marker to indicate how much money you want to give the partner, then click the Send button. In seconds you learn what the partner did, and whether you made money or lost it. There is no "right" answer for this game, but Polli has found that responses correlate with success in particular jobs. Those who send $5 or more tend to be team players suited to collaborative workplaces.

Psychometric games are part of a revolution in employee assessment. They center on so-called 21st-century skills, a catchall phrase embracing critical thinking, media literacy, entrepreneurship, collaborative prowess, ability to cope with change, and cross-cultural understanding. "Fluid, learning-intensive environments are going to require different traits than classical business environments," Polli explains. "And they're going to be things like ability to learn quickly from mistakes, use of trial and error, and comfort with ambiguity."

These are components of so-called *creative problem-solving ability.* In 2017, psychologists Beno Csapó and Joachim Funke wrote that

problem-solving is one of the key competencies humans need in a world full of changes, uncertainty and surprise. It is needed in all those situations where we have no routine response at hand. Problem-solving requires the intelligent exploration of the world around us, it requires strategies for efficient knowledge acquisition about unknown situations, and it requires creative application of the knowledge available or that can be gathered during the process. The world is full of problems because we strive for so many ambitious goals— but the world is also full of solutions because of the extraordinary competencies of humans who search for and find them.

Those who land interviews at innovative companies are often confronted with questions testing these extraordinary competencies. Here are two examples, asked at Bloomberg and Apple respectively.

? I've got an ordinary deck of 52 cards. I put a joker, face up, into the deck and shuffle and cut repeatedly. Then I start dealing you cards, continuing until the joker appears. What's the chance that the cards I've dealt you contain all four aces?

? You go up the mountain one day and come back down the next. In each case you leave at the same time. Will you ever be at the same place at the same time of day?

These are sometimes called *out-of-syllabus* questions. They are not a test of how well you remember textbook rules. It may not even be clear where to begin in answering. This is the realm of creative problem solving.

Many employers value problem-solving skills because this proficiency fits in with the view they have of themselves as innovative and disruptive. They are looking not just for employees with a narrow domain of competence but those who can learn new skills. Out-of-syllabus questions nudge the applicant out of a comfort zone. That does not mean that anything goes in answering them.

Imagination must be channeled through the question's constraints. The interviewee should brainstorm possible approaches to answering the question; identify the best approach and pursue it; communicate her logical train of thought to others; and finally, wrap it all up with a definitive answer.

This can be easier said than done.

How is anyone expected to tackle interview games and puzzles? There are some rules. I'll give you three.

1. Problems posed in interviews are often easier than they appear.
2. Think several moves ahead.
3. When all else fails, draw a picture.

Start with the question about the deck of cards. A common reaction is that it requires extensive calculation (and maybe a math course you never took). It doesn't!

Look at it this way: The only cards that matter are the four aces and the joker. The dealer might as well remove all the other cards. That would leave a packet of five; he could deal from that packet, and the outcome would be the same as dealing from the full deck. That's because you're asked only whether the aces come before the joker. The positions of the other cards don't matter.

Therefore, the question is equivalent to asking whether the joker is in fifth place in a shuffled packet of five cards. The chance of that is 1/5.

In the business world, there may not be anyone to tell you you're doing things the hard way. Employers value applicants with the knack of spotting quick, easy solutions.

The phrasing of Apple's question about the mountain is a tip-off. The interviewer probably wouldn't be asking whether you will be "at the same place at the same time of day" unless you will. Take that as a working assumption.

To develop it, go to the whiteboard and draw a picture. In this case the picture will be a simple chart of your travels up and down the mountain.

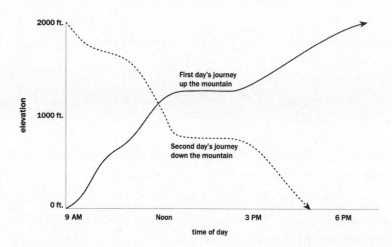

You set off at 9 a.m. the first day. Your elevation increases with time, though not at a constant rate. Some parts of the climb are steeper than others; you take a break for lunch; you will get tired toward the end of the day and ascend slower. Finally you arrive at the mountaintop. Your journey, charted as elevation versus time of day, is a wavy diagonal path from lower left to upper right (solid line). The horizontal part is lunch, when you stop for a rest.

The next day you again start off at 9 a.m. But now you're at the peak elevation and your path is a downward diagonal (dotted line). It's not an exact replay-in-reverse of the previous day. Downhill travel is faster, and you may take breaks at different times. You'll probably reach the bottom earlier in the day. But it's easy to see that the two days' lines must cross. They *have* to cross, so long as time keeps moving forward and you keep moving downward.

The point where the lines cross indicates when and where you were at exactly the same elevation at exactly the same time of day.

Those with a math or engineering background will recognize the diagram as an expression of the *intermediate value theorem*. This says (very, very roughly) that in order to get from Point A to Point B it's necessary to take on all values (elevations) between A and B. The intermediate value theorem is remarkably useful for proving math theorems, for solving certain logic puzzles, and for devising algorithms. Someone applying for a coding job at Apple should recognize the theorem as a tool of the trade. Thus an interview question that seems to have nothing to do with the job may actually have a lot to do with the job.

The psychometric game about splitting $10 differs from these logic puzzles in that there is no "right" answer. Yet it demands similar modes of reasoning, including thinking a move or two ahead. To make the most of this game, you must predict how the partner will react to your choice.

Because anything sent the partner is tripled, there is win-win potential. Sending money is collectively rational in that it grows the wealth that you and the partner may share. The partner can then reward you for your leap of faith. The thing is, you can't enforce this. The game does not allow you to communicate with the partner, not even to confirm that they have thought through the situation. The partner doesn't have to give back anything, and there are no repercussions for being a cheapskate.

Known as the *trust game*, this exercise has been a staple of behavioral economics since its publication in 1995. A team headed by University of Iowa economist Joyce Berg devised the game to demonstrate that people do not always act in the rational, self-interested way assumed by traditional economic theory.

That theory says you *shouldn't* trust the partner. You should keep all the money for yourself. But Berg and colleagues found that nearly everyone sent some money. The average amount was just over half the original bankroll.

Employers now use the trust game as a simple though nuanced personality test. It reveals deep-seated attitudes toward individualism, cooperation, and trust. It is used by firms hiring at-risk youth and those hiring computer science PhDs. Companies using this game first test it on their most successful employees. Job applicants are then scored on how closely their answers agree with those of the company's best employees in their field or position.

In most cases you can't go too far wrong by choosing $5 (half the sum you've been given). The $5 is tripled to $15. A generous partner might reciprocate by returning half of that ($7.50) to you. That, you might say, is the *least* the partner can do without being a jerk. Both you and the partner would be better off.

Accept the wisdom of sharing and you might ask yourself, *Why not send the entire $10 to the partner?* He'd then have $30 to split. You probably *would* do that, were the partner a friend, or were you able to communicate and strike a deal. But in this game you must depend on the kindness of strangers. Sending the full $10 is risky (or naïve?).

In hiring it's the extreme values ($0 or $10) that may raise red flags. Nevertheless, lower values of a few dollars may be optimal for more solitary or negotiation-intensive professions. Higher values are suitable for people-oriented lines of work where getting along is crucial.

Applicants who interview at selective companies can expect to encounter just about every common type of question, from the usual HR staples ("Walk me through your résumé," "Where do you see yourself in five years?") to grueling work assignments. But the most provocative and misunderstood questions are those that test 21st-century skills. This book will explore that phase of contemporary hiring: the use of logic puzzles, brainteasers, weird estimations, and psychometric games. It will help you understand why these assessment techniques are being used, and what employers hope to learn from them. Most of all it will tell how to succeed at them to win job offers.

This book is divided into three parts. The first is a quick history of attempts to predict job performance. It covers the rise and fall of intelligence and personality testing; the concept of adverse impact and attempts to eliminate bias in hiring; the development of behavioral interview questions, work sampling, and group interviews. It surveys scientific efforts to assess the value of hiring interviews as predictors of workplace performance. It explains why interviews are generally less predictive than most of us believe, and why this fact has done almost nothing to dislodge the custom. Both the successes and the failures of hiring science have led us to where we are today.

One chapter traces the use of puzzle-style questions in hiring, from World War II code breakers to Silicon Valley. Another chapter looks at how psychometric games have become an important part of hiring and analyzes the prospects for the field's most ambitious goal: the minimization of gender and ethnic biases in hiring.

Part II explores the psychometric games most commonly used in hiring. The games draw on well-known experiments from psychology, behavioral economics, and game theory. They say much about the taker's personality—and human nature as well. Despite the belief that applicants can't prepare for psychometric games, outcomes *can* be improved by knowing what to expect. At many companies, performance on the games determines who is invited to an interview and who gets a job offer.

Part III reveals and supplies answers to the most perplexing questions posed in interviews at selective employers. More than that, it is a tutorial on creative problem-solving. In the contemporary understanding, problem-solving is a learnable skill, valuable in the workplace as well as in job interviews. It is therefore important for job seekers to understand the unwritten rules of problem-solving. The interview questions are grouped into short chapters demonstrating shared approaches to a solution. By the time you complete this book, you will have learned a set of techniques that can help you answer questions you've never encountered before.

You don't have to be in the job market to enjoy this book. Games and puzzles say much about how our minds work. They challenge us to explore new ideas and to better understand other people — and ourselves.

Part I

A Short History of Assessment

Army Alpha

In 1917 Harvard's Robert Yerkes assembled a dream team of American psychologists in Vineland, New Jersey. Their mission was to devise a cognitive test for US Army recruits. The "Army Alpha" test was intended to help slot inductees into suitable positions. It would identify candidates for officer training and flag those not mentally fit for service. Because recruits differed greatly in educational background, the psychologists' assignment was to measure both "common sense" and intelligence while relying as little as possible on knowledge of schoolbook facts. The Army Alpha test drew heavily on the pioneering intelligence test devised by Alfred Binet in France. But it also tested knowledge of American pop culture trivia; and the ability, important in military life, to follow apparently senseless instructions to a T.

> If 4 is more than 2, then cross out the number 3, unless 3 is more than 5, in which case draw a line *under* the number 4.

> 1 2 3 4 5 6 7 8 9

Got that? The correct response is to cross out the number 3.

A second test, "Army Beta," attempted to transcend even language. Purely visual, it was administered to recruits who were illiterate in English or had flunked Army Alpha.

About 1.75 million inductees took the Army Alpha test in the World War I era. Scores were letter grades ranging from A ("very superior") to E ("very inferior"). Its French roots notwithstanding, the Army Alpha test was long considered a triumph of American ingenuity. After the war, the private sector took notice. For several decades intelligence ("IQ") tests were routine in American employment and widely endorsed by psychologists. In 1926, Princeton psychologist Carl Brigham adopted the Army Alpha test for college admission. This became known as the Scholastic Aptitude Test (SAT). As you may well know, the SAT is still around, albeit in greatly changed form.

Intelligence tests were never popular with job seekers. Almost by definition an intelligence test is difficult, and filling it out is work. Employers who used IQ tests seemed to be endorsing a one-dimensional view of human nature. It wasn't clear that intelligence even matters that much in most jobs—any more than the ability to do one-handed push-ups does.

The advent of widespread intelligence testing demonstrated one inconvenient truth: many high-IQ people never achieve much in their careers. This undercut the case for IQ as a predictor of job performance.

There was a more pressing problem. Yerkes, Brigham, and many other psychologists associated with intelligence testing were also leaders of America's eugenics movement. In a 1923 book, *A Study of American Intelligence,* Brigham wrote: "The army mental tests had proven beyond any scientific doubt that, like the American Negroes, the Italians and the Jews were genetically ineducable. It would be a waste of good money even to attempt to try to give these born morons and imbeciles a good Anglo-Saxon education, let alone admit them into our fine medical, law, and engineering graduate schools."

It's worth looking at a few of the Army Alpha questions underpinning Brigham's conclusion:

The Pierce Arrow car is made in... Buffalo, Detroit, Toledo, Flint?

Alfred Noyes is famous as a... painter, poet, musician, sculptor?

Velvet Joe appears in advertisements for... tooth powder, dry goods, tobacco, soap?

Like Thomas Edison, Army Alpha's creators assumed that smart people would know the things that they themselves did. The Army Alpha test trivia was taken from the culture of urban, affluent, white Americans who owned cars and radios, read newspapers, and were familiar with long-running ad campaigns. The Army tests, however, were given not just to urban elites but to draftees from rural communities with little exposure to consumer culture, and to urban immigrants who had arrived in the United States only a few years previously and spoke a language other than English at the dinner table. Unsurprisingly, these groups scored consistently lower on the tests. Nor is it surprising that nearly everyone reading these words today would qualify as an imbecile. The culture of the early 21st century is radically different from that of 1917.

In 1930 Brigham did something almost unprecedented in the history of American racism. He admitted he was wrong. Brigham published a paper, "Intelligence Tests of Immigrant Groups," explaining how the Army Alpha test was unsuited to cross-cultural comparisons and disowning his former belief that it could measure an abstract and ideal intelligence. He recanted his 1923 book "with its entire hypothetical superstructure of racial differences [that] collapses completely."

> This review has summarized some of the more recent test findings which show that comparative studies of various national and racial groups may not be made with existing tests, and which show, in particular, that one of the most pretentious of these comparative racial studies — the writer's own — was without foundation.

Intelligence is usually defined as the ability to learn. Learning, however, is a process that takes place over time. It is not easy to measure that process in a static test. For that reason Army Alpha and IQ tests settled for measuring what the test taker *had* learned. This may be a set of facts, or it may be skills such as forming verbal analogies or multiplying fractions. The core assumption is that those who are naturally good at learning things will have already learned many things. And they will have learned the things on the test.

But the things people learn depend on culture, economic class, and personality factors such as motivation and curiosity. By their nature intelligence tests confound these factors with cognitive ability, and it's hard to disentangle them.

The eugenic genie was not so easily put back in the bottle. One of the Army Alpha psychologists, Henry H. Goddard, established IQ testing at Ellis Island. He reported that most incoming immigrants were "feeble-minded" (though this applied only to those in steerage, not first class). Such claims, along with Brigham's book, influenced US lawmakers to discourage immigration from any but "Nordic" nations. In Germany of the 1930s Adolf Hitler came to power praising America for its support of eugenics. But the rise of the Nazi regime and the horrors of the Holocaust, filling the news and dominating the intellectual conversation, dampened whatever enthusiasm mid-century America had for eugenics and the racial theories behind it. Intelligence testing came under suspicion as well.

Adverse Impact

A 1971 Supreme Court ruling, *Griggs v. Duke Power,* proved to be the last straw for the widespread use of IQ tests in American hiring. The defendant was Duke Power, an electric company based in North Carolina. The firm long had a policy of segregating its work crews. African Americans were consigned to a separate division, with lower pay. This became illegal with the Civil Rights Act of 1964. Duke nominally opened the higher-paid divisions to all races, but it required that applicants have a high-school diploma or achieve a certain score on an IQ test. In practice Duke's Black applicants tended to be poorer and less educated than the whites, so few met the requirements. The Supreme Court found that the diploma and IQ scores were not material to a job consisting of tough outdoor labor in the Carolina backwoods. The IQ tests were being used as a loophole to perpetuate the kind of discrimination that Congress had outlawed.

The court therefore ruled that even neutral requirements or tests can be discriminatory, if they cause disproportionately few members of minority groups to be hired or promoted. This was termed *adverse impact.*

With *Griggs v. Duke Power,* the court weighed in on what "fair" means in hiring, an issue of some philosophical complexity. It affects contemporary companies that write diversity into their mission statements. Consider an archetypical Silicon Valley problem: a bro-culture company that is overwhelmingly male. Say it has 100 jobs to fill and there are 1,000 applicants, 400 of them women. Of the 100 best-qualified applicants (assuming this could be objectively determined), 55 are women. How many of those hired should be women?

(a)   About 40, because that reflects the gender breakdown of those who chose to apply to the company. Men applicants and women applicants should have equal chances of being hired.

(b)   About 50, because about half the world is female. The demographics of new hires should match those of the general population.

(c)   About 55, because that's the percentage of women among best-qualified applicants. The best-qualified people should be hired, regardless of gender.

(d)   All 100, because the company already has too many men. New hires should correct for old biases.

There is a case to be made for each of these answers. Most employers prefer the meritocracy answer (c) because they want the most capable workforce possible. They would like to believe that diversity can be achieved without ever passing over someone who is more qualified.

US law recognizes the right of employers to hire the most qualified people. But in the event of a discrimination complaint, an employer may be required to prove that its assessment methods can identify those who will succeed in a job. (It is not so easy to prove anything in the realm of hiring.)

In effect, the adverse impact doctrine endorses answer (a). The proportion of women hired should ideally equal the proportion of women among the applicants. An employer that meets this standard has an easy defense against discrimination complaints.

Today adverse impact is defined by the four-fifths rule, adopted by the Department of Justice in 1978. This advises large employers to hire similar percentages of applicants from all "protected classes." These are groups that are protected from employment discrimination by law. Examples include groups defined by gender, ethnicity, religion, national origin, age, and disability. That covers a lot of territory, and some states add to the set of protected classes.

The four-fifths rule asks employers to compute the percentage of applicants hired for each protected class. The smallest such group percentage should be no less than four-fifths of the largest.

That means, for instance, that the percentage of Blacks hired can range from 80 percent to 125 percent that of the percentage of whites hired. Should it fall below 80 percent, a Black applicant could claim discrimination by race. Should the ratio rise above 125 percent, a white applicant could claim discrimination.

Because the four-fifths rule supplies a little wiggle room, the (a) and (c) philosophies may not be too different in practice. But there's no guarantee of that. In practice, job applicants almost never have the data they would need to know whether adverse impact exists. Discrimination suits tend to be pursued only when the evidence is overwhelming.

Griggs v. Duke Power has had many consequences, some of them unintended. One was a practice known as *race-norming.* Say an aptitude test is known to be a good predictor of performance in a particular job. It's also known that the test is somewhat biased by race. With race-norming everyone is scored relative to their own race (or other protected class). The premise is that an Asian who scores in the top 10 percentile of Asians is presumed to be about as qualified as a white who scores in the top 10 percentile of whites, and so on. This avoids adverse impact while allowing companies to use familiar tests and assessment methods.

In the 1970s and '80s the US federal government and 38 US states adopted race-norming. But conservatives likened it to affirmative action and argued that it constituted reverse discrimination. The Civil Rights Act of 1991, signed by President George H. W. Bush, outlawed race-norming.

In some ways, US employment law is more specific about what

employers can't do to reduce bias than what they can. Adverse impact has made employers leery of intelligence and aptitude testing, even in jobs that clearly require mental agility. Whether adverse impact exists may depend on factors outside a company's control. Some American companies have many highly qualified applicants from overseas, resulting in high employment percentages of certain national-origin classes. This can create adverse impact even for normally favored groups like American whites. An opposite problem can occur if a disproportionate number of unqualified people from one protected class apply to a company.

Nevertheless, today's employers have considerable power to determine who applies. The job listings people see are based on what sites like LinkedIn or Facebook know about them. Generally speaking, that's a lot. "Just like with the rest of the world's digital advertisement, AI is helping target who sees what job descriptions," said Aaron Rieke, managing director at Upturn, a digital technology research group. A company that needs more qualified women or minority applicants has ways of reaching them.

The legal, scientific, and philosophical thinking about adverse impact has thrown into sharp relief a paradox. It is not too hard to devise assessment methods with considerable power to predict job success. But these methods will, in general, be expressed within a certain cultural frame of reference. Talented applicants with less exposure to the method's underlying culture will be at a disadvantage. Grappling with this is one of the foremost challenges of hiring today.

Personality Testing

In a 1996 essay psychologists Robert Hogan, Joyce Hogan, and Brent W. Roberts championed "a force for equal employment opportunity, social justice, and increased productivity." They were talking about personality tests for employment.

The psychologists argued that personality tests do not "systematically discriminate against any ethnic or national group," nor against the physically handicapped or aged. Thus personality tests are less likely to raise adverse-impact concerns than intelligence tests.

The personality surveys used for employment generally implement the *Five-Factor Model* (FFM), or *Big Five*. In 1961 Ernest Tupes and Raymond Christal, two US Air Force psychologists working at Lackland Air Force Base, Texas, identified "five relatively strong and recurrent factors" of personality. They had crunched data from inductees' self-reports of personality traits, looking for correlations.

"Big Five" isn't rocket science. It's more like a periodic table of personality. In theory each of us can be located somewhere in its five-dimensional space. The dimensions can be memorized as *OCEAN*: Openness, Conscientiousness, Extraversion, Agreeableness, and Neuroticism.

These are pretty much what they sound like, except for "openness" (to experience). Openness measures curiosity and interest in adventure, new or unconventional ideas, and cultural pursuits. More broadly, openness is identified with creativity, imagination, and the ability to think in abstract terms.

Each of the five dimensions is a scale measuring a fundamental trait and its opposite. The extraversion scale put extreme extraverts at one end and extreme introverts at the other. Most of us fall somewhere in the middle. That's true of the other four scales as well.

"Neuroticism" is the one scale given a negative (and Freudian-sounding) label. Some prefer Tupes and Christal's original name, *emotional stability.* That's considered the opposite of neuroticism, so either can be used as the name of that scale.

Tupes and Christal's 1961 publication, in an Air Force technical report, was scarcely noticed by academic or industrial psychologists. Over the following decades, a number of teams confirmed the Big

Five model. To be useful in hiring, personality-test results must predict future job performance. Data on that was thin and equivocal until the 1990s. Then a group of studies claimed correlations between test results and workplace productivity. Around the same time, it became possible to move personality testing from paper and pencil to online exams that are quick to take and quicker to score. By one estimate, 60 to 70 percent of American workers now undergo some kind of personality test in hiring. CVS, Home Depot, Lowes, Nokia, Walgreens, Xerox, and Yum Brands are among the many large employers using such tests. A 2014 estimate valued the personality-test business at $500 million a year.

Personality tests are usually self-reports. The applicant is asked to agree or disagree with statements such as "I am the life of the party." It's clear what most items are intended to measure. The obvious concern is that applicants can misrepresent themselves.

"Item endorsements are self-presentations, not self-reports," wrote Hogan, Hogan, and Roberts. They argue that the test taker is not necessarily saying who he is or even who he thinks he is. He is saying how he wants others to see him. A person who claims "I finish every task I start" may not actually do so, but he is endorsing that as a value.

Personality tests are long, and applicants usually rush through them. It's easiest to give up second-guessing and answer more or less candidly. It appears that most do. Commercial exams have been validated by comparing responses with psychologists' in-person evaluations. Items yielding unreliable answers are dropped from the questionnaire, leaving the ones that are the best indicators of personality.

Conscientiousness (roughly, "work ethic") is usually considered the most important Big Five attribute for hiring. Those low in conscientiousness might include the "high-IQ people who never accomplish anything"—the proverbial pet peeve of Microsoft hirers. A high extraversion score is vital for sales jobs and those dealing with the public. For other jobs it's OK to be in the middle or even the low end of the scale. Openness to experience is expected in creative fields such as design, consulting, and advertising.

"If something very bad happens, it takes some time before I feel happy again." Those applying for a job at McDonald's may encounter this statement. Clicking "agree" is said to correlate with neuroticism. Such applicants are presumed to be moody and to have trouble getting along with others and focusing on their work. It is easy to jump to the conclusion that such employees bring a disproportionate share of conflict, terminations, lawsuits, and "bad luck."

Ken Lahti, a vice president at CEB in Arlington, Virginia, claims that online personality tests can "screen out the 30 percent of applicants who are least qualified." In short, a quick, inexpensive test allows employers to bypass complainers, slackers, and troublemakers, while zeroing in on team players with the drive to get the job done. What can go wrong?

Barnum Effect

In 1947 psychologist Ross Stagner fooled a group of personnel managers by giving them a personality test and then reporting fake results—random statements lifted from astrology books. Stagner then asked the hiring professionals to rate the accuracy of his "findings." Most gave Stagner's report a high grade.

The following year Bertram R. Forer pulled an even better-known stunt. Forer gave a fake personality test to 39 students. Each then received the same bogus assessment, with statements such as

> You have a great need for other people to like and admire you.
> You have a tendency to be critical of yourself.
> Your sexual adjustment has presented problems for you.
> You pride yourself as an independent thinker and do not accept others' statements without satisfactory proof.

Just like Stagner's HR people, Forer's students overwhelmingly accepted these statements as descriptions of their own, unique personalities.

There is now such a substantial literature of gotcha studies that the topic has earned a name: the *Forer effect* or the *Barnum effect* (after P. T. Barnum, of "there's a sucker born every minute" fame). These proclaim the tendency for personality assessments, even baseless ones, to be taken as accurate, provided they are general enough to apply to almost anyone, more upbeat than not, and presented with authority.

There is cause to wonder whether the Barnum effect plays a role in the popularity of personality testing (and other assessment techniques as well). "It's intuitively appealing to managers that personality matters," explained Michigan State University management professor Fred Morgeson. Personality tests can be especially compelling to entrepreneurs, who often come from a technology background and are learning human resources on the fly. Online personality tests are quantitative, digital, and have almost zero marginal cost. Any modern manager wants to believe they work. But what test marketers rarely disclose is that no known means of employee assessment has the predictive power that managers (and the rest of us) typically take for granted. Morgeson holds that the connection between personality tests and job performance is "much lower than the field has led us to believe."

Behavioral Questions

Because in-person interviews remain the foundation of hiring, industrial psychologists have expended considerable resources in attempting to determine what interview techniques are most predictive of job performance. One enduring 20th-century innovation is behavioral questions. *Have you ever done something your boss told you not to do? How did it work out? Describe a time when you didn't have enough time to complete a work assignment. Tell me about a time you had to deal with a customer making an unreasonable demand.*

Interviewers see behavioral questions as an informal personality test. The rationale is that it's easy to check off good qualities on a test but harder to fabricate a coherent narrative. The stories that behavioral questions elicit tend to be truthful (more or less) and say something about how the applicant will handle similar situations in the future.

Behavioral questions have been updated with video interviews and artificial intelligence. HireVue markets a widely used video platform in which job applicants answer a set of behavioral questions as their phone or computer records video. "We capture tens of thousands of data points—emotions, words you use, active versus passive verbs, how often you say *um*," explains Loren Larson, HireVue's chief technology officer. "If you never smile, you're probably not right for a retail position."

The system is not exactly a lie detector, but it does parse tone of voice and facial expressions to judge sincerity and nervousness. Though a recruiter can review interview videos, candidates can be rejected without any human ever seeing their interview selfies. (How sad is that?) HireVue clients include the Atlanta Public Schools, Boston Red Sox, Delta Airlines, Carnival Cruise Lines, Ikea, Intel, Kohler, Kraft Heinz, T-Mobile, Unilever, and Urban Outfitters.

Whether in-person or virtual, behavioral questions are well regarded by the human resources profession. Job seekers may view them as relatively easy and low-pressure. They can be minefields, however. Behavioral questions offer an invitation to vent about bad bosses, conniving coworkers, and cruel luck. Unfortunately, the interviewer doesn't know your horrible boss, not unless his indictment was on the news. The more you complain about a bad boss, the more the interviewer may suspect there was fault on both sides. The interviewer may be concerned that people who complain a lot can be difficult; that the way you talk about your current boss and coworkers is a preview of how you'll be talking about your new company, if hired.

Behavioral questions are not immune to the Barnum effect. Interviewers may place too much faith in the ability of an offhand anecdote to reveal personality. These questions have also become a victim of their own popularity. "Anyone can talk about themselves for 15 minutes," observes Boston-based digital strategist Brett Rudy. He finds the standard behavioral questions "useless because everyone has prepared for them." All but the greenest job seekers are aware of the common questions and have been advised to walk into the interview with a set of well-polished anecdotes. As little as four might suffice, covering

- The time you didn't have enough time/money/resources to meet a goal
- The time a difficult colleague/customer/boss wanted you to do something unethical or stupid
- The time you made a big mistake (and learned from it or fixed it)
- The time you exceeded all expectations

Should an interviewer ask a *truly* original question, which is rare, a savvy applicant does what any politician does. "That's a good question. Let me say this…" — segueing to one of the canned anecdotes.

Work Sampling

Luis Abreu is a user-experience designer based in Brighton, England. After a 2014 conference he wrote an online article summarizing privacy and security updates in Apple's iOS 8. The article became popular with developers, and Abreu received an email asking whether he "might be open to exploring career opportunities at Apple."

Abreu replied, "Absolutely!"

This was followed by three phone interviews and five Face-Time interviews, each about half an hour long. Three weeks later Abreu received the coveted invitation to Apple headquarters in Cupertino. Apple paid Abreu's airfare and a three-night stay in a hotel.

The on-site interviews, heavy in sample work assignments, took the better part of a day: six hours, plus a working lunch, and a dozen interviewers. Abreu returned to Britain and a week later got an email saying, "We will not be moving forward with your application."

Many who have interviewed at Apple's Spaceship headquarters tell an all-too-similar tale: 1. Apple contacted the applicant out of the blue. 2. The decision process involved a dozen interviews spanning three months or more, with Apple springing for expensive travel and hotel. 3. Apple rejected the candidate in a curt email.

Such is the state of hiring at many selective employers. Companies are willing to interview many hyper-qualified people, only to reject most of them. This is the no-false-positives philosophy in practice. It seems to work for Apple—but not always for the job seeker. "My time was definitely a commodity for them," said another Apple applicant (who went through the whole process twice and was rejected twice).

Work sampling is another pillar of contemporary assessment. Applicants are given sample assignments, such as developing a marketing plan, coding an app, or drafting a contract. They are required to complete the work either in the interview or by a time limit. Microsoft pioneered work sampling—and with it the day-long marathon of interviews. Today work sampling is virtually universal in the technology industry and widespread in fields demanding specialized skills.

The premise of work sampling is that the proof is in the pudding. How an applicant performs on a technical task ought to forecast how that applicant would perform similar tasks on the job. Both common sense and research support this belief.

Work sampling is relatively costly for employers. It demands that multiple technical employees take time out of their day to conduct interviews or examine completed assignments. Consequently, Microsoft and other employers have ways of abruptly terminating unsuccessful interviews. SpaceX has a policy of halting the interview process the moment one interviewer decides an applicant is a bad fit. Elon Musk decreed that every hiring decision must be unanimous.

Work sampling has its discontents. "Even Mark Zuckerberg might not clear all the interview rounds because he might forget some library details of Java, and some interviewer may feel like he should know," explained engineer Deepesh Deomurari. In the real world, coders can work at their own pace and look up things they don't remember.

Another concern is teaching to the test. A standardized test may ask for the state capital of Nebraska, in the hope that a student who knows the answer to one state-capital question will also know the answers to others. But if everyone knows that the test asks for the capital of Nebraska only, teachers may skip the others. This improves scores, making teachers and students look good in a metric-obsessed age. But really the students haven't learned much.

The equivalent for software engineers is the "LeetCode interview." LeetCode is a popular coding and interview-prep website that offers engineers hundreds of typical technical questions and interview work assignments. The right side of the LeetCode window is a code editor allowing the user to type in code in a selected language. The code can be executed (to see how well it works) or critiqued by other users. LeetCode offers a path for anyone, from 10-year-old prodigies to mid-career switchers, to learn coding. It allows users to conduct mock job interviews with questions, rated by difficulty, that have been asked at specific companies. Other sites, such as HackerRank, InterviewBit, and Topcoder, offer similar features.

The result is that coders prepare by studying popular technical questions, and interviewers, who are often at a loss for good questions and work assignments, may source them from the code practice sites. This leads to "over-optimizing for one single thing," as one Cisco engineer put it. Candidates become good at answering the kind of questions that LeetCode poses. These typically involve finding efficient, counterintuitive answers to bite-size challenges. These can indeed be the building blocks of real applications. But LeetCode questions have been faulted for failing to address the big picture—"the ability to think about the overall architecture of the problem," one Google employee said. This ability draws on a much wider body of knowledge, intuition, and skill. Another engineer asked,

> Does anybody believe LeetCode-style problems are a good indicator someone is a good engineer in their specialized field? I've had this discussion with FAANG interviewers before, and every answer is always, "Do I personally think it matters? No, but I guess it can help you understand the way somebody solves problems." It honestly sounds like most interviewers don't even believe in what they're assessing the individual in, but are forced to defend the way they're asked to do it. Everybody is aware of the fact that FAANG interviews have become nothing more than LeetCode grinding sessions.

This has been a losing case. Work sampling is a noisy indicator (like everything else), but there does not seem to be a better way of measuring competence in a specific, definable skill set. Even a candidate who has crammed for the interview has learned something and demonstrated motivation.

Human resources people at selective companies don't lose much sleep over LeetCode. They speak rather the language of *false positives* and *false negatives,* coinages long used at Google. A false positive occurs when a candidate aces the interview and is hired, yet turns out to be an unsuccessful employee (a "regret hire"). The converse is a false negative: a candidate who would have been a good employee yet is rejected because of a bad interview performance.

It might seem that both cases are equally bad. Or it might seem that the false negative is the greater injustice. But the organizational mindset is different. "I'd rather interview 50 people and not hire anyone than hire the wrong person," Amazon's Jeff Bezos has said. No one gets blamed for a false negative. A company has no way of knowing it passed up a great applicant. But false positives become part of the team. Fellow workers have to work harder to clean up the underperformer's messes. Should it become necessary to fire a bad employee, that is a costly and emotionally draining process. A false positive reflects poorly on everyone who approved that hire, incentivizing caution. When a company has many qualified applicants, why take any chances at all?

Group Interviews

Unlike most tech firms, Apple is also a global chain of retail stores. New Apple Stores have been known to get 50 applicants for every open position. It's impractical to screen everyone one-on-one. Instead, Apple resorts to a *group interview.* Dozens of applicants are brought together in one large room for an exercise that melds personality test, reality show, and pep rally. Typically, a couple of Apple employees act as interviewer-emcees, posing questions or games to the group, with candidates answering in turn. One common example is, "Tell us something about yourself. The group will guess whether it's true."

Most people are bad liars (the basis of behavioral questions). The wisdom of crowds is fairly good at spotting deception. But it doesn't matter whether you "win" this game by fooling the crowd. Apple isn't going to hire you for being the most convincing liar.

Instead, a group interview is a speed date. Applicants don't have much time in the spotlight to impress the interviewers. A good strategy is to turn questions back to job-relevant qualifications whenever possible. If you started an Instagram account for a K-pop star in middle school and got 100,000 followers, this is an invitation to mention it.

You may have heard this advice for blind dates: watch how your date treats the waiter. That's what kind of person he or she really is. Apple's group interviews work much the same way. The interviewers will above all be watching how candidates treat other candidates. That says as much or more about their workplace performance as how they interact with the interviewer. Successful applicants will introduce themselves to others and mingle—and avoid bad-mouthing and backstabbing.

Oddball Questions

Group interviews, as well as the one-on-one kind, often include "oddball questions." This is a catchall term for any question that is out of the ordinary. Some oddball questions are, let's face it, silly:

What's your superpower?
Who's your favorite Disney princess?
You're a new crayon in the box. What color would you be?

Such questions have no right answer. You may be told (smugly) that there is no right answer. Interviewers ask such questions to signal how hip, creative, and youth-oriented they think they are. Questions like these are part of the cult of culture fit. The employer believes the company has a unique culture, and this culture must be preserved by hiring only those who will fit in, as revealed by answers to more-or-less frivolous questions. Though *culture fit* might be understood as the antithesis of *diversity,* both buzzwords are often mentioned in the same breath.

"What would you do in the event of a zombie apocalypse?" Ashley Morris, CEO of Capriotti's Sandwich Shop, asks this question of applicants. "There really is no right answer," Morris says. "The hope is that for us, we're going to find out who this person is on the inside and what's really important to him, what his morals really are, and if he'll fit in on the cultural level."

Larry Ellison, cofounder of Oracle, has recruiters ask, "Are you the smartest person you know?" Answer no, and the follow-up is, "Who is the smartest person you know?" Oracle's recruiters then try to hire that person. (So goes the legend.)

Warby Parker's signature question is, "What was the last costume you wore?" According to cofounder and CEO David Gilboa, this tests for the "fun and quirkiness" of the Warby Parker brand. "If we hire the most technically skilled person in the world whose work style doesn't fit here, they won't be successful."

Venture capitalist and PayPal cofounder Peter Thiel created a buzz by revealing that his favorite interview stumper is "Tell me something that's true that almost nobody agrees with you on." Explained Thiel, "It sort of tests for originality of thinking [and] for your courage in speaking up in a difficult interview context where it's always socially awkward to tell the interviewer something that the interviewer might not agree with."

Thiel reports that the three most common answers are "Our educational system is broken and urgently needs to be fixed";

"America is exceptional"; and "There is no God." He judges all to be poor responses. In the first two cases the opinions are hardly so unpopular that "almost nobody" agrees with them. Of the third Thiel (a gay Christian libertarian) says, it "simply takes one side in a familiar debate."

Like that old standard, "Name your worst fault," Thiel's question poses a dilemma. A good answer must be convincing, yet extremely unpopular. As at the Thanksgiving table, it's usually best to steer clear of politics and religion. You should also think twice before picking sides in a controversy in your line of work. The interviewer probably thinks he's more of an expert than you are, and he may hold the opposite view.

Thiel has written that successful companies are founded on "open but unsuspected secrets about how the world works." He cites Airbnb, Uber, and Lyft as companies that recognized the truth that many people have homes or cars they're willing to rent on a short-term basis, given a simple way of doing so. Good responses to Thiel's question are those that could be developed into a business pitch. Talk about what you believe people would be willing to share, lend, sell, or donate, could an app match them to a suitable recipient.

Venturing into similar territory is "Do you seek permission or seek forgiveness?" The interviewer is asking whether you get your superiors or authorities to sign off on novel initiatives ("seek permission"), or act first and deal with the consequences later ("seek forgiveness"). It's safe to assume that interviewers who ask this question see the "seek forgiveness" answer as more entrepreneurial. They're thinking of something like the electric scooter industry, which put its vehicles on urban sidewalks without waiting for regulatory approval.

That's not to say you should endorse the forgiveness answer wholeheartedly. This question bears comparison to one popularized by Tony Hsieh at Zappos: "On a scale of 1 to 10, how weird are you?" You're supposed to be weird, just not *too* weird.

In this case, all companies and organizations are hierarchies that expect their employees to go through channels. No one wants an employee who's *always* responding to the voices in his head. When an organization or a society's rules are clear, one should ask permission. Anything else will waste your time defending positions on which you are sure to lose. The sweet spot for disruption is when the rules haven't yet been invented. Then a bold, overall beneficial initiative has the best shot at success.

"If you were an animal, which would it be?" This must be the Platonic ideal of a dumb interview question. It should come as no shock that it's used at a wide spectrum of employers, from startups to the Fortune 500. Those who ask it take it seriously. Stormy Simon, former president of Overstock, recalled the time "an interviewee said they identified with a red panda because everyone thinks they are so cute and approachable, but it turns out they're just really lazy. We hired the candidate anyway despite that answer, but we parted ways within three weeks. It just goes to show how important the question is."

Uh, *right.* Anyone who examines the state of hiring today must agree that asking absurd interview questions has not prevented certain entrepreneurs and companies from achieving fantastic success. Whether those questions promoted that success is another matter.

Perhaps the takeaway is that rock-star entrepreneurs can ask any questions they want and are as susceptible as anyone else to the Barnum effect. But the applicant has cause to worry that scoring of responses may be idiosyncratic and inscrutable. Not every interviewer is as famous as Ellison or Thiel, but most have their own (harder-to-google) agenda.

Even at Warby Parker, oddball questions aren't a Halloween costume contest. You won't be hired because you had the most original or weirdest answer. You are expected to play along with the spirit of the question. Don't say, "I don't watch Disney movies" or "The animal I'd most like to be is a human, which is biologically an animal." That tells the interviewer his precious question is stupid. It is, but it's not your job to break the news.

Do Interviews Work?

Job interviews have been in widespread use for over a century. For most of that time they have been a topic of research by psychology, sociology, and management professionals. Investigators have assembled large data sets in the hope of teasing out connections between interviews and job performance. The studies span the use of traditional questions, behavioral questions, work sampling, and (to a much lesser degree) oddball questions and logic puzzles. Interviews have been compared to cognitive and personality tests as predictors of workplace success.

This body of research comes with a few caveats. We've all seen dueling studies on the health effects of chocolate. The trouble is that chocolate doesn't exist in isolation. The lifestyles of M&M consumers may be very different from those who eat artisanal truffles. Chocolate might have some health benefits while also contributing to unhealthy outcomes such as obesity and diabetes. It's impractical for study designers to control for every variable. The media play up studies saying chocolate is "good for you"— even if the study is poorly designed and financed by the S'mores Advisory Board. The disproportionate attention given pro-chocolate studies creates a skewed perception of where the science stands.

Similar issues apply to studies of hiring. Few employers use one interview technique exclusively and consistently. They are hardly in a position to hire a control group of random applicants and track how they perform on the job. Much of the scholarly data is taken from fake interviews enacted by college students or online volunteers. How well that applies to real-world workplaces is debatable. Yet promising techniques get written up in the business and popular media, leading to adoption and (often) disenchantment. This has been going on since Thomas Edison's time.

With these qualifications, let's look at what a century of determined research has revealed. The most important finding is that hiring interviews are poor at predicting job performance. Psychologists have been trying to tell employers this for decades—but employers don't want to hear it.

In 1994 Allen I. Huffcutt and Winfred Arthur Jr. reported that interview-based hiring decisions accounted for only 4 percent of the statistical variation in later on-the-job performance. That's better than flipping a coin, but not by much. Other studies indicate that when an interview is combined with other assessment methods (such as a personality or cognitive test), the interviewer's judgment actually *decreases* the validity of the decision.

Studies of *thin slicing* show how easily interviewers are swayed by first impressions ("thin slices" of an extended interaction). In a 2000 experiment, University of Toledo psychologists Tricia J. Prickett, Neha Gada-Jain, and Frank Bernieri trained three volunteers in standard interviewing techniques. The volunteers then conducted 59 mock interviews, asking HR standards ("Where do you picture yourself 10 years from now?" "What is your biggest weakness?" "Have you ever had a difference of opinion with your superiors? How did you handle that?"). The interviews lasted about 20 minutes each and were captured on video. After each meeting, the interviewers rated the applicant on attributes such as likability, intelligence, ambition, trustworthiness, and whether they would hire that person.

Each video was edited down to a 20-second clip. The clip showed the applicant entering the room, exchanging greetings, and sitting down. These short clips were shown to another group of people with no prior knowledge of the applicant or the interview. This group was asked to rate the applicants on the same criteria *based on the 20-second clip only.* The group's ratings were remarkably similar to those of the trained interviewers, despite the fact that they had not heard the answers to *any* of the questions posed.

The psychologists' devastating conclusion was that "a personnel director's assessment of an applicant's skill, knowledge, and ability might be fixed as early as the initial greeting." Rarely does anything happen in a hiring interview that changes that first impression.

This does not prove that first impressions are wrong. (But seriously, how good do you think an assessment based on a greeting is going to be?) Thin-slicing studies do suggest that the asking and answering of some widely used questions don't add much value to the interview process.

Like all of us, interviewers believe they're good judges of human nature. They may have an exaggerated opinion of their own discernment and of the predictability of other people. They often expect to predict job performance with virtually 100 percent accuracy. These credos are, if anything, even more ingrained at A-list companies, where elevated self-esteem is part of the air people breathe. Successful businesspeople often see themselves as experts on every topic, hiring included.

But the evidence reveals a huge element of chance in hiring. No known interview technique is able to eliminate that uncertainty.

What *does* predict job performance? There's an answer, but it's not one that employers or applicants especially want to hear. "All large-sample studies through the years have shown that paper-and-pencil tests are excellent measures of abilities and that other kinds of tests are usually more expensive and less valid," wrote John E. Hunter and Ronda F. Hunter in 1984. They were talking about cognitive and personality tests (today likely to be on-screen).

Tests aren't perfect, as the Hunters were well aware. They are biased against those falling too far outside the cultural bubble of those who created the tests. But cognitive and personality tests have considerable power to measure what they claim, and what they measure correlates to job performance.

Tests collect a lot of data. The same test is given to every applicant, and scoring is objective. That removes much of the noise. An interviewer, on the other hand, may ask different questions of each applicant. She may unconsciously seek to confirm a first impression, lobbing softball questions to liked candidates and more difficult ones to others. The snap judgment becomes a self-fulfilling prophecy.

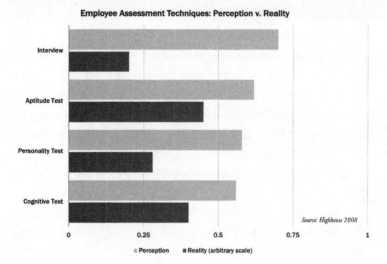

Employee Assessment Techniques: Perception v. Reality

Source: Highhouse 2008

In a 2008 survey article, Scott Highhouse of Bowling Green University compared the perception and reality of employee assessment. Surveys show that people believe that traditional ("unstructured") interviews are better than tests in predicting job performance. The empirical reality is the opposite.

When a job requires a particular skill, an aptitude test for that skill is, reasonably enough, a good predictor. But tests of general cognitive ability do almost as well. This is true even for occupations such as sales, which are more people-oriented than intellect-oriented. Better salespeople tend to score higher on cognitive tests.

Research finds that personality tests have predictive power, too. They are generally less informative than aptitude or cognitive tests but more informative than interviews.

"The notion that analysis outperforms intuition in the prediction of human behavior is among the most well-established findings in the behavioral sciences," wrote Highhouse. We resist the idea that mere tests can take the measure of ourselves or others. Human insight is essential (it must be!). And, as Highhouse noted, "Relying on expertise is more socially acceptable than relying on test scores or formulas."

In one particularly impressive demonstration, Highhouse and colleagues Filip Lievens and Wilfried De Corte asked groups of retail-store managers to make hypothetical hiring decisions. One group was told that applicants had taken an intelligence test, and their personality was assessed in an interview. Another group was told the opposite: that the applicants had taken a personality test, and their intelligence was gauged in an interview. The managers were then asked to rate hypothetical candidates using their scores for personality and intelligence. Both groups' decisions showed that they placed more faith in interview assessments than test scores. Intelligence was felt to be more important than personality, provided it had been judged in an interview.

Ask a psychologist how to improve job interviews, and you'll probably hear about *structured interviews*. In this format each candidate is asked the same set of questions, and off-topic conversation is minimized. The interviewer grades the candidate's answers as they're given. (Otherwise, memories can be unreliable and biased in favor of liked applicants.)

Studies indicate that structured interviews are more predictive than the usual, freewheeling kind. This research has been compelling enough to cause a handful of employers to adopt structured interviews. But the idea has gained limited traction at best. Taking questions from a list, with no small talk, comes off as stiff. Should a popular company always use the same list of questions, the full set would soon be posted online, providing a cheat sheet. This is one reason why high-profile companies mix up their interview questions—and why their interviews remain unstructured.

The false belief that interviews are more valid than impersonal tests has long influenced public policy. The National Commission on Testing and Public Policy's 1990 recommendations for school and workplace testing advised, "Test scores are imperfect measures and should not be used alone to make important decisions about individuals." The commission had tech-industry credibility, with Apple's vice president of education, Bernard Gifford, as its chair. Said Gifford: "We just believe that under no circumstances should individuals be denied a job or college admission exclusively based on test scores."

It's hard to imagine anyone disagreeing with that—except the psychologists who study such things. "Although these positions sound reasonable on the surface," wrote Highhouse, "they represent fundamentally flawed assumptions. No one disputes that test scores are imperfect measures, but the testing commission implies that combining them with something else will correct the imperfections (rather than exacerbate them)."

A more important policy was the one established by the Supreme Court on affirmative action (*Gratz v. Bollinger*, 2003). The University of Michigan used a point system for admission. Applicants who were members of underrepresented groups got 20 extra points. By comparison a perfect SAT score was worth 12 points, and the maximum point total anyone could get was 150. In a 6-to-3 decision, the court ruled this system unconstitutional. Despite that, Chief Justice William Rehnquist's opinion maintained that race *can* be a legitimate factor in college admission; what the court found objectionable was the point system. Candidates need to be judged on a personal basis, in interviews, rather than via an impersonal formula.

In 2019, Joe Biden, then running for president, vowed to ban the use of standardized tests in public schools. That sentiment has proved to be good politics. Almost no one likes standardized tests, and the socioeconomic biases of tests are well known. The error is in thinking that any alternative — such as interviews — must automatically be better. It is the biased judgments of those in positions of power that motivated standardized tests — and affirmative action — in the first place.

Most hiring science attempts to aid the employer in predicting future job performance. But that's a narrow view of what a hiring interview is. There are other stakeholders to an interview, notably the applicant and the firm's current employees.

Interviewers are often the employees who would be working alongside the candidate if hired. The chosen candidate's success may depend not just on her qualifications but on how the new colleagues feel about the selection process: whether the candidate was foisted on them by an inscrutable HR department, or whether they feel ownership in the decision. The objective is not just to find the "most qualified" candidate but also to assure current employees that their voices have been heard.

Anyone who accepts a new job is taking a leap into the void. No one wants to make a life-changing decision without performing due diligence. This means meeting potential colleagues and seeing the workplace. For all its failings, the hiring interview is "an effective means of establishing rapport between a potential employee and organization," as Prickett, Gada-Jain, and Bernieri conceded. For that reason, if nothing else, interviews are here to stay.

Bletchley Park

In the waning days of the First World War, German engineer Arthur Sherbius invented a secret weapon. It was an enciphering machine whose messages resisted the most skilled code breakers. After failing to interest the German navy in the machine, Sherbius started his own company. He marketed the device under the brand name *Enigma*—Greek for *riddle*. It achieved some success in peacetime as a way to keep business and governmental messages secure.

As the Second World War commenced, Britain recognized the Enigma threat. The machine had never been defeated, so it was likely that the Nazis would be using Enigma for their wartime communications. The British set about recruiting a team of code breakers to decipher the German messages. In September 1939, the Government Code and Cypher School moved from London to Bletchley Park, a Victorian-Gothic country estate whose isolation was better for keeping secrets.

The site had the further advantage of being halfway between Cambridge and Oxford, homes to scholars in many fields. Alan Turing, the most famous Bletchley Park recruit, was a Cambridge mathematician. But the organization found it had to cast its net far beyond math and Oxbridge. It hired language experts, classics scholars, musicians, governesses, and poets. The connecting thread was an interest in puzzles.

Cambridge and Oxford were already known for "Oxbridge questions," brainteasers posed in admission interviews:

? Why don't animals have wheels?

? What would happen if you drilled a hole all the way through the Earth and jumped in the hole?

? If today is Tuesday, what is the day that follows the day that comes after the day that precedes the day before yesterday?

(Answers appear at the end of the chapter.)

Bletchley Park asked similar questions of potential code breakers. Meanwhile it took advantage of the then-new phenomenon of crossword puzzles. The first London *Times* crossword had appeared in 1930, and the difficult, wordplay-dense cryptic crosswords had only just become popular. Bletchley Park requested that applications for war work contain a question asking whether the applicant enjoyed solving crossword puzzles. Applications saying "yes" were passed on to the code-breaking operation. In 1941 the *Daily Telegraph* ran a contest offering £100 to whoever could solve its cryptic crossword puzzle in under ten minutes. Five people succeeded. They were contacted by the government and offered secret work at Bletchley Park.

The Germans improved Enigma throughout the war and changed its settings daily. High-speed computing was essential to decrypt each day's messages. The British built the Bombe, a special-purpose machine devised by Turing, and later the Colossus, considered the first programmable electronic digital computer.

Historians have suggested that the British code-breaking operation shortened the war by two years.

In the decades after the war, the importance of Bletchley Park to the Allied effort and computer science gradually came to be appreciated. Britain's technical triumph was noted by the postwar computer industry on both sides of the Atlantic.

In the US, International Business Machines had begun marketing computers to private industry. IBM needed to recruit and quickly train programmers. At the time, the job was hard even to talk about. The term *software* did not exist until 1958, when statistician John Tukey coined it. Tukey remarked that software was already "at least as important" as the "'hardware' of tubes, transistors, wires, tapes and the like."

Gwen Lee saw an ad for data processors in a Toronto newspaper in the early 1960s. She showed up for an IBM-conducted group interview, finding herself the only woman and the only Black person there. She was given a test consisting of logic puzzles, some "the kind where you have to figure out that it's the baker who rides a bicycle and the mechanic who lives in the house with a red door."

After the tests were graded, Lee was called into a room with two male IBM associates. They could not believe that she had scored in the 99th percentile. One man accused her of being sent there for a prank. But they asked her some further questions and realized she was legitimate. Lee was hired for the most senior position offered and went on to a long career as one of the first women software engineers in Canada.

The early computer industry's attitude toward women was ambivalent at best. But there is at least anecdotal evidence that the use of puzzles resulted in the hiring of women when this was highly unusual in American engineering.

Interview puzzles became a custom of early Silicon Valley firms and Microsoft. Those who don't code may suppose coding to be a supremely logical task. It is no less a matter of finding bugs. "It was like working logic puzzles—big, complicated logic puzzles," said Mary Ann Wilkes, a Wellesley graduate tapped to program an IBM 704 computer for MIT. "I still have a very picky, precise mind, to a fault. I notice pictures that are crooked on the wall."

Noticing what's wrong is central to puzzle solving. The first or most obvious approach to a goal almost never works. The puzzle solver must expect to hit several roadblocks (much as the coder must expect bugs). The solution typically involves a leap of insight—a novel approach, simple in retrospect, that makes everything else fall into place. Solving a logic puzzle requires persistence, patience, and (when doing it in a job interview) the ability to function under pressure.

? You're standing on the surface of Earth. You walk one mile south, one mile west, and one mile north. You end up exactly where you started. Where are you?

Elon Musk long had a policy of interviewing every Tesla and SpaceX employee personally, even janitors. He cited this as his favorite interview question. It's an old brainteaser with a long history of use in tech interviews. The question has been so widely reported that you're unlikely to encounter it at Musk's companies today.

Like many brainteasers, Musk's question poses a paradox. Walking a mile south, a mile west, and a mile north ought to leave you a mile west of where you were. But instead it's said you end up where you started. Something weird is going on.

The classic answer is the North Pole. That satisfies the question's conditions because the four compass directions are relative to the curved surface of the globe. From the North Pole, every direction is south. The tricky part is the westward leg of the journey. Going west means following a line of latitude. Of these, only

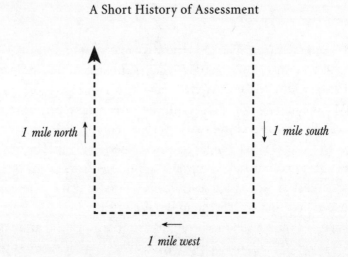

1 mile north *1 mile south*

1 mile west

the equator is a great circle spanning the Earth's circumference. All the other lines of latitude are smaller and more obviously curved. In the immediate vicinity of the North Pole, lines of latitude are small circles centered on the pole. The westward part of the journey would follow one such circle, and the northward leg would return to the North Pole.

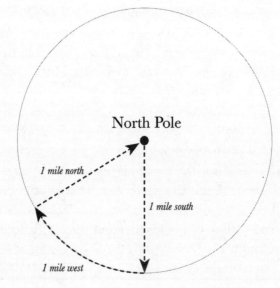

North Pole

1 mile north *1 mile south*

1 mile west

That solves the riddle. But if you stop there, you've not done as well as you might think. Some logic puzzles have more than one solution. This one has an infinite number.

Suppose you're in Antarctica, a bit more than a mile from the South Pole. You go a mile south, then make a tight westward circuit of the South Pole, in a circle exactly one mile in circumference. This will return you to where you were after the southward leg. Then you go north a mile to end up where you were originally. This fits the question's requirements.

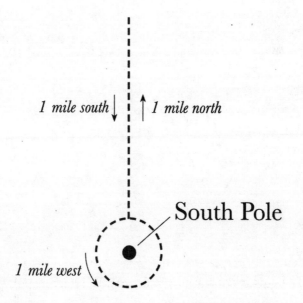

A circle with a one-mile circumference would have a radius of $1/2\pi$ miles. (Pi or π is the circumference of a circle with unit diameter, about $3.14159\ldots$) You would therefore have to start at a point $1 + 1/2\pi$ ($1.15915\ldots$) miles from the South Pole. Any point that distance from the pole would work, so there is a circle of solutions.

There are still other answers. You could start a little closer to the South Pole, so that you would travel a mile south, then travel west in a smaller circle of 1/2 mile circumference, covering it *twice*—and then travel a mile north to the original starting point. Or you could start a bit closer and cover a smaller circle three times, or four times, or any whole number of times.

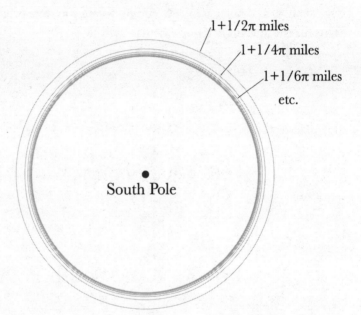

$1+1/2\pi$ miles
$1+1/4\pi$ miles
$1+1/6\pi$ miles
etc.

South Pole

This yields a family of solutions. The starting points all fall on circles about the South Pole, of radius $1 + 1/2n\pi$ miles, where n is any positive whole number. The circles converge on one with a radius of one mile. That would be the limit if the westward jag was an infinitely small circle, traversed an infinite number of times.

This question can be seen as a metaphor. In the real world there is no way to be sure that a particular solution is the only one (or the best one). The innovator needs to keep looking for ways to improve a product or business.

According to Musk, most engineers get the North Pole answer. Should they stop there, Musk asks, "Where else could it be?"

In 2018 a CNBC reporter posed Musk's question to random people on the street, with predictable results. No one got it right. The closest was a man who said "one of the poles" and then guessed the South Pole. The most popular (wrong) answer was the center of the Earth.

Do Interview Puzzles Work?

Puzzles and brainteasers have long been established in interviews in the financial, consulting, and internet retail industries, and are encountered at almost any selective employer that values creative thinking. Yet there is scant research addressing the value of such questions in hiring. These questions are generally asked along with more conventional ones. It is difficult to isolate their role in hiring decisions or even to tell if they have a role.

A 2007 paper by Jeremiah Honer, Chris W. Wright, and Chris J. Sablynski reported an experiment involving puzzle-style interview questions, apparently the first of its kind. Student volunteers were asked to solve six brainteasers. (The questions were taken from my 2003 book, *How Would You Move Mount Fuji?*) Videos of their answers were graded independently by three scorers. Honer's team found that the scorers agreed reasonably well in their ratings. This is important because there is always subjectivity in judging verbal responses.

No one was being hired for anything in this study. Subjects' puzzle-solving ability could not be compared to later, on-the-job performance. However, the volunteers also took the Wonderlic Personnel Test, a cognitive test used for hiring. There was a correlation between performance on the interview puzzles and that on the Wonderlic test. This supports the idea that interview brainteasers could be a cognitive test of sorts for employers who don't want to use an actual test.

The researchers asked the volunteers to agree or disagree with statements like "I felt good about the way the interview was conducted and administered." The puzzles received a respectably high average rating—6.2 out of 10. Not surprisingly, those who did well on the brainteasers were more likely to say they felt good about them. The group of volunteers, students from Northern California, was ethnically diverse, and 68 percent were women.

Puzzle-style questions inherit the usual failings of interviews. Evaluations based on them may reflect confirmation bias. Astute interviewers use such questions to *challenge* their own snap judgments. The puzzles are a way of hedging bets, of making sure employees who have demonstrated core competency can also handle new problems and learn new skills.

"Something that I learned very early on in information technology is that, regardless of the level of the position, experience and knowledge of specific systems tends to be overemphasized," explained David Agry, an interviewer who uses problem-solving questions. "Because information technology changes, you have to run to stand still. Having the desire and drive to continue learning and updating knowledge as well as excellent problem-solving abilities and customer-service mindset were far more important than prior knowledge. When I asked a variety of weird and random everyday life problems they had to genuinely think about, the person's natural problem-solving abilities and process would come to the fore."

Answers

? Why don't animals have wheels?

A wheeled animal is neither a contradiction in terms nor a physical impossibility. The fact that animals haven't developed wheels suggests that wheels are an extremely unlikely outcome of evolution.

A practical wheel must be able to rotate freely on an axle. You would have to imagine an animal growing wheels and axles that detach from the main body so they can rotate, yet are held in place so they don't fall out. The axle would probably require a biological lubricant. The animal would also need a way to harness muscle power to turn the wheels. This is especially hard to imagine. A creature might have wheels in front and hind legs for propulsion, but it's not clear how this would offer any advantage over having four legs and no wheels.

Darwin marveled at how something so perfectly optimized as a bird's wing could evolve. The answer, biologists now believe, is that every incremental step on the evolutionary path to flight conferred an advantage. The ancestors of birds evolved feathers for warmth, then acquired the ability to glide like a flying squirrel, to forage for food or escape predators. An increasingly streamlined body allowed powered flight for short distances. Ultimately birds were capable of flying long distances, allowing seasonal migration to secure food.

The big problem with wheeled animals is that a partially functional wheel doesn't appear to offer any survival advantage. A wheel/axle/power-train system either works as a finely tuned machine or it's deadweight. The chance of all the necessary elements evolving in simultaneous random mutations is infinitesimal.

Maybe we should ask why humans think wheels are such great things. One reason is that trains, cars, bicycles, and scooters *aren't* permanently attached to our bodies. We can use them when it's convenient and park them when it's not. Another reason is that we've paved our paradise to accommodate wheeled vehicles. Wheels are ill-suited to navigating forests, mountains, high grass, and seashores. Unless a species has the ability to build paved roads, wheels are useless.

? What would happen if you drilled a hole all the way through the Earth and jumped in the hole?

The Earth's outer core is molten and at incredibly high pressure. Liquid iron-nickel would flow explosively into any planet-spanning hole, closing it.

Let's suspend disbelief on that. Pretend the hole is kept open by a force field. Then jumping into the hole would not be so different from jumping into a deep well. You would fall with ever-increasing speed toward the Earth's center.

Unfortunately, you would retain the rotational velocity of the Earth's surface. As you approached the Earth's center, the hole's walls would have less rotational velocity than you do. That means you'd smack into the hole's walls, again and again and again.

This is a consequence of the *Coriolis effect*, the inertial force due to a rotating frame of reference. The Coriolis effect makes hurricanes spin counterclockwise in the northern hemisphere and clockwise in the southern. It (theoretically) influences the spin of water draining out of a basin and governs the Foucault pendulums that mark time in many science museums.

There's one easy way to avoid the Coriolis effect. Drill the hole from the North Pole to the South Pole. Because the hole would follow the axis of rotation, you'd be able to jump in at either end, free of rotational velocity. No more banging into the walls! But if the hole contains air, like what you need to breathe, you'd burn up like a meteor from friction.

All right: The hole is a vacuum, you wear a spacesuit, and the hole's North Pole and South Pole openings are sealed with glass domes so the vacuum doesn't suck in the whole atmosphere and suffocate everybody. You jump in at the North Pole opening.

Then your motion would be like a pendulum's: You would accelerate toward the Earth's center but overshoot it and decelerate, ascending to the Earth's surface at the South Pole end. At that point your momentum would be exhausted. You would fall back into the hole, again accelerating toward the Earth's center, repeating the process ad infinitum.

Nothing good comes of jumping into a hole drilled through the Earth.

? If today is Tuesday, what is the day that follows the day that comes after the day that precedes the day before yesterday?

It's best to work backward. Start with the last word in the question.

"yesterday" = Monday (since we're told it's Tuesday)

"the day before yesterday" = Sunday

"the day that precedes the day before yesterday" = Saturday

"the day that comes after..." [etc.] = Sunday

"the day that follows..." [etc., etc.] = Monday

The answer is Monday.

This is harder in an interview than it reads here.

The Blind Audition

I just don't think women should be in an orchestra," said Zubin Mehta, longtime conductor of the Los Angeles and New York philharmonic orchestras. Mehta wasn't alone in his opinion. The Berlin Philharmonic did not hire a woman until 1982, and Vienna held out until 1997. The rationales were legion. It was said that playing a horn distorts a pretty face, and it's unseemly for a woman to place a cello between her legs. There was even a maxim: "the more women, the poorer the sound."

But starting in the 1970s, American orchestras made a small change in their hiring practices. It resulted in a large change in the hiring of women musicians, from less than 5 percent in 1970 to 40 percent in 2019. The change was the "blind audition."

In this a musician applying for a job performs behind a screen or curtain for a panel of orchestra members. The applicant is identified only by a number and performs an assigned piece without speaking to the judges. The panelists are not shown a résumé or told anything of the applicant's education or experience. They judge on the performance—the one thing that really matters.

Blind auditions were one part of a cultural revolution in which attitudes shifted and glass ceilings shattered. A 1997 study by economists Claudia Goldin and Cecilia Rouse attempted to disentangle the many confounding factors. The authors estimated that the switch to blind auditions was itself responsible for 30 to 55 percent of the increase in the proportion of female new hires from 1970 to 1997.

Goldin and Rouse also reported that the screen had a substantial effect even when used only for a preliminary audition. Orchestras typically have three rounds of auditions. Some used the screen for the first round only. But even that increased the chance of a woman making it to the final round by 50 percent.

This fits in with a body of evidence that hiring bias is largely unconscious and front-loaded. When an organization has many applicants for a job opening, most of the eliminating is done in the earliest stages, which tend to be rushed and intuitive. It's easy, even for well-meaning recruiters, to pass over those who don't match an expected profile. But when a hirer is introduced to a woman or minority applicant who has already proven her merit, they may have a more open mindset.

Psychometric Games

Why not have blind auditions for regular jobs? This idea has motivated the fast-growing psychometric games industry.

The word *psychometric* describes any type of psychological measurement, including written tests. But in today's hiring the term increasingly refers to fast-paced, on-screen games and puzzles that gauge applicants' reactions, wits, and judgment. The word *game* is used to sound fun and nonthreatening. But the games are not frivolous. They are well-studied tasks, puzzles, and experiments discussed in the literature of psychology, recreational math, and economics. Among them are the balloon analog risk task, the dictator game, the marshmallow test, and the Tower of London puzzle. (I'll explain all of these in the coming chapters.)

Firms such as Arctic Shores, HireVue, MindX, Pymetrics, and Revelian package psychometric games with colorful animations and electronic or hip-hop soundtracks. The games begin easy and grow progressively more challenging, much like the levels of a video game. At the completion of each round applicants are rewarded with a snippet of fortune-cookie insight ("You are often skeptical of others, which can help you accurately assess situations"). A battery of a dozen or so games can be completed in about half an hour.

Psychometric games usually replace résumés as the basis for an initial screening. "Most recruiters agree résumés are terrible," said Pymetrics' Frida Polli. They contain a mixture of relevant information and "proxy variables" indicating gender, age, ethnicity, and other attributes that employers try to ignore. There is much evidence that this is a problem.

The title of a 2004 study by Marianne Bertrand and Sendhil Mullainathan asked the question: "Are Emily and Greg More Employable than Lakisha and Jamal?" The researchers sent fake résumés to real employers in Boston and Chicago. They found that résumés with white-sounding names got 50 percent more callbacks than those with Black-sounding names. This was observed even though the résumés listed the same levels of education and experience. Firms advertising themselves as equal opportunity employers were as biased as others.

In practice, those making hiring decisions have a strong tendency to favor people like themselves. If relatively more employers are Gregs and fewer are Lakishas, that puts Lakisha at a disadvantage.

One remedy is to strip out the applicant's name and other personal data. The screener (human or software) would work from the redacted résumé. But that isn't as simple as it sounds. An applicant who lists a Wellesley degree is saying something about the quality of her education, while incidentally supplying a hint about her gender and ethnicity. Names of colleges can hardly be stricken from consideration. There is a difference between a degree from a prestigious university and one from a diploma mill.

Proxy variables can be subtle. Older workers have the problem of too much experience. Their résumés give hirers an idea of their age, even when years are removed from work history.

At large companies, résumés tend to be vetted by artificial intelligence. In one widely publicized incident, Amazon devised a machine-learning bot to scan résumés, training it with information about a group of successful Amazon employees. It found that the test bot greatly favored men applicants over women. Guess what? Most of Amazon's successful hires had been men. Machine learning can be like a child that follows what its parents do, not what they say. The humans, at least, realize it would be terribly wrong to hire only men. AI is not so PC.

Machine learning is highly dependent on the training data (in this case, the group of successful Amazon employees). It's helpful for this to be balanced by gender, ethnicity, and other protected classes. But this raises a bootstrap problem. A company that doesn't have many female, Latino, or Black employees to begin with may not be able to supply enough company-specific training data for these groups.

There must be enough training data to produce meaningful results. In another much-circulated tale, a bot identified the two best predictors of job performance as being named "Jared" and having played lacrosse in high school. These correlations happened to exist in one employer's too-skimpy set of training data. A human would have immediately understood that these attributes are unlikely to apply in general. So far bots don't have that awareness.

Psychometric games promise to start with a blank slate. The initial candidate screening is based on games that do not come with the baggage of cultural expectations. In Polli's term, the games are "nondirectional"; a high score is not necessarily better than a low score. The scores are just data, used to identify applicants best suited to a particular job.

From the applicant's perspective, games may be more engaging than a written test. They are perhaps less likely to trigger test anxiety or interview jitters. The applicant can start a game at any time that's convenient and take a break between tests. There's no need to schedule a phone call for an interview on a day off (or try to take it at work without the boss finding out). The games are not as much of a chore as a work sample, nor are they snoopy like a personality questionnaire. They are less open to faking. "If I wanted to figure out how much you weigh, I could ask you," said Polli. "You might not know. You might not want to tell me. You might have changed since the last time you got on the scale. But if I just put you on a scale, it's going to tell me."

Too often recruiters default to the brand mystique of certain schools and employers. Psychometric games offer direct, quantitative comparisons between candidates, regardless of background. "A lot of our clients want to feel like they're tapping the broadest set of candidates out there and really finding the people that are best suited for them," Polli explained. "They're saying, 'I want to look everywhere, and with the same power that I have to find a great candidate from Harvard or Google.'"

Games can be tailored to specific companies and positions. One client, Unilever, needed to hire about 200 people for seven job descriptions, said Lauren Cohen of Pymetrics. "We then had [Unilever's] top employees in those roles play our games. We analyzed their trait data on the back end, looking at the traits they shared in common with one another and the traits that differentiated them from a much larger baseline group. All of that information was used to create a composite profile of what success looks like for those seven different roles. The composite acts as training data for our predictive algorithm."

The data often identifies attributes that human resources might not be looking for. After profiling top salespeople at a large New York financial institution, Pymetrics found that their most distinguishing characteristics were impulsivity, short attention span, and willingness to take risks. As Polli notes, that's three things you'd never see in a job description.

Promoters of psychometric games make two audacious claims. The first is that mere games are relevant to hiring and can predict job performance as well as or better than traditional criteria. For most employers, this demands a leap of faith.

There is a large body of open research on the psychometric tasks that companies such as Pymetrics use. But this research rarely addresses the games' use as a de facto personality test for hiring. It's the game marketers who say that their private research demonstrates that successful employees consistently score differently from others. They also claim this correlation is meaningful, of course—that the games' high scorers are not just lacrosse-playing Jareds.

In one sense, there is a low bar for success in this field. Those who sift through résumés generally focus on experience. Some studies have found only a modest correlation between experience and job performance, while others have found none at all—and still others have reported a *negative* correlation (those with *less* experience perform *better*). Elon Musk, whose companies have used Pymetrics' games, has questioned the connection between formal education and job performance and said that "there's no need to have a college degree at all, or even high school" for a job at Tesla or SpaceX.

The second claim, no less provocative, is that it's possible to predict job performance well with little or no gender or ethnic biases. It's not the first time that claim has been made of personality tests for hiring, but psychometric games offer some new tools for achieving it.

How someone performs on an on-screen game has no obvious connection to gender, race, age, religion, national origin, or physical disability. That doesn't mean there isn't one. In statistics, when you look hard enough for a correlation, you generally find one.

In deciding which psychometric tasks to use, Polli ruled out some known to have gender bias. It's been widely reported that men do better than women on tests of spatial reasoning, and this difference has been connected to a gene on the X chromosome. Spatial reasoning tasks—where you're shown drawings of 3D geometric figures and asked which can be rotated to coincide with a target image—have been used on cognitive tests going back to Army Beta. This ability is important for specialized jobs like architect but is less relevant for the vast majority of occupations.

"In the model-building process, we weight and de-weight different trait inputs until all different gender and ethnicity groups have the same chance of matching to the model," explained Priyanka Jain, Pymetrics' lead product manager. "What we consider de-biased is based on the Equal Employment Opportunity Commission standard of the four-fifths rule."

Pymetrics' bias-testing algorithm, known as audit-AI, is open source. It is conceived as a general tool for measuring and mitigating bias in machine-learning applications. Pymetrics offers this example. A company has a large number of applicants, split evenly among Asians, Blacks, Latinos, and whites (each a protected class in the US). A test or game that is known to be predictive of job performance passes 25 percent of the Asian applicants, 27 percent of the Blacks, 24 percent of the Latinos, and 26 percent of the whites. Is it OK to use that test?

The *bias ratio* is the proportion of passes for the group that does least well on the test, divided by the proportion for the group that does best. In this example, Latinos had the lowest proportion of passes (24 percent). Blacks had the highest proportion (27 percent). The bias ratio would be 24/27, or 88.9 percent. The four-fifths rule sets 80 percent as the minimum bias ratio, so this test would meet the standard.

Pymetrics' 12 games measure millions of data points bearing on 90 distinct traits. Cohen says that the games collect so much data that they are able to identify sets of attributes that are effectively bias-free across protected classes, yet highly predictive of job success. In effect, they use data mining to achieve a sort of equal-opportunity meritocracy. The chosen candidates are the top scorers on a set of game scores known to be predictive of success at the employer. No one is passed over in favor of someone with a lower score in order to meet a quota of protected classes.

Is there a catch? This takes us into new ethical territory. To give a concrete example, suppose a company has two ways of judging applicants: by whether they have a college degree and by whether they have at least two years of related experience. The data shows that both the degree and the experience are equally predictive of performance in a particular job at that firm. But the applicants with college degrees tend to be white, whereas those with two years' experience are much more diverse, approximating the makeup of the general population. The company decides to use experience as the hiring criterion and ignores whether the applicant has a college degree.

Is that fair? A new college graduate—of any ethnicity—might not think so. Maybe the graduate went into debt to get a degree, believing it would make it easier to get a job. But clearly a degree isn't essential for this particular job.

Now try this. Suppose the criteria are performance on two games, A and B. Both are equally predictive of success on the job. For some reason white people are better at game A, on average, while all ethnicities are equally good at game B. The company chooses to use game B in deciding who to hire. It ignores game A.

This is much easier to accept. No one took out a six-figure student loan to excel at game A. Hardly any applicant had even heard of games A and B before. Game A just seems to be a flawed predictor because of its bias.

It might still be objected that the employer is ignoring information. If games A and B are both predictive, then a hiring decision based on both criteria might be more predictive yet. Is the company ethically obligated to use all the information available?

Presumably not. In the real world all hiring indicators are imperfect, and each comes with a cost (of sorting through résumés, conducting interviews, scoring tests and games, and so on). No one expects an employer to use every possible assessment method. Achieving a sufficiently accurate predictor with minimal bias is the holy grail of hiring.

It would be no little irony if the fraught history of adverse impact has culminated in algorithms achieving the impartiality that has always eluded humans. Whether the marketers of psychometric games have achieved that goal is yet uncertain, as important parts of the data are proprietary. What's clear is that a broad cross-section of Fortune 500 and global companies have bought the pitch. With offices in New York, London, and Singapore, Pymetrics provides psychometric games for such firms as Accenture, Colgate Palmolive, Hilton, Hyatt, KraftHeinz, LinkedIn, MasterCard, and McDonald's. A 2017 Deloitte report found that 29 percent of global business executives were using games and simulations in hiring.

Creative Problem-Solving

The games and puzzles encountered in hiring connect to decades of research in creative problem-solving. The term describes the mental process of responding to unfamiliar challenges and arriving at successful solutions. Solving a puzzle, developing a new product, composing a film soundtrack, and writing a legal brief are held to be examples of creative problem-solving. Proponents of the concept maintain that there are analogies between all these things, and the analogies are not facile.

That raises the question of how creative problem-solving differs from plain old (discredited) intelligence. Carl Brigham was among the first to suggest that intelligence test scores were an example of *reification*. That word comes from the German expression for *making into a thing*. Academy Awards are reifications of filmmaking. They encourage us to imagine that the little gold statues are important and worthy of our attention, and that the sort of cinematic craftsmanship they honor is itself a well-defined thing. Likewise, IQ is the reification of a certain set of cognitive skills. Because there's a word or number for something, it's easy to assume that something is a thing (even when it's not).

An alternate view is that intelligence is an inherently vague concept, like beauty or justice, that resists precise definition. Knowing little-known facts could be a sign of intelligence (or just a sign of watching too much *Jeopardy!*). Ditto for performing analogies, writing essays, or solving puzzles.

The concept of creative problem-solving ability entails fewer grand assumptions. It is simply the ability to solve novel problems. It is not claimed to be an innate attribute (as was intelligence). In fact, it's recognized that problem-solving is, to an important degree, a learnable skill. It might be likened to playing a musical instrument. Not everyone is a Mozart, but virtually everyone can learn to play an instrument.

It might seem that an unchangeable attribute, as intelligence is supposed to be, would be more valuable to employers than one that anyone can learn. But employers have always hired for learned skills. If a company needs an attorney, it hires someone who has learned corporate law.

Problem-solving has become an active area of educational research. Experiments using on-screen games help scholars understand how children solve problems, tracking each step of the solution. A digital game can incorporate real-world features such as objects or rules that are ever-changing, or solutions that require collaboration with others. These elements are seen in psychometric games used for hiring.

Assessment of creative problem-solving ability has become a guiding principle of hiring at selective employers. So: How do you learn to solve unfamiliar problems?

Pappus, Simon, Pólya

One of the first to weigh in on that was Pappus of Alexandria (about 290–350 AD). In his *Collection*, Pappus describes a problem-solving technique that is usually translated as *analysis* or *the heuristic*. Pappus did not claim to have invented it. He attributed it to the very famous Euclid (of five centuries earlier) and the now-obscure Apollonius of Perga and Aristaeus the Elder.

Analysis, says Pappus, is "a special body of doctrine for the use of those...desirous of acquiring the ability to solve mathematical problems." Its essence is to work backward. Problems, both schoolbook and practical, typically ask how to get from an initial state of affairs (A) to a goal (B) while obeying certain rules. Pappus observed that it is often easier to start with the endpoint (B) and consider how to backtrack to (A). "In analysis," Pappus wrote, "we start from what is required, we take it for granted, and we draw consequences from it, and consequences from the consequences."

It's remarkable that Pappus attributes this to Euclid. For millennia Euclid's *Elements* has epitomized a tidied-up view of reasoning, ignoring the mental struggles and skipping to the pristine conclusions. Pappus gave voice to the messy, more halting course by which real people reason.

The modern study of problem-solving is often traced to Herbert A. Simon (1916–2001) and Allen Newell (1927–1992). Simon was an economist at Carnegie Mellon University, and Newell was a grad student who had worked at the RAND Corporation. The pair are now considered pioneers of both cognitive psychology and artificial intelligence. Their discipline-spanning work examined how humans solve problems in the hope that this would reveal how to design machines to do the same.

"Problem solving was regarded by many...as a mystical, almost magical human activity—as though the preservation of human dignity depended on man's remaining inscrutable to himself, on the magic-making processes remaining unexplained," Newell and Simon wrote. Their 1972 book *Human Problem Solving* describes efforts to program computers to perform tasks that humans find difficult, such as playing chess or proving mathematical theorems. In the Newell-Simon vision, problem-solving is a more-or-less efficient search through a space of potential solutions.

For any formidable problem, the number of possible solutions is exponentially vast. Human thought is too plodding to make an exhaustive search through all the possibilities. Instead we use heuristics (mental rules of thumb) to narrow down the scope of possibilities. "We need not be concerned with how large the haystack is," Newell and Simon wrote, "if we can identify a small part of it in which we are quite sure to find a needle."

Another 20th-century champion of problem-solving was Hungarian-born Stanford mathematician George Pólya (1887–1985). Though he published on a wide gamut of topics (and three mathematical prizes are named for him), Pólya is most widely known for his remarkable slim volume *How to Solve It* (1945). Directed at least in part to the general reader, the book's original cover promised "A system of thinking which can help you solve any problem."

How to Solve It has become the ultimate nerdcore self-help book. Computer scientist Marvin Minsky cited it as an essential inspiration. MacArthur "genius" Terence Tao used it to prepare for the International Mathematical Olympiad (he began competing at age 10 and went on to win bronze, silver, and gold medals).

According to Pólya, the thing that makes a problem a problem is that you don't know where to start. There is no formula to fall back on, no algorithm guaranteed to lead to a solution. In Pólya's view, adding a column of figures is *not* a problem, provided you've learned arithmetic or have a calculator handy. But a good logic puzzle leaves most clever solvers unsure where to begin.

Pólya says that the first step of problem-solving is to understand the problem. The second is to make a plan. The third is to carry out the plan. With luck, it succeeds. When it does, Pólya suggests looking back at the problem and its solution to ask whether you can learn anything from the experience. Problem-solving is a lifetime thing, and you should try to learn from every success or failure.

In outline this may sound like one of the more dubious TED talks. But Pólya develops his thesis into a compelling case. The problem-solver is like a picklock, trying one thing after another from a bag of tricks. The process is necessarily one of trial and error. But the best solvers are those who have the most tricks in their bag, and the best intuitions about which one to try next.

How to Solve It is a series of short essays describing problem-solving hacks. They are not mutually exclusive, nor need they be tried in any particular order. Some problems are objectively harder than others, but others are hard because they require surmounting mental blocks. Pólya's counsel is grounded in psychology as much as logic.

All theorists of problem-solving have noted the importance of drawing analogies. In order to understand our complex world we resort to *mental models*—handy paradigms that connect otherwise unlike situations. Here are some mental models: *Murphy's Law, catch-22, opportunity cost, reversion to the mean,* a *win-win situation,* and the *tragedy of the commons.* Such concepts encapsulate an important part of our shared practical wisdom. Those who recognize a catch-22 when they see it have an advantage over those for whom the concept is alien. They know that neither fork of the dilemma is going to work, and there's no use beating one's head against the wall. You need to move on.

Mental models come from somewhere, whether a Joseph Heller novel or fields such as economics, art, biology, politics, physics, and pop culture. Mental models are the raw material of analogies, and the most useful ones have applications far beyond the field that coined them (such as the examples above). You don't have to be a genius to use mental models. You do need a well-curated education, whether formal or autodidactic. One proponent of mental models is Charlie Munger, longtime business partner of Warren Buffett. It's Munger's view that "80 or 90 important models will carry about 90 percent of the freight in making you a worldly-wise person."

Problem-Solving Techniques

The chapters that follow are structured around 20 broadly applicable problem-solving techniques. Most are long known, described by Pappus, Pólya, Newell and Simon, and many others. I have emphasized those techniques most likely to be useful with the games, puzzles, and oddball questions encountered in contemporary hiring.

This book's Part II describes the most commonly encountered psychometric games. It introduces three problem-solving techniques that apply not just to the games but to other challenges you may come across:

Take a detour. Solving a problem is generally not so simple as making a beeline to the solution. You should expect to have to do something counterintuitive—something that seems to be wrong or to take you further from the goal.

Explore, plan, act. This is Pólya's template. First, explore your options and learn about them. Second, use what you learned to formulate a plan. Third, put the plan into action.

Put yourself in someone else's place. Successful problem-solving often depends on having an accurate conception of what other people are thinking and feeling. This is central to psychometric games that test emotional intelligence, and it is often a factor in logic puzzles.

Part III continues with logic puzzles and more open-ended questions asked in interviews. Seventeen chapters illustrate further problem-solving techniques:

Your first reaction is wrong. A problem is a problem because the answer *isn't* obvious. When a quick, easy answer pops into your head, be skeptical.

Pay attention to unexpected words. In brainteasers, every word counts. When a problem mentions an unexpected detail, it usually means that detail is crucial.

Use an analogy. The problem at hand might be similar to one you've encountered before. The analogy may suggest how to proceed. Those with experience in games and puzzles will be able to draw on many potential analogies. That is one reason why creative problem-solving is learnable (and why this book can help you to solve problems and, with a little luck, land job offers).

Break the problem into parts. Many big problems can be split into smaller ones that are easier to solve. This is the key to solving weird estimation questions such as "How many pennies are in Denver?"

Draw a picture. Most of us are visual thinkers. Sometimes a tough problem's solution becomes apparent once you make a drawing, diagram, or chart.

Try a simpler version of the problem. Sometimes you can invent a simpler (or more extreme or more general) version of the problem that is easier to solve. You may then be able to adapt its solution to the original problem.

Ask good questions. Some interview questions are interactive. You're given an incompletely specified problem and are expected to pose questions to the interviewer, filling in the missing information. You'll be rated on how pertinent your questions are—as well as on how you shape what you learn into a compelling solution.

Use a process of elimination. Though this doesn't always work, it is sometimes feasible to list all possible actions, strategies, or answers. You may then be able to run down the list and rule out all but one possibility, which must be the correct one.

Work backward. Pappus's 1,700-year-old advice can be interpreted several ways. A problem may ask how to achieve a goal, in which case you start with the desired outcome and go backward in imagined time. You may also work backward more conceptually, by taking the problem's unknown as a given and drawing conclusions from it.

Beware of trick questions. Some questions send solvers on a wild-goose chase for a solution that is either right under their noses or nowhere to be found. Trick questions are uncommon in hiring interviews (and arguably shouldn't be used at all). But you should be aware of them as a possibility. Heed any clues you get that a question is simpler than it appears.

Guesstimate and refine. When an interview question calls for calculation of a quantity, it's good practice to start with a quick, inexact estimate. Your final, more exact answer should be close to the estimate — or else you should understand why it's not.

Set up equations. Some brainteasers are glorified story problems. Once you understand the problem, you can translate it into equation(s) that can be solved the way you learned in algebra class. (Assuming you remember algebra class.)

Don't follow the wrong footsteps. We fall into mental ruts — ways of thinking that have served us in the past. Some games and puzzles are difficult because they require us to disregard an old mental path and forge a new one.

Ignore the MacGuffin. A problem may trick you into thinking that you must first learn or deduce a particular unknown (Alfred Hitchcock's famous "MacGuffin") in order to arrive at a solution. But the MacGuffin is misdirection, and you don't need it to solve the problem.

List, count, divide. Many interview questions require the estimation of a probability. One technique is to list possible outcomes of equal probability, count how many obey the given conditions, then divide by a total to get the answer.

Look for a parallel to the job. Many puzzles and oddball questions have a hidden connection to the job — to important principles of business, finance, engineering, or coding. You're expected to recognize that connection and use it in your answer.

Introduce a new feature. Try adding a new element to the problem. It might clarify the situation and point to a solution. This is one of the more advanced problem-solving techniques, requiring intuition as to when and how to use it.

Ready to match wits with employees of today's most innovative companies?

Part II

Mind Games

Take a Detour

For six years, German psychologist Wolfgang Köhler was marooned in the Canary Islands with nine chimpanzees. Köhler had accepted a one-year stint as director of the Prussian Academy of Science's primate center on Tenerife, beginning in 1913. As war broke out, ships refused to transport him back through the British-controlled Atlantic.

Köhler spent some of his time on Tenerife studying how chimpanzees solve problems. A chimp would be shown a banana and have to figure out how to get it. In the simplest experiments, a fence or other barrier separated chimp from banana. The ape could see the fruit but couldn't grasp it. Instead the chimp took a long detour around the barrier to get the food. Köhler was impressed because previous experiments had reported that dogs and cats did not do that. They stood at the barrier, gazing at the food.

Köhler's apes were acquainted with what might be called the core technique of problem-solving: the *conflict move*. This is an action that seems to take the problem-solver further from the goal but is actually necessary to attain it. Conflict moves are counterintuitive and, as such, are the central gimmick of many logic puzzles and even toys. Think of the toy known as a *Mädchenfänger* in Germany and Chinese handcuffs in the US. It's a cylindrical braid of bamboo fiber. Two people insert a finger in either end. As they try to remove their fingers, the toy grips tighter. To release the fingers, you must do what seems exactly wrong: push the fingers toward each other.

Problem-solvers learn to embrace conflict moves. Psychologists test the principle with a puzzle known as the Tower of London. It's now one of the more common psychometric games for hiring.

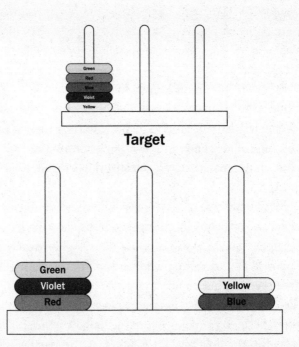

Target

? You'll be shown three poles with colored disks on them. The goal is to rearrange the disks to match the target image (at top) in as few moves as possible. You can move only one disk at a time, and it must be the uppermost disk on its pole. Click a disk to lift it, then click the destination pole to put it there. If needed, on-screen buttons let you undo a move or start the game over.

This game will remind hard-core puzzle fans of the Tower of Hanoi, a popular toy for over a century. In physical form the Tower of Hanoi consists of a board with three vertical poles, one threaded with eight disks of descending size to form a cone. The goal is to move all eight disks to either of the vacant poles. The rules say you must move one disk at a time and cannot ever put a disk on top of a smaller one.

First marketed in 1883, the Tower of Hanoi has no known connection to the Vietnamese capital. It was originally attributed to a certain "Prof. Claus." That turned out to be an anagram of "Prof. Lucas," meaning Édouard Lucas, a prominent French mathematician of the time. Lucas devised many brainteasers, one of which we'll encounter as a job interview question (page 148).

Over the years the Tower of Hanoi has been offered in many forms: physical and virtual, dollar-store and deluxe. It's become a cliché of puzzle-style video games. In 1982 University College London neuropsychologist Tim Shallice adopted Lucas's puzzle as a tool for diagnosing lesions of the brain's frontal lobe. This part of the brain controls planning, initiative, and problem-solving. Shallice used a simplified version of the toy with three colored balls, all the same size but of different colors, on three posts. Patients were asked to rearrange the balls, one at a time, to match a target configuration. Shallice dubbed his test the Tower of London (TOL).

In 1997 Geoff Ward and Alan Allport introduced a more challenging five-disk Tower of London, suitable as a general cognitive test. When you encounter the Tower of London in hiring, it will be this version. You'll find that the game is a little like coach airline passengers trying to get into window, middle, and aisle seats. Someone has to get out for someone to get in.

There is a simple trick for solving the Tower of London. It does not always yield the solution with the minimum number of steps, but it's easy to remember. In brief, you assemble the target configuration starting with disk(s) that, once placed, won't ever have to be moved again.

Look at the diagram's target image. It has all five disks on the first pole. The bottom disk is yellow. That's the one to start with.

Now look at the main image with the movable disks. The yellow disk is ready to move, being the topmost disk on the third pole. To place it where it needs to go, it's first necessary to move the three disks occupying the first pole. These should go on the second pole, as we don't want to put them on top of the yellow disk. Moving them takes three moves, leaving them on the second peg in reverse order (green, violet, red from bottom up). Note that these are conflict moves because we're moving three disks from the first pole, where they must ultimately end up, to the second pole, where they don't belong.

Now we're free to move the yellow disk to its destination on the first pole. That's the fourth move. The yellow disk will never have to be moved again, so we can forget about it. It as if we're starting over with four disks rather than five.

Consulting the target image again, the violet disk needs to go on top of the yellow. The violet disk is now sandwiched in the middle of a three-stack on the middle pole. Move the red disk above it to the third-pole. Then we're free to move the violet disk on top of the yellow disk.

That's two disks in place, and this took only two more moves (4 + 2 = 6 total).

Next up is blue. Move the red above it to the middle pole, above green. Then blue goes on violet, on the first pole. That's another two moves (4 + 2 + 2 = 8) to place another disk.

Red is next, then green. Each can be achieved in a single move. This solution uses 4 + 2 + 2 + 1 + 1 = 10 moves.

The Tower of London measures the ability to think multiple moves ahead. That seems to be important in many different types of jobs. The difficulty of any particular TOL configuration depends in part on the number of conflict moves required. For almost any job, you want to achieve the target configuration as expeditiously as possible. It's especially important for jobs requiring planning and managing complex projects.

There is a body of opinion that it's impossible (or pointless) to prepare for psychometric games. There are no pat answers to crib. Some games test attributes that are not easily changed: eye-hand coordination, reaction time, and memory. You can't prepare for those any more than you can for an eye exam—and why would you want to?

Employers using psychometric games are not looking for superhero reflexes or a photographic memory. Not many jobs require that. They are concerned with traits predictive of job success such as the ability to plan ahead, the willingness to accept risk, and the ability to understand other people's feelings. The job applicant benefits from knowing the backstory: what a particular game is intended to measure; how others usually respond; how responses affect suitability for particular jobs. Learning about a game beforehand allows the job seeker to approach it with more confidence. It also helps ensure that the applicant understands the rules. Too many players skim a screen of instructions on their phone and plunge in. If the player misunderstands the game, that doesn't help her or the employer.

Those taking an on-screen psychometric exam are often required to agree that the results may be made available to other employers for a specified period, often a year. This can be helpful, for the applicant doesn't have to keep taking the same exam, and results can be matched to other employers offering jobs for which the applicant is qualified. But it also means that subpar game play (for one employer) may stick with you like a ding on your credit rating. Psychometric games demand being taken seriously.

* * *

Three tips apply to anyone playing these games. First, *you can use a phone, but don't.* The code underlying the games grades players on milliseconds of response time. For that, a full-size keyboard with moving keys remains superior to a phone touchscreen. You won't have to worry about dropping the phone, and you'll appreciate the unimpeded visibility of a computer's larger screen.

Don't skip the disclosures. The games usually start with a form allowing you to indicate whether you are color-blind, dyslexic, or have attention deficit disorder. Although you might be reluctant to disclose such personal matters so early in the process, it's hard to avoid doing so. One common game asks players to distinguish red and green dots. That's a nonstarter for someone with red-green color-blindness. Publishers offer an alternate version of the game, and anyone who's color-blind will want it.

Take a break. You're allowed to take a break between games. There's no downside and some upside. Walk the dog, do yoga, have some coffee. You'll probably come back to the next game fresher.

Coordination and Memory Games

There are dozens of commonly used psychometric games. The ones you encounter will depend on the employer and the job you're seeking. Some "games" are little more than IQ test questions with animated graphics. Geometric designs tumble on-screen, and you're asked which two are the same. Or you're shown numbered tiles and asked to click on a set that totals 22. The graphics don't change how these questions work.

The more novel games are time-based. In the *keypresses task* you are asked, upon a cue, to hit the space bar as many times as you possibly can until told to stop. (Or else you click a button on your phone's touchscreen. *Please* don't use a phone.)

Employers don't care how many times you can pound a

space bar. This is a measure of general stamina. For some the game triggers a competitive urge, and they go all out to get a high score. Others makes a good start but slack off well before the game ends. Still others can't get into a basically meaningless task. They may be slackers, or they may be independent thinkers. An average or low score may be fine for some creative jobs.

The *digit span test* measures short-term memory. A succession of digits flashes on-screen, one at a time: 4...9...0...You're asked to type in the digits you saw.

Get it right and you'll be presented with a four-digit number. Get that right and the next one is five digits. This continues until you choke—and you will, soon enough.

Digit span tests have long been part of verbally administered cognitive tests. Number memory seems a specialized thing, yet it correlates surprisingly well with IQ and is a far more concrete, readily measurable concept. Most people can remember a seven-digit number without much trouble. That's why many nations' telephone numbers have seven digits or thereabouts.

Digit span matters for accountants and others working with numbers. It's better to be able to remember a number than to have to keep looking back at a source. But digit span is primarily a test of short-term memory. It correlates with recall of words, facial expressions, and body language, all of which are vital in parsing the human world around us.

Digit span isn't about identifying memory savants. Remember eight or more digits, and you're in good shape.

The more complex games involve conflicting impulses. Here's one example.

? You'll see a sequence of red or green dots, briefly flashed on-screen. Hit the space bar every time you see a red dot... but not when the dot is green. When the dot is green, do nothing.

This is a *go / no-go task*. It's psychology's version of "Simon Says." You're asked to perform a repetitive action on cue, *except* when a signal tells you not to. Like "Simon Says," it's harder than it sounds. This version adds in cognitive dissonance, for green normally means "go" and red means "stop"—but here it's reversed.

Go / no-go tasks were designed to measure impulsiveness. Those who click the instant they see a dot, getting many wrong responses, are impulsive. They tend to be risk-takers as well.

There are many other go / no-go tasks, and a set of psychometric games often includes several. Each complicates the go / no-go decision in a different way.

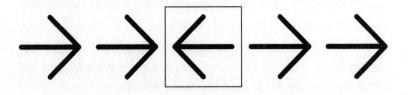

In one game you're presented with five colored arrows in a horizontal row. The center arrow may or may not point in the same direction as the other arrows. You're instructed:

> If arrows are *blue or black,* use arrow keys to indicate which direction the *center arrow* points.
>
> If arrows are *yellow,* use arrow keys to indicate which direction the *side arrows* point.

Huh? By design, the instructions are arbitrary. The blue-or-black business is difficult to absorb. One trick is to mentally frame the colors as *yellow* and *dark color.* Tell yourself to indicate the direction of the side arrows for yellow, and the center arrow for "dark color."

Small mouth   **Big mouth**

Another go / no-go game borders on the absurd. You're asked to distinguish between "small mouth" and "big mouth" faces, indicating which you see with arrow keys. The big mouth is about 5 percent wider. The difference is almost subliminal. Nonetheless you'll probably do better than random guessing.

Don't worry too much about these games. Everyone finds them difficult. As game publishers unpack it, these games measure not only impulsiveness but attention span. Some people keep up their focus and may improve through the game's duration. Others get bored and zone out. Low impulsiveness and long attention span are good for air traffic controllers and accountants. The opposite can be true for salespeople.

? Which would you rather have?
  (a) $55 now, or
  (b) $75 in 61 days

? Which would you rather have?
  (a) $54 now, or
  (b) $55 in 119 days

This is the famous *marshmallow test* of Stanford psychologist Walter Mischel. In the early 1970s, Mischel and Ebbe B. Ebbesen presented nursery-school children with a dilemma. They could have one marshmallow to eat immediately...or two marshmallows, provided they could wait 15 minutes to eat them. Mischel set the first marshmallow on the table within easy reach. The child could eat it at any time, but if he did, there would be no second marshmallow. Mischel and Ebbesen timed the children with a stopwatch. Few managed to hold off the full 15 minutes. The average child lasted about six minutes before giving in to temptation.

The marshmallow test has since become a pop-psychology meme. We're all kids in a marshmallow test. We live in a culture that tempts us 24/7 to buy, consume, and take it easy. We know we should skip the dessert, go to the gym, and save for retirement. But it's easier to do what feels good right now. You only live once.

Deferring gratification can be the ultimate conflict move. Mischel and colleagues did follow-up studies of the children who had participated in the first marshmallow tests. They reported that those who had been able to resist temptation were more successful and less troubled in later life. They had higher SAT scores and lower rates of divorce, obesity, and drug abuse.

This psychometric game is a grown-up version of the marshmallow test. You're presented with a series of binary choices about money and time. The questions may be interactive, like an optometrist's exam. How you answer one determines which choice you're offered next.

Take $55 now versus $75 in 61 days. The case for (a), the immediate option, is that you might really, *really* need the money now (you're being evicted or something). Also, an immediate payment is a sure thing, and life is uncertain. You can't be entirely sure the benefactor will be around in 61 days. You can't even be sure *you'll* be around. Carpe diem already.

But if $55 isn't going to make or break you, and you take the offer at face value, there's a lot to be said for the delayed option, (b). An accountant would say that's a 36 percent return in two months' time—equivalent to an annualized return of a stupendous 543 percent.

The second choice, $54 versus $55 in 119 days, is more of a toss-up. It's not so clear it's worth waiting almost four months for an extra dollar. The premium for waiting is equivalent to an annual return of 5.79 percent. That's no better than average returns for other readily available investments (stocks or mutual funds, say), so there's no compelling case for waiting.

I mention returns here, but you won't have time to run the math while playing the game. The point is to gauge knee-jerk reactions. Being relatively willing to delay rewards is associated with the Big Five trait of conscientiousness. It's vital for occupations demanding self-starters who can pace themselves on long-term projects. In fact, every job requires self-discipline, if only to put in the hours to get the paycheck.

Explore, Plan, Act

A psychometric game is a little world. It's not as detailed as the usual sort of video game, but like video games it plunges the player into unknown territory. The first thing to do is explore. Try out the game's options and learn how they work. Then use what you learn to formulate a plan to maximize your score. Finally, execute the plan. This embodies George Pólya's all-purpose prescription for problem solving: *explore, plan, act.*

Psychometric games may collect thousands of data points. The score is just one. The code also documents how that score was achieved. It records how players confront unknowns and learn from experience; whether they got discouraged from an early stumble or triumphed after a string of failures. A human interviewer would likely forget many of the details and contrive a narrative justifying the final score. The code remembers everything.

? You're shown a balloon attached to an air pump. Click a button to add a puff of air. Each time you do, the balloon expands, and you add 5 cents to a potential jackpot. You can stop any time you want and collect the jackpot. But every puff risks bursting the balloon. Should that happen, you collect

nothing from that balloon. The game will give you the opportunity to inflate a number of different-colored balloons, allowing you to learn from experience and adjust your strategy. Once collected, money goes into a permanent bank account and is not at risk.

This game is the balloon analog risk task (BART), devised by a team of psychologists led by Carl W. Lejuez of the University of Maryland and published in 2002. BART measures attitudes toward risk—specifically, the trade-off of risk and reward. (The marshmallow test, complementary in some ways, is time versus reward.)

We've all blown up toy balloons or bubble gum. The goal is to get it as big as possible without it bursting in your face. That requires a middle ground between caution and ambition. We have some idea of the physical limitations of rubber balloons and bubble gum. Not so with a virtual balloon on a screen. You can play it safe, settling for a few cents, or you can keep pumping to learn the breaking point. But you don't know whether there is a fixed breaking point or it varies.

The standard BART score of the psychology literature is the

average number of clicks on balloons that hadn't exploded (the burst balloons aren't tallied). This is typically around 30. Lejuez's team found that high BART scores correlate with risk-seeking behavior, including cigarette smoking, gambling, alcohol and drug abuse, unprotected sex, and shoplifting. BART is a bad-boy (bad-girl) index. Yet risk-taking isn't always bad. In many lines of work the willingness to take risks is essential. The optimum varies among occupations, and that makes BART useful in hiring.

Here's a BART cheat sheet. The colors of the balloons make a big difference. In the original 2002 experiment the colors were orange, yellow, and blue. The orange balloons burst in anywhere from one to eight pumps. Yellow balloons were good for up to 32, and blue for 128. The colors may vary in a hiring game, but you should assume that they indicate different likelihoods of bursting.

Within its color's limits, a balloon's bursting point is random. The BART software essentially draws balls from a virtual urn in order to decide whether the balloon will burst on a given click. For a yellow balloon in the 2002 experiment, there would initially be 32 balls in the urn—one black and the rest white. Each time the player pumps, the algorithm draws a random ball and sets it aside. When it draws the black ball, the balloon bursts. This can happen on the first click, the 32nd, or any other, all with equal probability.

"The goal of this game is to collect as much ($) as possible by pumping balloons," says the instruction screen for Pymetrics' BART game. Take that at face value, and you want to play the odds like a smart gambler. You should try to learn the behaviors of the colors and adjust your strategy accordingly. Recognizing that burst balloons are part of the game, you shouldn't be overly cautious.

On the other hand, you don't want to press your luck too far. Say you've got a purple balloon and suspect it has a maximum of 128 pumps. As you approach that limit, you should be aware that you have more to lose than to gain. You've already earned most of what's possible with that balloon and stand to lose it all if it bursts. It would be unwise to take that risk to squeeze out a few more nickels.

As Lejuez's group pointed out, the optimal strategy is to pump each balloon up to half its color's maximum and then call it quits (assuming you know the maximum, and the balloon hasn't already burst). With this strategy the balloon bursts half the time, and that's OK. The other half of the time, you collect five cents for each pump. The expected earning is half that (2.5 cents) because you collect only half of the time. The table shows payoffs for the original color scheme. The game's profit resides mainly in the hardest-to-burst color (blue here).

	Optimal strategy	Expected earnings
Orange	Pump 4 times and quit	10 cents
Yellow	Pump 16 times and quit	40 cents
Blue	Pump 64 times and quit	$1.60

By the profit criterion, most people are too timid. They worry too much about bursting the balloons and settle for less money than they could have earned. Lejuez's team reported that the average number of pumps for blue balloons was about 30.

The game's goal is not necessarily *your* goal. You are not trying to maximize Monopoly money; you're trying to land an interview or a job offer.

Jobs involving negotiation, finance, and entrepreneurship require a comfort level with risk-taking. If you're applying for a position where "no guts, no glory" is the ethos, you should be willing to burst some balloons and adopt a maximizing strategy based on color. If you're applying for a position where risk-taking is more likely to be seen as a problem—a schoolteacher, nurse, or accountant—don't try so hard to maximize.

The *explore, plan,* and *act* phases can overlap. You will be earning money as you learn the behavior of the balloon colors. You will continue learning throughout the game and may adjust your plan as needed. With BART, the three phases happen simultaneously, and this is true with many other types of problem-solving.

? You'll see four decks of cards. Click on any deck to draw a card. Some cards win and earn you money. Others lose and cost you money. You start with a $2,000 virtual bankroll. You're free to switch decks as often as you want. The goal is to end up with as much money as possible.

Think of the four decks as slot machines. You're not told the odds. That's for the casino to know and you to find out (expensively). Some machines pay out more often, though the amounts are modest. Others dangle the prospect of a huge jackpot that almost never comes up. You have to play the machines to get an idea of their behavior, but most slot players switch too frequently to learn much.

Here you can expect to find that at least one of the decks is "safe." By that I mean it has modest wins and no big losses. Click repeatedly on this deck and you'll probably end up about where you started.

At least one deck will be "high-risk." Click on it and you'll probably score a big reward (say, $100). Click again and again for similar outcomes. But sooner or later you'll get hit with a loss big enough to sting (say, $1,150).

Regardless of the job you're applying for, you should try out all the decks. For all you know, one could be a gold mine. (It won't be, but you're expected to leave no stone unturned.)

Should you be willing to play the high-risk deck? It would be easier to answer that if we knew its expectation—what gain or loss can be expected in the long run. The trouble with this game is that there is no "long run." Pymetrics' card game allots the applicant only 80 clicks. That doesn't allow much scope to sample each of the four decks, form a confident statistical conclusion, then exploit it by clicking on the deck believed to be best.

Those comfortable with risk tend to pick the high-risk deck repeatedly. They take it on faith that their willingness to accept risk will be rewarded (the way the stock market offers higher returns than bonds). This behavior is suitable for jobs in the financial industry, sales, and other high-risk undertakings.

Others avoid the high-risk deck after their first big loss. This shows an aversion to risk and is more suited to jobs with steady paychecks.

? You will be given a series of choices between an easy task and a hard task. With the easy task, you must hit the space bar five times in three seconds. With the hard task, you must hit the space bar 60 times in 12 seconds.

Choose a task

Probability of winning
Medium (50%)

$1.00 Easy

$2.77 Hard

? If you complete the easy task, you may earn $1. With the hard task you can earn more: from $1.24 to $4.30. You are not certain to win anything, however. At the start of each trial, you'll be told the probability of earning the money by completing the chosen task.

Once you complete a task (or fail to do so), you'll be told how much you've won and presented with a new choice. The goal is to earn as much money as possible in two minutes.

On each trial, if you don't decide between the easy and hard task within five seconds, a choice will be made randomly.

This is a test of how well you manage your time. The first thing to understand is that, once you begin the game, the clock is ticking. You've got two minutes total, and that includes dilly-dallying. If you spend five seconds choosing, the choice will be made for you—but you never want that to happen, because that's five seconds in which you could have been playing. Another important point is that the three-second easy task takes less time than the 12-second hard task. Should you favor the easy task, you get to play more times.

The tasks are accurately labeled. The easy task is a cinch, whereas the hard task requires real effort and not everyone succeeds every time. Take the example above. The hard task's prize is $2.77 to the easy task's $1. With either, the chance of being paid for successful completion is 50 percent. We can better compare the choices by calculating a "wage" per second of game time. Pick the easy task and you have a 50-50 shot at winning $1 (a $0.50 expectation). Divide by the three seconds of time required, and that's an average of $0.17 per second.

With the hard task, you have a 50 percent chance of earning $2.77 (an expectation of $1.39, *assuming* you succeed). That eats up 12 seconds of precious game time, averaging $0.12 per second. On a per-second basis, therefore, the easy task pays better than the hard task—and that's before you factor in the real possibility of failure on the hard task.

Choose a task

Probability of winning
High (88%)

For comparison, here's a choice where the hard task is *marginally* attractive. There's a good (88 percent) chance of getting paid, and the hard task is worth the maximum of $4.30. That means the hard task pays an average of $0.32 per second, versus $0.29 per second for the easy task.

Because the hard task takes four times as long, it can't possibly make sense unless it's paying more than four times as much money. Most of the time, it isn't. Even the maximum payment of $4.30 may not compensate for the risk of failure.

I'm doing the math here so you don't have to. You shouldn't spend time on calculations during the game. Note that there is a simple strategy for maximizing the score: *always* pick the easy task. Don't even slow down to ponder the choices. Just click on the easy $1 button. That way you spend more time playing and earning.

As with all psychometric games, the object is not necessarily to get a maximal score but rather to get one similar to those of successful people in the job you're seeking. Many players go in assuming the hard task is difficult but "worth it." One of the things the game can measure is how long it takes the player to learn that the hard task isn't all it's cracked up to be. There's nothing wrong with trying the hard task once or twice, especially early in the game; you can then segue to the optimal all-easy strategy.

High monetary winnings are likely to be associated with success in jobs requiring self-starters. Many people spend their workdays doing things the hard way or wasting time on boondoggles. The less you do that in this game, the better.

Put Yourself in Someone Else's Place

There is a type of logic puzzle involving colored hats, nations of liars and truth-tellers, and "perfect logicians." This genre presents a highly artificial, pinball-machine view of human nature, in which "I can deduce X because that perfectly logical guy deduced Y and didn't deduce Z." Such puzzles nonetheless invoke an important problem-solving technique: put yourself in someone else's place. You need to figure out what another person knows, feels, or will do.

This imperative is perhaps more realistically addressed in tests of so-called emotional intelligence. Such tests cover a grab bag of skills, but common to nearly all are items measuring empathy, cooperation, and the ability to read emotions.

? You've been matched with a partner and have been randomly selected to receive $5 for participating in this game. You now have the option of sharing some of that money with your partner. It can be any amount from nothing to the full $5, in increments of $0.50. How much, if any, would you like to give your partner?

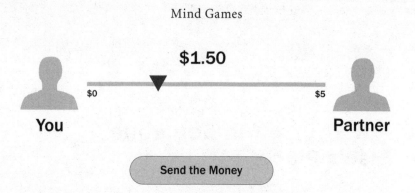

This is the dictator game, another widely studied experiment of behavioral economics. It's simpler than the trust game discussed earlier. Here you split the money, and that's that. Playing this game is like deciding how much to tip a waiter or donate to a public-radio pledge drive. You don't have to worry about what the partner will do. You just have a chance to be generous. Or not. It's called the "dictator" game because the person who splits the money has all the power. But you should put yourself in the other person's place before hitting the Send button.

Daniel Kahneman, Jack L. Knetsch, and Richard Thaler published the dictator game in 1986. (Kahneman and Thaler are Nobel laureates, giving this game an unusually distinguished provenance.) They sought to understand the nature of altruism. Do diners leave tips out of generosity, or habit, or just because they don't want other people to think they're cheap?

In typical experiments, only 1 in 5 dictators give their partner nothing. The average donation is about 30 percent. With a $5 bankroll, that would be $1.50.

Behavior in the dictator game is known to be highly dependent on *whether someone is watching.* When the split is made under rigorously secret conditions so that no one, not even the partner, can learn the dictator's identity or choice, about 60 percent of people keep all the money for themselves.

A game for employment is hardly private. The employer, or at any rate an algorithm, *will* be judging you on how you split the money. Let's run down some options.

Keep everything for yourself ($0 to the partner). This maximally self-interested response is common among people who are successful in finance.

$1.50 to the partner. This corresponds to the typical 30 percent offer of dictator games. It shows a balance between empathy and profit. This is a good answer for a wide range of jobs.

$2.50 to the partner. This is a 50-50 split. It says you care about others, something important in highly collaborative work and jobs that deal with the public.

$3.00 or more to the partner. Extremely generous offers are rare. But entrepreneurs often show unusual altruism in this game.

In economics, the dictator game has been used to explore attitudes toward wealth inequality. A 2018 study by Norwegian economists Björn Bartling, Alexander Cappelen, and Mathias Ekström had volunteers play one of two versions of the dictator game. In one version, the person receiving the money was said to be randomly chosen. Surveyed players generally felt that the lucky partner should share his wealth. Furthermore, the opinions of political conservatives and liberals were remarkably aligned on this.

In the other version of the game, the money was described as a prize for the partner who had performed better on a cognitive test. Then the consensus was that the winning partner had earned the money and had less or no obligation to share it.

Dictator-game research suggests that people across the political spectrum are open to redistributions of lucky windfalls, yet accepting of merit-based wealth, even in winner-takes-all contexts. Attitudes on income inequality have much to do with the stories we tell ourselves about wealth. Do the rich succeed by pluck or luck? There are prominent examples of both, and it's not hard to find stories that fit in with whatever you want to believe.

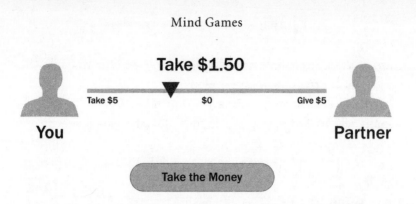

Take $5 $0   Give $5

You   Partner

Take the Money

? This is the same setup as the dictator game above, except that you can give — or take — any amount, up to $5 in increments of $0.50, from the partner. How much would you like to give or take?

Psychometric exams often follow up the dictator game with the *heaven dictator game.* Created by Spanish economist Aurora García-Gallego and colleagues, it offers the twist that the dictator can take from as well as give to the unseen partner.

You might feel that your response to this game should be the same as it is to the regular dictator game. If the partner deserved a share of your $5 before, he or she does now. If you just thought it would be nice to share the money, you can still do it.

Indeed, García-Gallego's team reported that the vast majority of subjects give the partner a share of the $5. But about 12 percent opted for zero, and another 13 percent took money from the partner.

What is fair in the heaven dictator game? It's a little easier to justify the zero option. ("The partner should feel lucky I didn't take anything…") Yet zero is actually less popular in this game than in the standard dictator game. Some of the people who stiff the partner in the standard game are apparently the ones who take money in the heaven dictator game.

This game demonstrates the power of framing. When offered

a range of options, it's common to favor the middle choice—particularly when the situation is unfamiliar or ambiguous. Many digital receipts make it easy to enter tips of 18, 20, or 25 percent. Customers take the on-screen options as hints and often pick the middle value, 20 percent—which, by design, is higher than most people tip otherwise.

It's okay for your choice on this game to be a little greedier than on the standard dictator game. For a job involving finance or dealmaking, a low or negative offer is acceptable. In other positions, a negative offer can raise a red flag. "Taking someone else's money because I can" can correlate with corner-cutting, self-serving, and other ethical mischief that no employer wants.

What is this person feeling?

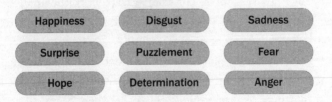

Happiness Disgust Sadness

Surprise Puzzlement Fear

Hope Determination Anger

? You'll be shown photographs of people with different facial expressions. Pick the word that best describes the expression.

Some of the photos are accompanied by short stories. Read the story before choosing a description.

The *facial emotion recognition (FER) task* was originally developed to help diagnose autism and Asperger's syndrome. Perceiving emotions accurately is an important skill for those dealing with the public and for managers and negotiators. But if you're on the autism spectrum, you'll probably find this game difficult.

We evaluate facial expressions holistically, paying attention to context and tone of voice. It's harder when working from a headshot alone. Take *happiness*. We expect a big smile. Batman's nemesis the Joker has a big smile. Nineteenth-century French anatomist Guillaume Duchenne showed that authentic expressions of happiness involve the eyes as well as the mouth. The muscles around the eyes raise the cheeks and create crow's-feet in smilers of a certain age. We recognize this intuitively but find it hard to articulate. Without the upper-face cues, a smile comes off as insincere. (Hence the selfie advice to squint a little at the camera. It converts a "say cheese" grin into something more authentic.)

Two expressions easily confused are fear and surprise. With surprise the eyes open wide, the eyebrows arch, and the jaw drops. With fear the eyebrows are more flat and the sides of the mouth are pulled sideways.

The short texts that accompany some faces in this game introduce a context. "A woman went to a horse race and put all her money on a favorite horse. For the bet to pay off, the horse has to come in first or second. As the horses make the final turn, the woman's horse is in second place."

Even without the picture, you'd expect "hope" to be the correct answer. In the photos with stories, the words suggest one feeling, while the photo may be closer to another. These faces with stories gauge whether you rely more on expressions and intuition or on words and logic.

You won't have much opportunity for analysis in this game, as each expression comes with a time limit. Many find they're better at this exercise than expected. Go with your instinct, and you'll often find that you "magically" click on the right word.

For what it's worth, a 2013 study by David Comer Kidd and Emanuele Castano reported that reading literary fiction improved performance on an emotional intelligence test that included recognition of facial expressions. It's possible that reading about richly realized fictional characters primes readers to be more attuned to clues about other people's emotions.

Part III

Puzzles and Problem-Solving

Your First Reaction Is Wrong

Jeff Zwelling, chief operating officer of ZipRecruiter, says this is his favorite interview question:

? A hammer and a nail cost $1.10, and the hammer costs one dollar more than the nail. How much does the nail cost?

You might want to say your answer aloud before reading on.

"Some candidates will instantly blurt out 10 cents," Zwelling says, "which is obviously wrong." Maybe it's not so obvious, for many interviewees give that answer. But the right response is five cents. The hammer is a dollar more ($1.05), and that adds up to $1.10.

This question isn't about math so much as impulsiveness. It reveals whether the candidate thinks before speaking. According to Zwelling, the question comes with a built-in hint. "Ten cents is too easy of an answer, and if it was that easy, I wouldn't be asking it."

Brainteasers are, by their nature, difficult. This means that when a quick and easy answer pops into your head, it's almost certainly wrong. You should doubt your first impulse. Doing so is an especially useful tactic in a job interview, where you're expected to narrate your thought process. You can begin by saying that the obvious answer is so-and-so, but obvious answers are usually not right in this sort of question. You then attempt to prove that obvious answer wrong. This is a good way to get acquainted with the problem and confirm that you understand it. With luck you'll see a more promising approach. Even if you don't, the interviewer should give you some partial credit just for appreciating that the problem might be subtler than it appears.

Try this Oxbridge question, now asked in interviews at Apple and other tech companies.

? You've got a cup of hot coffee and a small container of cold milk (just out of the refrigerator). You plan to drink the coffee in five minutes. When should you add the milk, to make the coffee the coolest in five minutes' time?

Someone in a hurry to cool coffee should be in a hurry to add the thing that's going to cool it, right? But apply the first-reaction-is-wrong rule, and it's probably the other way around. You should add the milk at the last possible moment.

The first-reaction rule can at best point you in the right direction. You're expected to explain *why* the milk should be delayed, and that takes a little knowledge. When Isaac Newton wasn't tackling gravity and motion, he studied cooling. *Newton's law of cooling* says that the rate of heat transfer is proportional to the temperature difference between an object and its surroundings.

A cup of hot coffee is surrounded by air and a countertop at room temperature. Because hot coffee is much warmer than its environment, its temperature will begin dropping quickly. This in turn will reduce the temperature difference, causing the rate of temperature decrease to diminish. The coffee will approach room temperature ever more slowly. It can take an hour to reach lukewarm.

When you put cold milk in hot coffee, it immediately reduces the coffee's temperature. It thereby reduces the temperature difference between the coffee and its environment, slowing the rate of cooling. This leads to the surprising conclusion that adding cold milk ASAP keeps the coffee warmer longer. Delaying the milk to the last moment results in the coolest beverage.

In 2007, Britain's *The Naked Scientists* podcast tried it out with hot tea and confirmed that the beverage was cooler after delaying the milk.

The phrasing of the interview question adds a further complication. The milk is "just out of the refrigerator." It will be cooler than its surroundings and will be getting warmer as the coffee is getting cooler. After five minutes the milk will be less cold than it was in the refrigerator. This will tend to counteract the effect just described.

But it doesn't make enough difference to change the conclusion. Hot coffee is going to be 100-plus Fahrenheit degrees warmer than room temperature. Refrigerated milk is only about 30 degrees cooler than room temperature. All else being equal, the coffee will cool much more quickly than the milk will warm. The modest change in the milk's temperature over five minutes won't make much of a difference.

? How would you tell whether this is aluminum or steel? [The interviewer is holding a silvery object.]

Are you thinking, *use a magnet*? Join the club. But for this question, asked of engineers at Apple, using a magnet is not a particularly good answer.

To see why, take a magnet from your stainless-steel refrigerator and try to stick it on your matching dishwasher or oven. It probably won't stick. Steel is an iron-carbon alloy of variable composition. Some steel is magnetic, and some isn't. The fronts of refrigerators are formulated to hold magnets because consumers demand a way to post notes and children's drawings. Otherwise, high-end stainless steel usually isn't magnetic. Neither is aluminum, so the magnet test is indecisive.

There are many ways of distinguishing steel from aluminum. A good response will name as many as possible. Density provides one sure test. Aluminum is much lighter than steel. It has a specific gravity of about 2.7, versus about 7.8 for steel. (These numbers compare the weight of the metal to that of an equal volume of water.) That means that a one-inch cube of steel is nearly three times heavier than a one-inch cube of aluminum.

It's possible to detect that difference by hefting it in your hand. Otherwise there are devices for measuring specific gravity. You don't need anything more than a good kitchen or postal scale, a cup, and a pan. Fill the cup to the brim with water and set it in the pan. Then slowly lower the metal object in the cup until it is fully immersed. Water will spill out of the cup, and the volume of this water will equal that of the metal. Take the cup out of the pan and weigh the overflow water. (You'll probably do that by weighing the pan with the overflow water in it, then pouring the water out and weighing the dry pan. The difference is the weight of the water.) Finally, fish the metal object out of the cup and weigh it alone.

Suppose the water is 24 grams and the metal object is 186 grams. Both have the same volume. That means the density of the metal must be 186/24, or 7.75 times that of water. That rules out aluminum and is well within the range expected of steel. This experiment won't be too accurate, but with a threefold difference, it doesn't have to be.

Neither magnets nor specific-gravity tests are used much in scrapyards, where nonmagnetic stainless steel commands higher prices than aluminum. Salvagers favor the grinding machine test. Put the unknown metal against a spinning grinding wheel. Steel throws sparks; aluminum doesn't.

A handy alternative is the key test. Take a house or car key and try to scratch the unknown metal. If it scratches easily, it's aluminum (which is as soft as silver and gold). If the metal doesn't scratch, it's steel.

It's not impossible to distinguish the two metals by appearance. Though a lot depends on the surface treatment, aluminum tends to be duller, and steel tends to be more silvery. Iron oxidizes as orange, flaky rust. Though most steel is relatively rustproof, a metal object with specks of orangish corrosion is likely to be iron or steel.

Aluminum oxidizes to a thin, hard surface layer of aluminum oxide. This is whitish and, unlike rust, almost impossible to chip off. A whitish bloom is reason to think a metal object is aluminum.

This question is a test of practical knowledge, but also the ability to brainstorm. Do you settle for the first answer that sounds reasonable, or can you be prolific with ideas? That's important because, in creating a new product or business, the first idea often has to be rejected or sidelined. Apple started making computers; they're now less than 10 percent of its business. Starbucks was founded as a chain of Seattle boutiques selling gourmet coffee beans and grinders. It became a global success only when its founders realized they could serve coffee ready to drink.

? What weighs more on the Moon than on Earth?

The Moon's surface gravity is about one-sixth that of the Earth's. That means that things weigh about one-sixth as much, and there really aren't any exceptions. The obvious answer is "nothing." Those who know physics may feel especially sure of this. But the interviewer wouldn't be asking the question unless he had some answer in mind. It's your job to think of it.

Take an object that weighs X on Earth. Its Moon weight will be about $X/6$. The only way $X/6$ can be greater than X is for X to be a negative number. We need something that has negative weight on Earth, something that falls up rather than down.

Like a helium balloon. That's the intended answer. Whether it's strictly correct is more a matter of semantics than physics. A physicist would say that a helium balloon *does* have a small weight, on both the Earth and the Moon, due to the mass of its helium and rubber and the pull of gravity. But helium is lighter than air, so on Earth a helium balloon displaces a weight of air greater than its own. This creates buoyancy, an upward force larger than the downward force of gravity.

The Moon has no air and no buoyancy. There a helium balloon would simply have weight, and it would fall at the same rate as anything else. You could measure the balloon's weight by setting it on a postage scale (which would have to be recalibrated for lunar gravity). Thus a helium balloon arguably has more weight on the Moon than the Earth.

Note that a rubber helium balloon would burst in the lunar vacuum. There are YouTube videos demonstrating that rubber balloons pop in a vacuum chamber. A Mylar balloon might stand a better chance.

? You are shown two identical envelopes. Both contain cash, and one envelope contains twice as much money as the other. You are given one envelope and are allowed to keep however much money is in it. But you are offered the opportunity to switch envelopes. Would you switch or not? Why?

The commonsense answer is no, there's no point in switching. Your envelope has a 50 percent chance of being the better one. Switching won't change that. But because that seems so obvious, you ought to expect a trap.

Known as the "two envelopes problem," this puzzle has its origins in one described by Belgian mathematician Maurice Kraitchik in 1943. In Kraitchik's original telling, two men are given neckties as presents. They argue over whose tie is more expensive and agree to settle the matter with a wager. They will find out how much the ties cost, and the man with the cheaper tie will win the other man's more expensive tie.

Each man can reason that he stands to lose the tie he's got, but he stands to gain a tie that's more expensive. This makes the wager look favorable—but a bet can't be favorable to both sides!

The version with money in envelopes became popular in the 1980s. Since then the problem has sparked decades of controversy in mathematical and philosophical journals. It is asking a lot of a job applicant to give a definitive answer to a question that perplexes scholars.

Let's start with the case for switching. Call the envelope you've got A and the amount it contains $A.

The other envelope, B, has either half $A or twice $A. Each is equally likely. By switching, I stand a 50 percent chance of ending up with $A/2 and an equal chance of getting $2A. That comes to

$$1/2 \times \$A/2 + 1/2 \times \$2A =$$
$$\$A/4 + \$A =$$
$$\$1.25A$$

I expect to do 25 percent better by switching.

Most find this conclusion suspect. Here's another way of looking at it. For the sake of concreteness, say that one envelope has $100 and the other has $200. I don't know which amount is in my envelope, A.

Should I have the $100, then by switching I'd be trading up to $200, for a gain of $100. Should I have the $200, switching would mean trading down to $100, a loss of $100. I stand a 50-50 chance of gaining or losing $100. It's a wash. There is no point in switching. This is easier to accept.

What went wrong with the argument saying I'd gain 25 percent on average? I called the amount in my envelope A and decided that I either lose $A/2$ or gain A. But these two outcomes are not independent of the value of A. They are *determined* by the value of A.

As a switcher, I lose $A/2$ if and only if A is the larger amount. I gain A if and only if A is the smaller amount.

When I say $A/2$, what I really mean is "half of the larger amount (whichever envelope it's in)," that is, $100. When I say A I mean "the smaller amount," which is also $100. I stand to lose or gain the same amount.

The trouble with the above case for switching is that the mind freely reinterprets Xs and Ys according to context. Here the A describing my loss does not refer to the same quantity as the A describing my gain. Algebra doesn't work unless the same letters refer to the same quantities.

In short, there is no point in switching.

Most interviewers will be satisfied with this explanation. But scholars have pointed out that there is a legitimate case for switching. Like paradoxes big and small, this one hinges on what is left unsaid.

"One envelope contains twice as much money as the other." We need to know who decided which envelope and how. It makes a difference.

Here's one interpretation: A "banker" first decides how much she's willing to commit to this odd little game. Say it's $300. Then $100 goes in one envelope and $200 in the other. A coin toss decides which envelope is labeled A and handed to the player. All this occurs backstage, before the game begins.

In this setup there is a fixed sum of cash in play. The coin toss does not change that. Should the player switch, he is equally likely to trade up as trade down. In either case the gain or loss will equal the difference between the two envelope amounts ($100 in this example). This leads to the conclusion that switching is pointless.

But here's another interpretation that is equally consistent with the problem as described. Backstage, the banker first decides how much to put in Envelope A, the one that will be handed to the player. *Then* she tosses a coin. If it's heads, she puts double the A amount in Envelope B. If tails, she puts half the A amount in B.

To the audience, this game looks identical to the previous one. Two envelopes, same explanation, same choice. The (subtle) difference is that the coin toss has determined how much money is in the other envelope, B. The player holds A, the envelope whose contents were chosen before the coin toss. With this understanding, the switching logic is flawless. You risk losing half of whatever you've got but stand to gain as much as you've got. You really can expect to gain 25 percent by switching.

It follows that the problem is ambiguous as stated. It's possible to imagine situations in which switching makes sense, and others in which it doesn't.

This question has become popular with interviewers because it resonates. Every business is a portfolio of bets on an uncertain future: product launches, new markets, IPOs, mergers. A new venture may have a good chance of succeeding (in which case the sky's the limit) and also a good chance of failing (but you can't lose more than what you've got). It's easy to jump to the conclusion that the venture is worth pursuing. But the ruinations of many products and companies suggest otherwise. It's not that companies shouldn't attempt daring things. It's just that they need to be aware that they can't see all the backstage machinations of the market and the world. When faced with ambiguity, we tend to favor the reading we want—the one that makes an appealing venture look more attractive than it is.

Pay Attention to Unexpected Words

It's not the easiest thing in the world to invent a logic puzzle. Popular ones are told and retold, becoming streamlined in the process. As with a riddle, every word counts. You should therefore pay attention to odd, unexpected, or "unnecessary" details. It's safe to assume the unexpected details are crucial and that they offer a hint. Here's a question that's been asked at Apple.

? You're blindfolded and wearing rubber gloves. In front of you is a table with a hundred coins on it. Ninety of the coins are heads, and 10 are tails. You can't see or feel which is which. How would you split the coins into two groups, so that there are the same number of heads in each?

You might expect that the goal is to sort the heads from the tails. That would be no mean feat with the blindfold and rubber gloves, but no one expects an Apple question to be easy! However, that's *not* what this question asks. It sets forth an almost legalistic demand: "split the coins into two groups, such that they contain the same number of heads."

Let that sink in. There are 90 heads. The interviewer could say, "split the coins into two groups with 45 heads each." That would be clearer. That the interviewer didn't phrase it that way is significant. It probably means that the solution does not involve having 45 heads in each group.

As it turns out, that supposition is right. So how do you change the number of heads?

Well, you could remove a few coins from the table, or add a few coins from your pocket. But the question says to split *the* coins, strongly implying it's the hundred on the table. There's no mention of adding or subtracting coins, and it's hard to see how that would help.

There is one other way to change the number of heads. *It's to flip over some coins.* If a coin was heads, it will now be tails, and vice versa.

Say we divide the hundred coins into two groups. There are X coins in the first group and $100 - X$ in the second.

We know there are 90 heads in all, but we have no idea how many are in each group. Define another unknown, Y, as the number of heads in the first group. Then the second group must have $90 - Y$ heads (because there are 90 heads total). Got that?

We can also say that the first group, with X coins and Y heads, must have $X - Y$ tails.

Now use your rubber gloves to flip over all the coins in the first group. Instead of having $X - Y$ tails, this group will now have $X - Y$ heads.

We want to choose the unknowns X and Y so that the number of heads in the turned-over first group $(X - Y)$ equals the number of heads in the second group $(90 - Y)$.

$$X - Y = 90 - Y$$

That's possible only if $X = 90$. The solution is to split the hundred coins into groups of 90 and 10; then turn over the group of 90. The two groups will then have the same number of heads.

Try it out. Say there are 82 heads in the group of 90. That means there are 8 heads in the group of 10. Turn over the group of 90, producing 82 tails and 8 heads—the same number of heads as in the other group.

Notice that the smallest possible number of heads in the first group is 80. In that case all 10 of the other group would have to be heads, in order to make 90 in all.

When confronted with a puzzling question, you should think like an attorney examining a contract for loopholes. If a word or phrase isn't boilerplate, it's probably there for a reason. A useful trick in the interview is to repeat the question in your own words. This helps to confirm that you haven't left something out. Should you omit a crucial element, even the most flint-hearted interviewer ought to point that out—and maybe steer you in the right direction.

? Name three previous Nobel Prize winners.

The crucial word here is *previous*. Would it be too easy to ask for this year's winners? No, the Nobel laureates are not exactly household names...except when they are. The Nobel committee has been awarding prizes since 1901. Some of the past winners are very well known and not too hard to figure out.

Start by asking yourself, who was a famously smart person who ought to have won a Nobel Prize if anyone did? Are you thinking Albert Einstein? Bingo. He won (Physics, 1921).

There is a Peace Prize. Who are the most noble humanitarians of the past century? For Americans, the names Martin Luther King Jr., Nelson Mandela, Mother Teresa, and Mahatma Gandhi are likely to trip off the tongue. The first three won, and Gandhi almost did. He was assassinated in January 1948, and the Nobel committee declined to award a Peace Prize that year. The rules say recipients must be living.

There's a literature prize. Who are some famous literary authors of the 20th century? Many Americans will think of Ernest Hemingway, William Faulkner, and Toni Morrison. All three won.

There are fewer household-name winners in the sciences and economics. But don't forget James Watson and Francis Crick (who could supply two of the three needed names), Ivan Pavlov (guy with the dog), or Erwin Schrödinger (guy with the cat).

So, as an example, a correct answer to the question could be Einstein, Martin Luther King Jr., and Ernest Hemingway.

Want to celebrate women's achievement? Try Marie Curie, Mother Teresa, and Toni Morrison.

You could answer using only US presidents: Theodore Roosevelt, Woodrow Wilson, Jimmy Carter, and Barack Obama all won Peace Prizes.

Other well-known winners are Albert Camus, Winston Churchill (for literature, not peace), T. S. Eliot, Richard Feynman, Al Gore, Werner Heisenberg, Rudyard Kipling, Henry Kissinger, Doris Lessing, Thomas Mann, Guglielmo Marconi, Alice Munro, Eugene O'Neill, George Bernard Shaw, and W. B. Yeats.

? If you had $2,000, how would you double it in 24 hours?

There is a type of interview question in which you're told that Jeff Bezos (or whoever) is offering you money to start a new business. What would that business be? This is not that kind of question. The operative phrase is *in 24 hours*. As a grown-up, you're supposed to know that no business venture can be expected to double capital in 24 hours.

There is a trade-off between risk and return. A 100 percent gain in 24 hours is an insanely great rate of return, so it's going to come with insane risk. It's going to be a gamble.

You could, for instance, buy $2,000 worth of casino chips and place them on red in a high-stakes roulette game. It's double or nothing.

You could buy a futures contract expiring in 24 hours. (This allows you to bet on an uptick or downtick in interest rates, the S&P 500, or the Chinese renminbi—with outcomes not so different from the roulette example.)

Bottom line: There are many ways you *could* double your money in a day, but none of them make much sense. Someone in the habit of accepting that kind of risk would not be solvent for long.

? You work in midtown. Your parents live uptown, and your romantic partner lives downtown. After work you go to the subway station and get in the first train that arrives, whether uptown or downtown. You find that you end up at your parents' 90 percent of the time. But the schedules show that the uptown and downtown trains are equally frequent. How can that be?

The detail that stands out is the "equally frequent" schedules. Strike the "equally frequent" sentence, and there's nothing to explain. It could be that 90 percent of the trains are uptown trains (at that particular station at evening rush hour). Then, of course, you'd expect to travel uptown 90 percent of the time.

Another thing "equally frequent" tells us is that we are to place more faith in the schedule than riders of public transit are accustomed to doing.

One thing that's inescapably random is the moment you arrive at the train station. This is determined by all the minor delays of your day. You arrive at a random moment and wait until the first train pulls up. Finding 90 percent of trains to be uptown implies that, for 90 percent of random arrival moments, the next train is an uptown train. There is a simple explanation for that. It could be the uptown train always arrives a little before the downtown train does (and both run like clockwork).

Example: Each train runs every 10 minutes. The uptown train arrives on the 10s: 5:10, 5:20, 5:30, etc. The downtown train arrives on the 1s: 5:11, 5:21, 5:31. You are nine times more likely to arrive between 5:11 and 5:20 (in which case the next train is the 5:20 uptown) than between 5:10 and 5:11 (when the next train will be the 5:11 downtown).

This puzzle dates at least to the 1950s and was described by math popularizer Martin Gardner.

Use an Analogy

History doesn't repeat itself, but it rhymes. When confronted with an unfamiliar problem, you should ask yourself, *Is this like any problem I've confronted before?* It may not be the same problem, but it could be close enough to provide guidance.

? Would you rather fight one horse-sized duck or 100 duck-sized horses?

This internet meme has become a ubiquitous interview question. As early as 2003, Reddit users began submitting it to "Ask me anything" sessions. It was posed to President Barack Obama in a 2012 session, though White House staffers ignored (ducked?) the question. The BBC asked it of 2016 London mayoral candidates. In 2017, Senator Jeff Flake used it as a softball question at the Supreme Court confirmation hearing of Judge Neil Gorsuch. This provoked a demonstration at Flake's Phoenix, Ariz., office, complete with a protestor in a horse-sized-duck costume. You can find videos online of Bill Murray, Aaron Paul, Bruce Springsteen, and other celebrities weighing in on the issue.

There is, needless to say, no one right answer. The interviewer is looking to see how you justify your choice. It's safe to assume the horse-sized duck is a metaphor. It represents something else, and one analogy is to the workplace. Maybe you've worked in a fast-food place or at a retail counter. Some customers have small complaints; others have big ones. Many of these complaints are a complete waste of time, but every complainer must be dealt with. It's usually easier to deal with one customer with a big complaint than 100 customers with small ones (for everyone thinks their complaint is big). That's reason to choose the horse-sized duck—the one big problem—rather than 100 small problems.

It's possible to take this question more literally and use a completely different analogy. You may have heard the claim that the giant creatures of some science fiction films (Godzilla, giant insects, and their ilk) would collapse under their own weight. This is due to *change-of-scale effects* that are often discussed in high school science classes.

The weight of any creature is proportional to the cube of its linear dimensions. Its muscle and bone strength, however, are proportional to the square of those dimensions. Because of this, very small creatures, such as ants, can lift several times their own weight. But very large creatures struggle to support their weight against gravity. This effect limited the size of dinosaurs and explains why the largest whales can be bigger than dinosaurs: the water helps support the whale's weight.

Change of scale would similarly apply to horse-sized ducks (HSDs) and duck-sized horses (DSHs). A duck has two pencil legs supporting a Butterball-turkey body. That's all it needs, as a normal-sized duck. But those relatively thin legs would be inadequate for the 1,000-pound weight of a duck scaled up to horse size. A HSD would plop down and be unable to get up.

Nor would it be able to fly. There's a reason you don't see flying horses. Wing area is proportional to the square of length. Most flying creatures are small (insects). Even among birds, the largest ones don't fly.

The one thing a HSD might be able to do is swim. Scaled up proportionately, it would still float, and the water would do the heavy lifting. But a swimming HSD would still be woefully underpowered. The paddling area of its webbed feet scales up only as the square of linear dimensions, yet it would need to overcome the inertia of the HSD's cube-scaled mass. To sum up, a HSD isn't going to chase you on land, water, or air. Stay out of pecking range and you'll be fine.

But duck-sized horses would gain many advantages from their smaller size. Their legs would be able to support many times their weight, and they would be able to jump at you like grasshoppers. A pack of DSHs would be a holy terror.

Bill Murray went with a HSD, "figuring that the neck is mostly feathers. I'd act like I was trying to ride it, and then I'd strangle it from behind."

Interview riddles often work like essay questions—for a class where you didn't study the material. You are expected to draw connections, tell a story, and come to a conclusion, all without saying anything too obviously wrong or stupid.

"It is hard to have a good idea," George Pólya wrote, "if we have little knowledge of the subject, and impossible to have it if we have no knowledge. Good ideas are based on past experience and formerly acquired knowledge. Mere remembering is not enough for a good idea, but we cannot have any good idea without recollecting some pertinent facts; materials alone are not enough for constructing a house but we cannot construct a house without collecting the necessary materials."

? Why is a tennis ball fuzzy?

Watch out for questions that ask *why?* Why do golf balls have dimples? Why are footballs shaped like Stewie Griffin's head? Why does [familiar sporting good] have [a feature that's kind of weird when you think about]? Such riddles have become popular with interviewers. They are treacherous because there is no pat answer. With this question the thing to address is that tennis balls are not just fuzzy; they are *uniquely* fuzzy. Baseballs, soccer balls, billiard balls, and bowling balls are not fuzzy. Other racket sports, such as squash and racquetball, use fuzz-free rubber balls. Badminton uses shuttlecocks with real or plastic feathers (but no fuzz!). Why are tennis balls different?

Think of other fuzzy or fluffy things that move through the air: feathers, snow, dandelion and milkweed seeds, gossamer. They move slowly due to air resistance.

Imagine two identical rubber balls. Glue faux fur to the surface of one. Which is going to move through the air faster? Which is going to bounce better?

Obviously, it's the one without the fur. The fur would present more resistance to the air, slowing the ball, and it would cushion the rubber on impact, diminishing the bounce. Both effects apply (to a lesser degree) with tennis-ball fuzz. This is well known to serious players. Given a choice of balls, pros look for those with flattened felt. They will rebound more.

Tennis balls weren't always fuzzy. The earliest examples, going back to the 1400s, were leather, and the game was played on a lawn. In the 1700s, cloth balls (enclosing wool and a cork core) became popular. Not until 1870 was rubber used. Cheap, durable, and uniform, rubber balls quickly supplanted the traditional kinds.

But rubber is much bouncier than the balls it replaced. Along with clay courts, rubber balls produced a faster game, making it harder for players to react and increasing the risk of injury. All else being equal, more bounce creates a need for larger courts. But most tennis courts are located in affluent suburbs, where real estate is costly.

The fuzz is a way of dialing back the bounce. Not just balls but racquets, courts, rules, and players have coevolved over time. All are related. You can't change one thing about the game without affecting other things. Adding fuzz to rubber balls helped keep tennis interesting and playable.

Fuzz has other effects too. By increasing friction with the air, fuzz renders spin more important. A skillful player can apply spin that causes balls to curve while in flight. This adds a further level of strategizing and is now an essential part of the game.

Here I've thrown in some tennis history and trivia that most job seekers won't know. If you know this stuff, great; if not, maybe you can relate tennis-ball fuzz to something you do know. An engineer could go further into the weeds of fuzz aerodynamics. But the interviewer is looking for the big picture.

? If there were a machine that produced $100 a year for life, what would you be willing to pay for it today?

Money now is better than money later. This is a fact of business life, and some employers want to make sure their job candidates have a working understanding of the concept. In financial terms, the money machine is an *annuity*—a stream of income for life (or some other specified period). This analogy is crucial to answering the question, for there are ways to calculate the value of an annuity. There's even a way to calculate it in your head.

Buying the money machine, or any annuity, is a gamble. As income for life, it inherits the uncertainties of our mortal existence. In setting a fair price, age and life expectancy ought to matter. The machine is worth more to a millennial than to a boomer. Say you're 30 and figure you have a life expectancy of 50 years. Then you could expect to receive about $5,000 in all.

That doesn't mean you should be willing to fork over $5,000, though. Actuaries express the worth of an annuity as a *present value.* This is the lump sum, payable right now, that is equivalent in theory to a future income stream.

Lottery jackpots are one example (and another pertinent analogy). The winner of a $100 million jackpot never gets a check for $100 million. Instead he's offered the choice of an immediate lump sum, which is always much less than the jackpot, or a series of payments over many years that will add up to $100 million. The lottery board wants to avoid a big up-front payout by encouraging the winner to take the series of payments.

To calculate a present value, you need a *discount rate.* This is like an interest rate, expressing the time value of money for a person or business. For a business, the discount rate might be the interest rate a company is paying on its debts or the return it expects to make from other ventures. For an individual, the discount rate might be the anticipated return on investments. But if you really need or want the money now, your personal discount rate might be higher than any realistic investment return.

Let's say you can save extra cash in a mutual fund believed to offer a 5 percent average return. Then getting $100 right now is better than getting it a year from now, if only because you could invest the $100 and expect to have about $105 in a year's time.

In fact, if you have a bit more than $95 now, you could invest it at 5 percent and have $100 in a year's time. For that reason, $95 could be considered the present value of a $100 payment a year from now.

Every spreadsheet has a present value (PV) function. You plug in some information, and it computes the present value for you. For someone who collects the first $100 immediately, expects 50 payments in all, and has a 5 percent discount rate, the present value of the money machine is $1,926. That, rather than $5,000, might be a reasonable price.

You probably won't be allowed to use a spreadsheet in the

interview. There is a shortcut well suited to mental math. The present value of a long-term annuity roughly equals the annual payment divided by the discount rate. In this case you'd have

$$\text{Present value} =$$
$$\text{payment/discount rate} =$$
$$\$100/5\% = \$100 \times 20 = \$2{,}000$$

This shortcut formula applies to a perpetuity—a type of annuity intended to pay out forever. But most of a long-term annuity's present value comes from the first couple of decades of payments. The shortcut formula is therefore a decent approximation when there are many expected payments, as with a young person who expects to collect for many years. For a lifetime annuity, the actual value is always less than this formula's value (in this case, $1,926 rather than $2,000).

Products, research programs, and acquisitions have an up-front cost. If the innovator is lucky, they become a cash cow. A good answer to this question will show you're aware of the trade-offs and can evaluate them, or at least speak the language of those who do. A point to make is that present values of "money machines" are highly sensitive to the choice of discount rate. This gauges expectations and desires about the future. Discount rates are one of the great imponderables of finance and deserve careful attention when evaluating a business proposition.

? There's a long line for a blockbuster movie. The theater announces that the first person in line whose birthday matches that of someone ahead of them in line gets a free ticket. You don't know the birthdays of any of the people in line and can't put your twin in front of you. But you can choose any particular position in line. What position gives you the greatest chance of winning the free ticket?

This question may remind you of the *birthday problem*. In this math-class exercise, students announce their birthdays in turn until two discover they have the same birthday. The point is to show that shared birthdays are a lot more common than most imagine. The chance of at least one match in a classroom of 23 students is just over 50 percent. For a group of 50, a match is 97 percent certain.

The birthday problem is an important analogy here. But the interviewer is not asking about the birthday problem per se. She's asking, what position in line offers the best chance of winning the ticket?

You don't want to be first in line, for there's no one in front of you to match. The chance of person #1 winning the free ticket is zero.

Person #2 has only a sliver of a chance. He would have to share his birthday with person #1. The chance of that is about 1/365.

("About"? Should you press the issue, the interviewer will confirm that you don't have to bother with leap-year days, nor with the fact that births are more common at certain times of year.)

The chance of winning a free ticket increases with numerical place in line. But at some point, the chance must hit a maximum and decrease. The last position at which you could possibly win is #366. There would be 365 people ahead of you. It's *barely* possible that they could all have different birthdays. Then your birthday would have to match someone else's (again, ignoring leap years).

There is a trade-off. You want to be far enough back that you have a decent number of people in front of you (who might match your birthday), yet not so far back that the first match will likely be between two people in front of you.

Unless you're a calculating prodigy, you're not going to get the exact answer in your head. But anyone who remembers the birthday problem from school can give an approximate answer. Given that the chance of a match is 50-50 with a smallish classroom's worth of people (about 23), you don't want to be too far from position #23. But the trade-off isn't symmetrical. It's better to be a little ahead of #23 than a little behind it.

Here's why. Once a match happens to two people in front of you, it's game over. You lost. But there's no immediate penalty if you fail to match anyone ahead of you. You still have a chance, as good as anyone's, of matching someone behind you. So, you want to be a few places ahead of position #23 — maybe around #20.

Should the interviewer let you use a computer, you can create a spreadsheet to get the exact answer. Make four columns. The first is your position in line, n. The second is the probability of no birthday match among the first n people. Third is the chance of at least one match in the first n people. Finally, the fourth column is the chance that person #n is part of the first match. Schematically it would look like this:

Position in line, n	Chance of no match in the first n people	Chance of at least one match in the first n people	Chance that person n is part of the first match
1	100%	1 minus the cell to the left (= 0%)	0%
2	364/365 times the cell above (= 99.73%)	1 minus the cell to the left (= 0.27%)	Cell to the left minus the cell above it (= 0.27%)
3	363/365 times the cell above (= 99.18%)	1 minus the cell to the left (= 0.82%)	Cell to the left minus the cell above it (= 0.55%)
...			
n	$(365 - (n-1))$ /365 times the cell above	1 minus the cell to the left	Cell to the left minus the cell above it

Inspecting the third column of the full spreadsheet, you would find that the chance of at least one match first exceeds 50 percent when there are 23 people (it's then 50.73 percent). This is the answer to the classic birthday problem.

But to answer the interview question, we use the fourth column (as shown in the chart). The curve peaks at position #20. At that point the chance of winning the free ticket is about 3.23 percent.

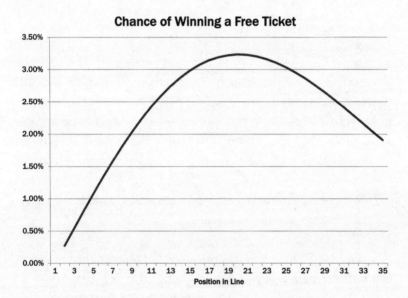

Chance of Winning a Free Ticket

Break the Problem into Parts

A near-universal problem-solving strategy is to break a difficult problem into smaller, easier-to-solve parts. This strategy is used in grade-school arithmetic and was encoded into early attempts at artificial intelligence. It's something everyone tackling a big project does, either instinctively or with project-management software.

? Imagine you're turned into a mouse and trapped in a water bottle. How would you escape?

Asked at Goldman Sachs, this question plunges the applicant into an alternate reality without giving many details. You're a rodent in a bad situation—so how do you break *that* into parts?

This problem stumps people because of its unknowns. One is *whether the bottle has a cap on it.* A grown mouse can wriggle through a pencil-diameter hole. But it can't open a tightly sealed water bottle from the inside, and it can't survive long without air.

Most likely a human will have to uncap the bottle. As a sentient mouse, your greatest asset may be the alarm that humans feel at seeing a rodent in one of their precious beverage containers. Therefore, another significant unknown is *whether the water bottle is transparent.*

It's legitimate to ask the interviewer about both points. But even without further guidance, these two binary unknowns create a two-by-two grid of four possibilities. You'll probably find it easier to devise a strategy for each contingency than for the original, underspecified problem.

	Bottle is transparent	Bottle is opaque
Bottle has no cap	"Eek!" says rodent-hating human. The human will see you and toss the bottle away or hold it at arm's length while trying to find a suitable place to dispose of it. The bottle is open, so you make your exit.	Stupid human doesn't know you're in the bottle until you're in its mouth. The human will not want to eat you; they will spit you out, way too dramatically. You scurry to safety.
Bottle is capped	This is dicey. The human may throw away the capped bottle with you in it. No good. Should you find yourself in a capped transparent bottle, it's best to hide from human eyes. You may be able to make yourself inconspicuous by nestling under a label or logo. Otherwise, try to look adorable, pawing the bottle to inspire pity. Maybe you'll luck out with an animal lover who will set you free.	Thirsty human will uncap the bottle and then…(see the no-cap case above)

A clever mouse can expect to escape in three of the four cases here — and has a shot at it even in the fourth.

*   *   *

Breaking a problem into parts is particularly useful with interview questions asking for weird estimates. How many cars have a flat tire on the Fourth of July? How many yoga instructors are named "Arlene"? How many Snickers candy bars are there in the world? Questions like these were popularized by Enrico Fermi (1901–1954), the Nobel laureate physicist. Fermi demanded that his University of Chicago physics students estimate quantities like the number of piano tuners in Chicago.

Today we can look up needed statistics in seconds. Yet Fermi-style questions remain as popular as ever in hiring. Interviewers invariably say they are more interested in the applicant's thought process than in the final number. This thought process generally involves breaking the problem into parts. You should express the unknown in terms of quantities that are known, can be looked up, or sound like they could be looked up.

? I see you're from Denver. How many pennies are in Denver?

A good reply is to confidently announce that

The number of pennies in Denver =
The population of Denver ×
The average number of pennies per capita

The Census Bureau tracks the population of Denver, and it's easy to google. If you're really from Denver, you should know the city's approximate population, anyway. You should also have a vague notion of how many pennies are in your change jar, under your couch cushions, or in your car. The equation expresses the required unknown in terms of two easier-to-evaluate quantities.

This isn't the only possible way of breaking down the problem. You might say:

The number of pennies in Denver =
The number of coins in Denver ×
The percentage of coins that are pennies

This isn't wrong. It just doesn't get us any closer to the goalpost. The number of coins in Denver is as much an imponderable as the number of pennies. The first formulation is better.

With a question like this, the interviewer probably won't let you google Denver's population. An answer to a Fermi estimation is expected to be a verbal performance, with any needed math done extemporaneously. The first rule of mental math is to use round numbers. Census figures are inconveniently precise. The population of any metropolitan area is usually several times that of the population within city limits. This supplies scope for adopting a round figure. For a midsize city like Denver, a population of one million is a safe guess. (The 2010 Census put Denver's population at 600,158. The metropolitan area is about three million. So yes, one million is a defensible number for "the population of Denver.")

How many pennies does the average Denver resident have? You're from Denver, and the interviewer probably isn't. Whatever you say carries a certain authority. And this estimate will also be fuzzy enough to justify a round figure. Pennies are in home change jars, at banks, in cash registers, and in the Denver Mint. A reasonable estimate might be an average of 500 pennies per Denver resident.

Taking one million as the Denver population and 500 as the average number of pennies, multiply to get 500 million as the number of pennies in Denver.

Almost any interviewer would give you an A for that. Whether this estimate is accurate is another matter (and beside the point for getting a job offer). My online search revealed that even the US Mint has only a vague idea of how many pennies there are, anywhere. The Mint knows how many pennies it produces (some 13 billion a year), and it melts down old, damaged coins that pass through the banking system, but most of the pennies produced are simply never seen again. Pennies get tossed into drawers, forgotten, and not circulated for a long, long time. The number of pennies in active circulation is estimated at 130 billion. With 325 million Americans, this would be 400 per person. But a large proportion of the coins are AWOL. (Indeed, sanitation officials complain of people throwing pennies in the trash.)

Bottom line: Not even the director of the Denver Mint knows how many pennies are in Denver. Talk a good game, and no interviewer can say you're wrong.

? How many people could you fit in Texas?

Does the interviewer envision packing people in, like a crowded stadium...or stacked on top of each other, like a Dubai skyscraper...or what? You should ask. But no matter what the interviewer says, within reason, you'll find that you could easily fit everyone in the world in Texas.

The answer can be expressed as the product of two quantities:

area of Texas × packing density

These quantities should be measured in compatible units. If the area of Texas is in square miles, the packing density should be the number of people per square mile.

The nation's coast-to-coast width is something like 2,500 miles. Picture a map of the US; how does the width of Texas compare with that of the Lower 48? From El Paso to the Louisiana border, the state is maybe a quarter as wide as the distance from San Francisco to the East Coast. That would put Texas's width at around 600 miles.

Texas is about as tall as it is wide. Draw a bounding square around Texas, 600 miles on a side. The area of the square is 600 × 600 miles, or 360,000 square miles. But Texas has an irregular shape, so let's say it occupies about half the area of the bounding square. That would be 180,000 square miles. We might as well make it easy and call that 200,000 square miles.

Next we need to know how many people we could fit in a square mile. Let's take an extreme case of people standing shoulder to shoulder on a flat plain, all facing the same direction. You could fit an average-sized person into a two-by-one-foot rectangle. (That's two feet for the shoulder-to-shoulder distance by one foot.)

A mile is 5,280 feet. A square mile has room for over 5,000 rows, over 2,500 abreast, which comes to more than 12.5 million people. Call that 15 million.

Multiply by your estimate of Texas's area — 200,000 square miles — to get 3,000 billion, or three trillion. That's far more than the world population, now closing in on eight billion. There would be plenty of room to fit everyone in the world in Texas. In fact, this could be achieved at roughly New York City density.

Exact figure: Texas has a land area of 268,597 square miles.

? How many times would you have to scoop the ocean with a bucket to cause sea level to drop one foot?

This question can illustrate three tricks for answering estimation questions. One is to use any imprecision in the wording as license to pick a round number. The interviewer hasn't said how big the bucket is, so I'm going to say it's one cubic foot. (Metric units make the conversions easier, but I'll use English units to show it can be done.)

Now we need to know the area of the ocean, in square feet. This number will be the question's answer. That's because the volume that must be bailed is the ocean's area (in square feet) times the sea-level drop (one foot). That product will be X cubic feet, and since our bucket is one cubic foot, it will be necessary to scoop X times.

You're not expected to know the area of the oceans. You might know roughly how big the Earth is (something less than 8,000 miles in diameter); how much of its surface is ocean (about 70 percent); and the formula for calculating the surface area of a sphere (it's $4\pi r^2$).

Here's another trick. In doing an extended mental calculation, there will be a series of roundings. You don't want to always round each term up, for that would result in a product that is too large. Nor do you want to always round down, resulting in a too-small answer. A good trick is to remember whether a quantity was rounded up or down, and round the opposite way for the next multiplication. This is easier than it sounds and will become quite natural.

Say we're figuring the area of the Earth. It's 4 times pi (3+), times the planet's radius squared. The first two terms come to 12 and change. We'll want to round that down to an even 10. (Just *remember* that it's been rounded down.)

The Earth's radius is half its approximately 8,000-mile diameter, or about 4,000 miles. Square that for 16 million square miles. Multiply by 4 times pi, and we've got 16 million times 10, or 160 million. But wait, that 10 was really 12-plus, so the product is going to be bigger. That's cause to round 160 million up to 200 million square miles.

Seventy percent of that is ocean, so the oceans cover about 140 million square miles.

The next step is to convert square miles to square feet. A mile is 5,280 feet. Round that down to 5,000. A square mile is about 5,000 × 5,000 square feet (really more, especially now that it's squared). That's 5 × 5 = 25 times 1,000 × 1,000 (1 million), or 25 million. Since we rounded down and squared, we have good cause to round up to 30 million.

Now multiply 140 million by 30 million. The way I'd do it

while narrating is to cut the 140 in half and double the 30, to get 70 times 60, or 4,200 (times a million million). That's 4,200 trillion square feet, or 4.2 quadrillion.

The final step is to multiply that by 1 foot to get 4.2 quadrillion cubic feet, aka buckets.

A third trick is to not overstate the number of significant figures. It would be odd to claim that millennials account for 24.663 percent of the population. That's because *millennial* is an informal term that different people define in different ways. A statistic like "24.663 percent" implies a precision that doesn't exist. In general it is misleading, even dishonest, to report too many significant figures. For the mental estimates of an oddball question, one significant figure is usually all that can be justified (and even that might be pushing it). In this case, I'd probably round down the 4.2 and say it takes about 4 quadrillion scoops to lower the ocean a foot.

For the record, recent scientific estimates put the world's ocean area at about 361 million square kilometers. That's 139 million square miles (our estimate was very close), translating into 3.88 quadrillion square feet and a similar number of cubic feet to be bailed. The 4 quadrillion figure is admirably close, all things considered.

The wild card with this question is buckets. They come in various sizes. In the US, a five-gallon capacity is common for storage and mixing paint. That holds only 0.668 cubic feet, whereas our initial estimate envisioned a bucket that could hold an entire cubic foot. So with a five-gallon bucket, the answer would be half again bigger.

? How much does the Empire State Building weigh?

The Empire State Building is the edifice that launched a thousand Fermi questions. How many staplers are in the Empire State Building? How many Ping-Pong balls could you fit in the Empire State Building? How many people in the Empire State Building had avocado toast for lunch?

This question, asked by Apple interviewers, is one of the hardest of the lot. It can throw even those skilled at this type of question. A 20th-century skyscraper's mass resides in steel girders, concrete, plate glass, marble floors, elevators, drywall, plumbing, electrical wiring, sinks, toilets, and heating and air-conditioning units. All have different densities, and much of the construction fabric is invisible to the occupant. It's out of sight and out of mind.

Despite that, the break-into-parts technique works well with this question. You may want to use a whiteboard, though. The first thing to write is

weight = volume × density

You surely don't know the volume or density of the Empire State Building any more than you do its weight. But volume is easier to calculate, and it's not hard to set some limits on density.

A well-informed person knows that the Empire State Building (ESB) has about 100 stories (it's actually 102). The stories of a typical skyscraper are about 14 feet high, measured floor to floor (another useful statistic to know for Fermi estimates). Let's say the ESB is about 1,400 feet tall.

Were it a simple box, the volume would be the height times the area of the base. But since the ESB tapers to a point, we'll have to make allowance for that. Start by figuring the area of the base. The building occupies a full city block, and the block is distinctly rectangular because that's the way the Manhattan street grid was drawn. How long is a city block? New Yorkers will be aware of the size of Midtown's "short blocks" (about 20 to a mile) and "long blocks" (about 7 to a mile). But maybe you've never been to New York. You may have heard the rule of thumb that there are 16 city blocks to a mile. (Or not. In the latter case you'd have to make a wild guess, but it's probably going to be in that neighborhood.)

A mile is 5,280 feet. Divide that by 16 blocks. More mental

math: to make things easier, we can round down both the numerator and the denominator. 5,280/16 is roughly 5,000/15, which is 10,000/30 = 1,000/3 or about 333, and we round that down to 300. The block area (for a square block) would be 300 × 300 = 90,000 square feet. But since we rounded down, let's now round that up to a nice even 100,000 square feet.

That would count the sidewalk and adjacent streets, out to the center divider. The building's ground-floor area would in fact be somewhat smaller. And the ESB's higher floors are smaller than its ground floor. But if you conjure up a mental picture of the building, you'll see that it has a bullet-shaped profile without much taper throughout most of its height. You might say that the average floor is about half the area of a 100,000-square-foot block, or 50,000 square feet.

The volume of the ESB is then about 1,400 times 50,000 — or 700 times 100,000 — or 70 million cubic feet.

Now we need the building's density. Those who have visited the Empire State Building will remember art deco marble, hardwood, and gilding. These dense and expensive materials are veneers, only as thick as they need to be to look good. Obviously, most of the ESB's enclosed space is air and contributes almost nothing to the building's weight.

Densities can be expressed on a scale where the density of water is 1 (a specific gravity). For most woods and drywall, the density is a little less than 1. That's because wood is lighter than water and floats. Other common building supplies — concrete, brick, glass, marble, and aluminum (a stylish material when the ESB was built) — have densities between 2 and 3. That leaves steel, which is much denser at about 7.8. It's structural steel that made modern skyscrapers possible. But that's because steel beams can support many times their own weight. Steel constitutes relatively little of a skyscraper's volume.

Let's guess that the average density of the ESB's construction materials is 2. It can't be too different from that. That leaves the question of how much of the enclosed volume is empty space (air) and how much is construction fabric. A reasonable guess is that the building is 90 percent air and 10 percent construction materials by volume. Again, that may not be accurate, but it can't be wildly off.

Then the building's overall density would be about $0.1 \times 2 = 0.2$. That means the ESB weighs about 1/5 as much as a similar volume of water. Multiply 1/5 by our volume estimate of 70 million cubic feet to get that the ESB weighs about as much as 14 million cubic feet of water.

What does a cubic foot of water weigh? Good for you if you know it's 62.4 pounds. But the metric system is used throughout the world except in the US, Liberia, and Myanmar. Even in those outlier nations, STEM grads are more likely to know the metric system's density of water, because it's so easy. A liter of water weighs a kilogram.

A liter is a cubic decimeter, and a decimeter is very close to 4 inches. There are about 3 decimeters to a foot, and $3 \times 3 \times 3 = 27$ cubic decimeters (liters) to a cubic foot.

A cubic foot of water therefore weighs about 27 kilograms. This puts the mass of the ESB at

14 million $\times$ 27 kilograms

Another thing to remember is that a thousand kilograms is a metric ton, which is not too much different from the English ton. Dividing the first term by 1,000 and multiplying the second by the same factor, we have

14,000 $\times$ 27 tons

This is something less than $15,000 \times 30$, or 450,000 tons—let's say an even 400,000 tons. That's the answer.

According to the building's current owner, the Empire State Realty Trust, the ESB weighs 365,000 tons.

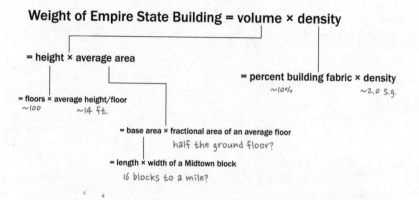

The diagram shows how the problem was broken into parts. Every unknown was expressed as a product of two other quantities. Keep doing that until you reach quantities that are known or easy to estimate.

In answering any estimation question, the goal is to make it look effortless. Fermi memorized scientific constants and population and economic data to aid in his displays of mental prowess. You can too. It's a good idea to know:

- the approximate population of the city, state, and nation where you're interviewing (for the US, it's 330 million)
- the world population (7.8 billion)
- the size of the Earth (a little less than 8,000 miles in diameter and 25,000 miles in circumference)
- unit conversions: a mile is 5,280 feet, a day is 24 × 60 × 60 seconds, a full circle's rotation is 360 degrees
- some financial data about the company where you're interviewing, such as number of employees, annual sales, stock price, and earnings per share

Draw a Picture

Interview rooms have a whiteboard. It's there for a reason.

? Every day at noon an eastbound ship leaves New York for Le Havre, France, and a westbound ship leaves Le Havre for New York. The trip takes exactly seven days. If you leave New York on an eastbound ship today, how many westbound ships will you meet during the journey?

Like many interview brainteasers, this one has a long history. It was devised by French mathematician Édouard Lucas (1842–1891), also known for the Tower of Hanoi. It stumped many of Lucas's colleagues.

Leaving New York and heading east, you are destined to meet the seven westbound ships then in the water. Hence the most popular wrong answer, seven. It's wrong because you must also meet the seven westbound ships that will depart from Le Havre in the course of your journey. That's 14 ships.

Drawing a diagram will help clarify the issue. It's a chart of arriving and departing ships. You start in New York at Day 0 and progress eastward (upward in the diagram) with time (to the right). Your journey is shown as the bold diagonal line. It crosses diagonal lines representing westbound ships. The dots represent crossings of your ship with a westbound ship. Though I've drawn just part of a complete, seven-day diagram, it's enough to see that you will meet two ships on the first day. One crossing will occur half a day out from harbor; that's when you will meet the westbound ship that is destined to arrive in New York a day after your ship departed. The other meeting will be a full day into your journey; it will be with the incoming ship that arrives two days after you left.

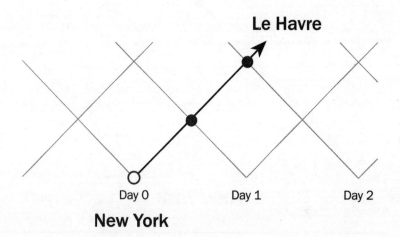

Le Havre

Day 0   Day 1   Day 2

New York

The pattern is that you meet two ships for every day you're at sea. Seven times two is 14, agreeing with the previous figure. In case you're wondering, see page 150 for what the whole diagram would look like. Obviously, you won't have time to draw a complete diagram in the interview.

Is 14 your final answer? The tricky part is dealing with the "edge cases," shown as hollow dots in the diagram. At the very instant you leave New York at noon on Day 0, a westbound ship pulls into harbor. Does that count as a meeting? Likewise, a westbound ship pulls out of Le Havre just as you pull in.

Le Havre

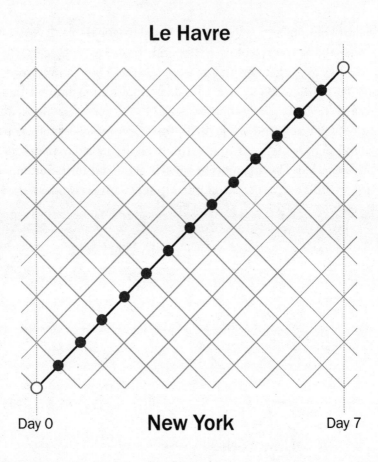

Day 0   **New York**   Day 7

The 14 answer counts one edge case but not the other. You might feel both cases ought to be treated the same way. This would lead to the answers 13 (counting neither edge case—only mid-ocean meetings) and 15 (counting both edge cases).

The question has an extra twist, and you can impress the interviewer by mentioning it. Le Havre is six hours ahead of New York. Though the question does not mention time zones, they make a difference.

We're told the ships leave both cities at noon. That would be local time, of course. The Le Havre–departing westbound ships actually have a six-hour head start on the New York–departing eastbound ships. If, as stated, the voyage takes exactly seven days, the westbound ships will arrive in New York six hours "early," at 6 a.m. local time.

Let's say it's 11:45 a.m. in New York. You've boarded a ship that's about to depart for Le Havre. Nearby is the ship that arrived from Le Havre early that morning and has been docked for almost six hours. Does that ship count as one you "meet during the journey"? I would say no. The ship was already there when you boarded your ship, and it has not moved since then.

Just before noon, the closest *moving* westbound ship is 18 hours out in the ocean. You will meet that ship in 9 hours (since it and your ship will be traveling toward each other at the same speed). Thereafter you will cross paths with another ship every 12 hours. Finally, your ship will pull into Le Havre six hours "late," at 6 p.m. That day's westbound ship left six hours earlier; you met it three hours out from Le Havre.

Allowing for time zones, there are no debatable cases in the harbors. All the meetings of moving ships occur well out from harbor, with both ships moving before, during, and after the encounter. There are 14 such meetings.

Taking this all into account, 14 is the best answer. It's the only one that applies when you allow for the time difference. Should you ignore time zones, the question is somewhat ambiguous. You can defend 13, 14, and 15 as valid answers.

It's possible to draw a picture for almost any problem, but not all pictures are helpful. Drawing a hundred duck-sized horses probably won't get you anywhere.

A picture is almost a given when a problem involves geometry ("a perfectly circular disk" — see below). But many of the most useful pictures are abstract. Lucas's problem is solved not by drawing ships but by making a schematic chart. When a problem involves changing quantities or multiple options, that's reason to consider a flow chart or decision tree.

? You're making a table from a perfectly circular disk. You attach three legs, each perpendicular to the disk, at random points on the disk's area. What is the chance the table will stand when you flip it over and put it on the floor?

A tripod is generally stable. The first thing to address is how a three-legged table could *not* be stable.

Picture the tabletop as a heavy marble disk, supported by perpendicular, toothpick-thin steel rods. One way the legs could fail to support the top is if they're in a straight line. Then the top would flip over on the axis defined by the line.

Another way the table could fail is if the legs are too off-center. Were the legs all near one edge of the top, it would fall over.

Draw a circle on the whiteboard. Add three random dots to represent attachment points for three legs. Try several different arrangements of dots to get a feel for it.

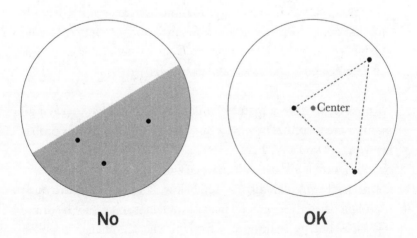

No   OK

Look at the diagram labeled *No.* This table would fall over. The three points of support are off center, in that they're in the same half-circle (shaded part). Half of the tabletop has no support at all. In fact, it's more than half, for the three points are each some distance within the shaded part.

In order to stand, the table needs support on all sides of its center. Look at the diagram labeled *OK.* It's not an optimal design, but it works. The tabletop can't pivot on any two points without most of its mass resisting. There is no half-circle that doesn't contain a leg.

Here's another way of describing that. Connect the three points with lines to make a triangle. As long as the center of the circle lies inside the triangle, the table will stand. Otherwise, the table will fall over.

This can be justified by physics as well as common sense. Objects act as if their mass were concentrated at a point, the center of gravity. For a uniform disk, the center of gravity is at the center of the circle (more exactly, in the midpoint of the disk's thickness, at the center of the circle). This center must be supported on all sides. The object will tip if all the support is to one side.

The next stage of the problem is to figure the probability that three points, each randomly chosen from the circle's area, will *not* be in the same half-circle (equivalently, will form a triangle enclosing the center).

Imagine picking the first point, anywhere in the circle. Is there any possible choice that would prevent the table from standing?

The answer is no, with a qualification. We don't want the first point to coincide with the table's center. That would mean that all three points would be in the same half-circle, barely. The tabletop would be on the verge of tipping over from the center pivot.

But the chance of a randomly chosen point coinciding with the exact center is infinitesimal. Essentially any random choice of Point 1 is going to be OK.

Step 2 is to select the second point. Again: Is there any choice that would prevent the table from standing?

As before, we would have a marginal case if the second point happened to be identical with the table's center. But now there's another issue. The table will not stand if the first point, second point, and table's center are all in a straight line. In that case any third point would define a half-circle containing all three points.

But once again, the chance of a random point coinciding with a center point or even being on a line running through that center point is effectively zero. Any random choice of first and second points is almost certainly going to be okay.

It's the third random point that determines whether the table will stand. This merits another diagram.

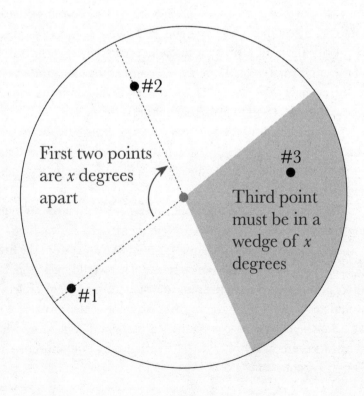

First two points are *x* degrees apart

#2

#3

Third point must be in a wedge of *x* degrees

#1

Point 3 must not fall in any half-circle that contains Points 1 and 2. We can describe the three points by their angular positions from one another, measured from the table's center. If there is an angle x between the first two points, then the third point must lie in a pie slice, also of angle x, in order for the table to stand.

When x is small—when Points 1 and 2 fit in a thin pie slice—then Point 3 is constrained to fit in an equally thin slice, opposite from it. When x is large—when Points 1 and 2 define a big pie slice—then Point 3 can be anywhere in a similarly generous slice.

Points 1 and 2 can be anywhere from 0 to 180 degrees apart. Given that all angles are equally likely for two randomly chosen points, we are justified in splitting the difference. On average, Points 1 and 2 are half the 180-degree maximum, or 90 degrees apart. This means that a stable Point 3 will typically have to fall within a 90-degree slice of the full 360 degrees. The chance of that is $90/360 = 1/4$. The table therefore has a 1 in 4 chance of standing.

This question, asked at Goldman Sachs and elsewhere, is a harder update to an old brainteaser specifying that the legs must be attached to the circumference of the tabletop. That qualification turns out to be unnecessary. Omitting it makes the problem more mystifying.

? You have your choice of three unmarked doors. Behind one is gold; behind another is nothing at all; and behind the remaining door is a secret passage to another set of three doors, with the same contents and rules. (But the contents are randomized, so you don't know what's behind any door.) What is the probability that you will find the gold?

A flow chart helps show what's going on. Represent the initial choice with three arrows. One points to gold, another to nothing, and the third to the secret passageway. Because the doors are unmarked, you have no way of knowing which is which. Each outcome is equally likely (a 1 in 3 chance).

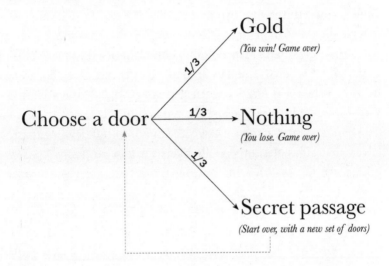

The first two outcomes, gold and nothing, are decisive. Pick either, and the game is over. Not so with the secret passage. Pick that, and you essentially start over. It's conceivable that you could choose the secret-passage door again and again, as in an endless video-game dungeon. That may seem hard to analyze, but look at it this way: The secret-passage door can only delay the inevitable. Sooner or later, you must pick a decisive door. Whenever that happens, the chances of choosing gold and nothing are equal. Therefore the chance of ending up with the gold is 50 percent.

You can bolster the visual argument with math. To do that, assign values to the doors. I'll say the gold door has a value of 1 (in bazillions of dollars). The nothing door, naturally, has a value of 0.

Call the probability of ending up with the gold, through any possible sequence of choices, P. Then the value of playing the game is P ($ bazillion). That must also be the value of the secret-passage door, for it's a reset equivalent to playing the game anew.

Reading off from the diagram, we can see that

$$P = (1/3 \times 1) + (1/3 \times 0) + (1/3 \times P)$$

Simplifying that,

$$P = 1/3 + 1/3 \times P$$
$$3P = 1 + P$$
$$2P = 1$$
$$P = 1/2$$

The math confirms that the player has a 50-50 chance of getting the gold.

Try a Simpler Version of the Problem

Estimation questions are often highly specific. *How many pizzas are ordered on St. Swithin's Day?* It's easy to panic about not knowing when St. Swithin's Day is.

You don't need to know! As a ninth-century AD English bishop-saint, Swithin has nothing to do with the consumption of pizza in the twenty-first century. The question is really no different from *How many pizzas are ordered on any given day?* That simpler question is easier to answer because you don't have to know when St. Swithin's Day is (July 15, in case you're wondering).

This introduces another important strategy: *Try a simpler version of the problem.* With luck, the simpler problem's solution may be identical to the original's. Otherwise the method used for the simpler problem may suggest how to tackle the original.

There are several ways to invent a simpler version of a problem. One is to eliminate a condition (such as "on St. Swithin's Day") to produce a more generalized problem (pizza on any random day). Another is to take one of the numbers in the problem and replace it with a smaller quantity. Here's an example.

? If I write down all the numbers from 1 to a million, how many times do I write the digit 2?

Try replacing the large number (a million) with a smaller one. Ask yourself: "If I write down all the numbers from 1 to 10, how many times do I write the digit 2?" It's obvious that 2 is the only number with a 2 in it. The answer is one.

Now scale up a little. "If I write down all the numbers from 1 to 100..." This is a little more complicated because most of the numbers have two digits. A 2 may appear in the 1s column or the 10s column.

Every 10th digit in the 1s column is a 2: 2, 12, 22, 32... up to 92 (that's ten 2s in all).

There are also ten 2s in the 10s column. This is due to the block of 10 consecutive numbers from 20 to 29. Notice that the number 22 gets double-counted, but that's as it should be; it contains two 2s.

The 100s column really doesn't matter. The only number that uses it is 100, and it doesn't have a 2.

That means there are 10 + 10 = 20 digit 2s between 1 and 100.

The pattern is coming into focus. Imagine writing all the numbers from 1 to 1,000,000, each underneath another, on a long scroll of paper. Include 0s for leading digits, giving every number exactly seven digits.

There are no 2s in the leftmost column. There can't be, because that column is all leading 0s, except for the 1 in 1,000,000. Since we're interested in 2s only, we can ignore the leftmost column. That leaves six columns that have 2s. It's easy to see that all ten digits are used equally in these columns. It's like running through the numbers on a combination lock. There are six columns with a million digits each, of which exactly 1/10 are the digit 2. The answer is $6 \times 1,000,000/10 = 600,000$.

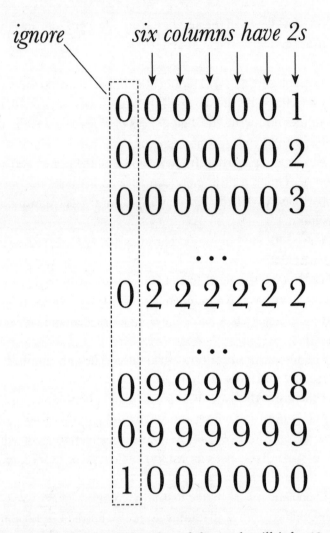

? Today is Tuesday. What day of the week will it be 10 years from now on this date? How confident are you of your answer?

Start with the simpler question, "What day of the week will it be a year from now on this date?" We know that birthdays, the Fourth of July, and Christmas usually advance one day of the week from year to year. This is because 365 cannot be evenly divided by 7. It's 52 whole weeks, plus a remainder of one day. That pushes this year's Tuesday birthday onto Wednesday next year.

Unless, of course, it's a leap year. Years divisible by 4 have an extra day, February 29. A leap year therefore has 366 days, with a remainder of 2. The day of the week jumps forward two days whenever a February 29 intervenes.

There are other adjustments that most people aren't aware of. A leap year is skipped in every year ending with *00*, except when the year divides evenly by 400. This will next be an issue in 2100, but it's unlikely you'll be interviewing for a job then.

So if today is Tuesday, this date will be Wednesday next year *unless* a February 29 intervenes—in which case it will be Thursday.

A given 10-year period may have either 2 or 3 leap years. This will advance the day of the week by 12 or 13 days. We can subtract 7 without changing the day of the week, so that's effectively 5 or 6 days ahead. If today is Tuesday, this date will be Sunday or Monday 10 years from now.

To decide which, we need to figure out when the next leap year is and also consider whether today is before or after February 29.

- If this year is a leap year and February 29 has yet to come, there will be 3 leap-year days in the coming 10-year period. That will add 3 extra days to the usual 10, making the answer Monday.
- If this is a leap year and it's after February 29, there will be 2 leap-year days in the coming 10-year period, for an increase of 2 extra days plus 10. The answer is then Sunday.

But we're not done yet. The current year may not be a leap year.

- If next year is a leap year, there will be 3 leap-year days in the coming 10 years. (The answer is Monday.)
- If 2 years from now is a leap year, then 10 years from now will also be a leap year. If the present date is March 1 or later, there will be 3 leap-year days in the next 10 year-period (so Monday is the answer).
- But if 2 years from now is a leap year and the present date is February 28 or earlier, we won't get to count the leap-year day in Year 10, so there are only two (Sunday).
- If 3 years from now is a leap year, there will be 2 leap-year days in the next decade (Sunday).
- There is one more edge case: You could be interviewing on Leap Year's Day. Then 10 years from now can't be another leap year, so there won't be a February 29. There is no "day of the week" for a date that doesn't exist!

Example: I'm interviewing on Tuesday, July 12, 2022. It's not a leap year. There will be 3 leap years in the coming 10 years (2024, 2028, and 2032). The 2032 leap year counts, as July 12 is after February 29. The leap years advance the day of the week 3 days on top of 10 years' worth of annual advances, for 13 days total. Subtract 7 to get a net advance of 6 days. In 10 years (2032), therefore, July 12 will be 6 days ahead of Tuesday, meaning a Monday.

Don't forget the second part of the question: *How confident are you of your answer?*

Research shows that people tend to be overconfident of their knowledge, skills, or accuracy. In a notorious example, a 1981 study found that 93 percent of drivers believed their driving skills to be better than average.

Predictive models are the lifeblood of the insurance, financial, and consulting industries. It is not just important for models to be accurate; it is necessary to know how accurate they are. All models fail, sometimes. Countless companies have gone under because some very smart people were too sure their predictions were right.

Even when you're as sure as sure can be, there is some non-zero chance you've made an error. In answering this question, you should acknowledge that. Having 99 percent confidence in a mental calculation—under the stress of a job interview, no less—would be impressive. Claiming 100 percent confidence would be unrealistic.

? You have two well-shuffled decks of cards. One is a regular deck of 52 cards. The other is a half-deck with just 26 cards (the hearts and spades only). You are to pick a deck and then draw two cards from it. If the cards are the same color (red or black), you win. Which deck would you choose?

Also: Suppose there were a third deck, consisting of 26 cards drawn randomly from a full deck. Which deck would you now choose?

Blackjack players know that decks are finite, and this has consequences. Drawing an ace depletes the supply of aces remaining in the deck. This decreases the chance of drawing another ace.

The same principle applies here. Suppose you draw a card from the regular deck. It's red. That leaves 25 red cards remaining in the deck (which now has 51 cards). The chance of drawing a second red card is 25/51. This is about 49 percent, less than the 50 percent that applied for the first card.

The half-deck of 26 cards is smaller and more affected by each card drawn. After selecting a first card, there will be only 12 cards of the same color in the remaining 25 cards. The chance of getting another card of the same color is 12/25, or 48 percent.

You should therefore prefer the full deck to the half-deck. It's not a huge difference, but there is one.

The follow-up question asks about a half-deck of 26 cards

drawn randomly from a full deck of 52. Because it's random, there is no guarantee of an even split of colors.

That's good. To see why, imagine a particularly simple case. Say all 26 random cards just happen to be red. Then you'd be sure to draw two reds and win.

The mix will surely not be so lopsided, but any imbalance works in your favor. If there are extra blacks, then you're more likely to get a black on the first draw and another black on the second. In fact, an even split of colors is the worst possible case for the color-matching game.

That means that the third deck is clearly preferable to the second deck. At worst the third deck has an even split, but probably it doesn't, and that increases your chance of winning.

The tricky part of the question is whether the third deck is also better than the first deck, with 52 cards. A slow, hard approach is to calculate the probabilities for the third deck. This can get involved, and it's easy to stumble. There's a much better way to look at it. *The third deck is essentially the top half of the first deck.* Remember, the first deck is "well-shuffled." There's no guarantee that its top half contains an equal representation of colors. So if you draw two cards off the top, there is no difference between drawing from the first deck or the third.

If that's still not clear, imagine an even simpler case: a "deck" of just two cards. These two cards were drawn randomly from a complete shuffled deck of 52. Now if you choose the first deck, you'll be drawing two random cards from it—and that's exactly how the two-card deck was created. The chances of winning must be equivalent.

The answer is that you should pick the first or third deck, which offer equal chances of winning, but avoid the second.

? Which is more stable, a four-legged chair or a five-legged chair?

Try asking yourself which is more stable, a two-legged chair or a three-legged chair? Two-legged chairs aren't really a thing. If you did build one, it would flop right over. But a three-legged chair or stool works. It's a tripod whose legs rest on three points without wobbling. This is true whether the floor is uneven or the three legs aren't exactly the same length (within reason). The tripod exemplifies simple-is-better design. By contrast, a four-legged chair can wobble on an uneven floor, and a five-legged chair has multiple ways to wobble.

So why aren't more chairs three-legged? Well, anyone who's spent much time sitting on a three-legged stool or chair knows it's easy to tip over.

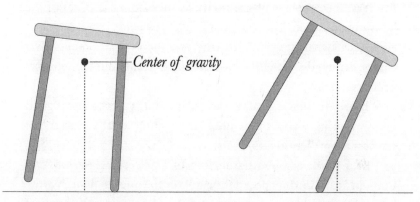

Will right itself   **Will tip over**

When you lean back in a chair, it balances on two adjacent legs. The points of contact of those two legs with the floor define a line. Once the chair's center of gravity moves over that line, the chair will tip over rather than right itself.

The diagram understates the point, for we should really consider the system of chair-plus-sitter. The sitter's weight and height raise the center of gravity, making the system even more top-heavy.

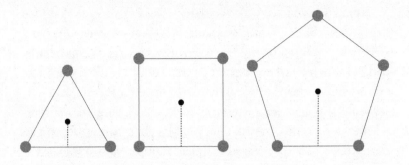

With a three-legged chair, the center of gravity is relatively close to the outside of the triangle defined by the legs. With four or five legs, the center is progressively farther from the edges of the bounding polygon. That means a five-legged chair is better able to right itself when tipped. This isn't just theoretical. Some swivel chairs are made with five casters rather than four, for greater stability.

There are then at least two kinds of stability. Fewer legs is good for preventing wobbling, while many symmetrically placed legs are best for preventing tip-overs.

Back to the wobbling issue. In a 1973 *Scientific American* column, Martin Gardner posed the riddle of the uneven floor. A four-legged table wobbles when placed on a slightly uneven floor. "If one does not mind the tabletop being on a slant," Gardner asked, "is it always possible to find a place where all four legs are firmly on the floor?" The answer is yes. Gardner supplied an intuitive proof that has since inspired a scholarly literature on the math of wobbling.

When a symmetrical four-legged table (or chair) wobbles, it flips between two quasi-stable positions. There are two diagonally opposite legs (call them A and C) that contact the uneven floor and act as a pivot. Push down on Leg B and it will touch the ground too, supporting the table on an A-B-C tripod. That leaves the remaining leg, D, in the air. Should you instead push down on D, that creates an A-D-C tripod and lifts B off the floor. This plays havoc with drinks at rustic cafés. Gardner showed that, by simply rotating a four-legged table about its center, it's possible to find a position at which all legs solidly contact the floor. A four-legged table can be as stable as a tripod.

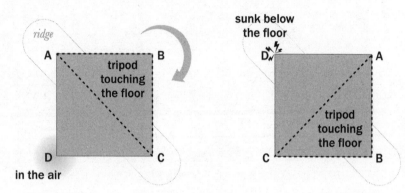

Gardner's proof stipulates that the four legs are in a square arrangement (the shape of the tabletop doesn't matter). It is easiest to visualize if you imagine the floor has a ridge or hump. Legs A and C sit on the crest of this ridge. Legs B and D are in "valleys" to either side of the ridge. Only one can touch the floor at the same time.

Now press down on Leg B so that it touches the floor and forms a tripod with A and C. This leaves the remaining leg, D, hanging in the air. Rotate the table 90 degrees about its center, *keeping legs A, B, and C in contact with the floor at all times.* Leg A will slide off the ridge into the upper-right valley (the position originally occupied by Leg B). Leg B, meantime, will move from its valley location up onto the ridge at lower right, while Leg C will slide from the ridge to the lower-left valley.

Leg D will end up on the ridge at upper left. But since its

diagonal opposite, B, is on the ridge, and the A-C pivot is at the lower elevation of the valleys, the tip of D will have to sink like the low side of a seesaw. It will plunge into the floor surface (you have to imagine the floor is made of soft clay). If the lower tip of D started out an inch above floor level, it will end up an inch below the surface. That's the only way to keep A, B, and C all just touching the floor in their new locations.

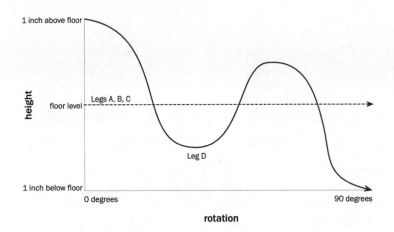

Now use the intermediate value theorem (page 13). We'll do the same thing we did with the puzzle about going up and down the mountain. Make a chart of distance above or below local floor level versus rotation. Legs A, B, and C remain at zero height throughout the rotation. Leg D starts an inch above the floor and ends up an inch below it. As long as the floor surface is continuous, the D line has to cross the A-B-C line in order to get from where it starts to where it ends. It may cross more than once if the floor's surface is more complicated than a simple ridge. At the point(s) of crossing, all four legs will be planted securely on the floor.

"The theorem is actually useful," Gardner wrote. "If you don't mind the table's surface being on a slight slant, you don't have to search for something to slip under a leg. Just rotate the table to a stable position. If you have to stand on a four-legged stool or chair to replace a light bulb and the floor is uneven, you can always rotate the stool or chair to make it even."

The result is probably more practical for tables than chairs. At outdoor cafés, the tables tend to be circular and can be rotated without inconvenience. Chairs, by contrast, are normally expected to point in a specific direction—toward the table, a desk, or a counter.

Should you have a rectangular table or chair rather than a square one, it may be necessary to rotate it as much as 180 degrees. But Gardner's proof *doesn't* work for five or more legs, no matter how they are arranged. It requires a single wobbling diagonal, and a five-legged table can have several of those.

To wrap up, a four-legged chair is more stable against wobbling than a five-legged one. Unlike the latter, it can be made to rest solidly on an uneven floor just by being rotated. But a symmetrically arranged five-legged chair is more stable against tipping over.

This question has been asked of engineers at SpaceX. It's worth adding that stability isn't everything. A squarish chair better fits the human body and architecture. Any cabinetmaker wanting to make a pentagonal seat would waste a lot of wood. Unlike squares or rectangles, pentagons cannot be cut out of sheets without wastage.

Ask Good Questions

A common corporate dysfunction occurs when employees complete their parts of a project in isolation and hand them "over the transom" to other employees with minimal communication. Too often the work has to be redone because someone had a misconceived notion of what was required. So it's smart to ask questions first.

A class of interview questions brings that to the fore. You're asked how you would perform a task or design a product. Unlike a logic puzzle, the question does not supply all the information you'll need to answer it. You're expected to fill in the blanks by posing questions of your own to the interviewer. The problem is interactive, and you'll be rated on the quality of your questions as well as the resulting answer.

? How would you solve problems if you were from Mars?

This has become a quintessential question at Amazon. As far as I can tell, it's relatively new and may have been inspired by the 2015 film *The Martian*. Matt Damon plays an astronaut stranded on Mars, who must solve a series of technical and human problems in order to get back to Earth. As asked at Amazon, this question is open to interpretation. The first thing to do is to disambiguate. Ask the interviewer if the question means,

(a) I'm an undiscovered Martian life-form consistent with current science. That would probably mean I'm an underground microbe and not going to do much problem-solving.

(b) I'm a Martian in the obsolete pop-culture sense: a fictitious intelligent extraterrestrial from the Red Planet.

(c) I'm a future human settler of Mars.

(d) I'm from Mars, Pennsylvania.

You'll be told (b) or (c), as they offer the richest field for answers. A no-less-significant ambiguity is what kind of problems you're to solve. Is the question asking:

(a) How do I, the Martian, solve problems in general?

(b) How would I, with my Martian perspective, solve the Earth's problems?

Here (b) is the more interesting case. It's appropriate for your answer to use any facts about Mars that might be relevant, but mainly you're expected to speak from the standpoint of a wise outsider. The question amounts to, *How would you solve the world's problems if you weren't encumbered by earthbound ways of thinking?*

There are a lot of ways to go with that. But you should keep your eye on the prize. The point is not what you'd do as a Martian; it's getting a job offer on planet Earth. For that there is a valuable cheat sheet: Amazon's mission statement. You should look it up on the company website before the first interview. Think mission statements are a bunch of homilies that no one reads? I hear you.

But Jeff Bezos at least read it and signed off on it. It's fair to assume that your interviewers have been drilled on the bullet points.

Amazon's job website lists a set of "Leadership Principles." I skimmed it, looking for statements that bear on Martian (?) problem-solving. Here are just a few that stood out:

> Leaders...think long-term and don't sacrifice long-term value for short-term results.
> Speed matters in business. Many decisions and actions are reversible and do not need extensive study. We value calculated risk taking.
> Accomplish more with less. Constraints breed resourcefulness, self-sufficiency, and invention.

This can be a template for your answer. And it's OK to say you're cribbing from Amazon's mission statement. The interviewer will be impressed that you took the trouble. You might say something along these lines:

"A year on Mars is almost two Earth years, so I'd take a longer-term perspective. One thing I see on Earth is that everyone is obsessed over next quarter. But solving big problems is a marathon, not a sprint, and most of the daily ups and downs are just noise. It's important not to get distracted—and to stay focused on the long-term goal.

"That doesn't mean time isn't precious. In trying to solve their problems, Earth people waste an incredible amount of time making even trivial decisions. I'd tell people about Fredkin's paradox: The more similar two options are, the harder it is to decide which is better—and the less it really matters. Martian problem-solving is dynamic. Be willing to take some risks, and also be willing to change quickly if and when the data changes.

"Mars is a small planet, so we value economy of means. The

best solutions are those that make the smartest use of what we've got. Maybe Earth could learn something from that too."

Wherever you're interviewing, look up the company's mission statement beforehand. It will often come in handy.

Interactive questions are often presented as exercises in design. One Microsoft question asks

? How would you make sure there is always milk in my refrigerator?

Don't take a whimsical premise as license to say anything. (The interviewer has heard, "I'd put a cow in the refrigerator!") As former Microsoft interviewer Joel Spolsky explains, "Smart candidates understand that design is a difficult series of trade-offs." A good answer will articulate those trade-offs. One place to begin is by asking what the goal of this milk-delivery system is.

- Is it so that customers never again have to go to the market for milk? OK, but then they *would* have to go to the market for cauliflower and granola and marinara sauce. There's not much point in focusing on milk when the real issue is the time spent on trips to the grocery store. There are plenty of online grocery-delivery services, and they're far more practical than something like a citywide system of refrigerated-milk pipelines.
- Is it so that customers never forget to buy milk? Then one solution is to have a scale built into a refrigerator shelf. Customers put the milk carton(s) on the scale. It measures the weight of milk, compares it with past consumption patterns, and reminds the customers when they need to buy milk.

- Is it so the customer never runs out of milk in an emergency? In that case, there's a low-tech solution: put a few cans of evaporated milk in the refrigerator. Or better yet, stock some ultra-high-temperature-treated (UHT) milk, which tastes much better and is sealed to last about six months unopened. It's cheap insurance against running out.

A popular answer to this question describes a "smart refrigerator." It would scan its contents, using machine learning to identify foods and read labels and UPC codes. The scanner might recognize a gallon container of low-fat, lactose-free milk, 37 percent full. It would inform the customer when milk is needed, or even place an order for home delivery. And it could do this for every regularly purchased food item.

A smart refrigerator would entail new hardware. There is a software-only solution that is nearly as good. The customer downloads an app and gives it permission to access charges on the credit card(s) used to buy groceries. The software analyzes patterns of consumption and uses them to send reminders. When GPS detects that the customer is at a market, the app texts a full shopping list. All of this would be free to consumers—and for an extra charge, groceries could be delivered.

In real life you're often dealing with a client or boss who hasn't thought a project through. The process of asking good questions may help you both discover what the goal is. ("People don't know what they want until you show it to them," as Steve Jobs said.) Your job is to work with the client to refine a conception that may be half-baked and even self-contradictory.

It's necessary to distinguish interactive questions from logic puzzles. A puzzle often seems to have insufficient information to permit an answer, but it actually doesn't (and it may be bad form to bug the interviewer for hints).

One clue is the word *how*. When a short question asks *how* you would do something complicated, that's a tip-off that you should be asking some questions of the interviewer.

More generally these questions involve optimization. You must find a design or plan that best serves human values. Your questions will often ask, *What is to be optimized*?

? How would you empty a plane full of Skittles?

Skittles are fruit-flavored candies that look like M&Ms and come in a hard candy shell. Were you to open the doors of a plane inexplicably packed with Skittles, the candy would pour out in a rainbow-colored torrent.

Interviewers who ask this question are interested in the ability to organize a big, labor-intensive project. A good response takes into account practical, economic, and even legal angles. One popular answer is to use cranes (or some gizmo) to tilt the plane back and forth, allowing the candy to pour out. Most interviewers do not consider this a realistic answer (not unless you're a mechanical engineer who can explain the crane setup in convincing detail).

A more amusing idea is to invite children to enter the plane and take away all the "free candy" they want. (Sorry, but no airline attorney would stand for that negligence-suit-waiting-to-happen.)

Rather than launching into some half-baked scheme, you should first ask a few questions of the interviewer. For instance:

- What is valuable here: the plane or the Skittles? Do we care about saving the Skittles at all?

The answers are likely to be "the plane" and "not really." A new Boeing 737 runs about $100 million. The resale value of candy removed from its packaging is zilch. Many of the recovered Skittles would be broken, and an airliner interior contains a constantly updated selection of the world's pathogens. Even donating the candy to a food bank raises legal and nutritional issues. Skittles are about as empty as calories get.

- Is the goal to remove every Skittle, or just 99+ percent of them?

Air travelers don't want to hear Skittles crunching under their feet or find them raining down from the overhead bins. A working airliner needs to be Skittle-free—or very, very close to it.

- Is the goal to empty the plane as quickly as possible, or as cheaply as possible?

The two goals are related ("time is money"). Pretend the plane costs $100 million and the airline makes a 3.65 percent annual return on its investment (you can probably see why I picked that number). Then the plane would earn $3.65 million a year, or an even $10,000 a day. That's a rough idea of the cost of each day's delay in getting the plane back into service.

A crack cleanup crew might run $100 per person per hour. If a team of 100 could clean the plane in an hour, the labor would cost $10,000 but would be well worth it. Delays are so expensive that it's worth hiring a lot of people, provided they can clean up the plane quickly.

A realistic plan is to open the doors and let as many Skittles as possible pour out under gravity. Then send in a team with snow shovels and brooms, to sweep the Skittles toward the doors. They should slide their feet across the cabin floor, to avoid stepping on and crushing Skittles.

Next the team uses industrial or handheld vacuum cleaners to pick up the whole or crushed candies. The plane, its upholstery, and carpets will then need a thorough cleaning.

Unlike M&Ms, Skittles dissolve in water (as many kids have discovered). The main ingredients are sugar, corn syrup, and hydrogenated palm-kernel oil. A standard carpet shampooing machine ought to be effective at dissolving pulverized Skittles. Your plan might also include steam- or pressure-washing the interiors of the cargo hold and passenger compartment.

? You walk into your office and find a time bomb on your desk. It's ticking with 90 seconds to go. You're on the 60th floor of a 100-story building. What would you do?

Asked at Dropbox, this question is a test of deduction as well as organizational ability. The interviewer has gone to the trouble of specifying three numbers: 90 seconds, 60th floor, 100 stories. These allow you to draw some tentative conclusions, and you should confirm them with the interviewer before devising a plan.

New York and Chicago are the only US cities that have hundred-story skyscrapers. Therefore, a 100-story building is probably not going to be in the middle of nowhere. It's going to be in the densest part of a major metropolis. (Ask the interviewer to confirm.)

Another deduction is that the windows on the 60th floor of a mega-skyscraper are not going to open. (Confirm.) Should your plan involve tossing the bomb out, you would have to smash the window. This probably isn't practical. Can you see yourself banging a chair against thick glass, waiting for it to shatter into thousands of shards, while a time bomb ticks just feet away?

Assuming you did succeed in breaking the window and throwing the time bomb out, it's going to hit a crowded street or another building. Even if you think you could time the throw so that the bomb detonates in midair, it would spray the cityscape with shrapnel.

Then there's the business about 90 seconds to go. It looks like the interviewer has been watching some action movies. In that genre, a time bomb is a device for creating tension. It is an alarm clock strapped to sticks of dynamite. Or it uses a watch, a digital readout, or a laptop computer to supply a visual countdown.

In the real world, bad guys do not make bombs that look like bombs. Nor do they set them out where they are likely to be discovered. But OK, you play along with the premise. Plan B is to evacuate the building. A hundred floors likely means thousands of people. You'd have to convince them that you're not crazy, and that there really is a bomb in the building, without causing a panic. This isn't going to happen in 90 seconds.

At best you might be able to herd your coworkers on the bomb floor to an adjacent floor via stairs. This is a halfway realistic goal that may not require crowd-control superpowers. Ask the interviewer: Would evacuating just one floor, the one with the bomb, be enough to prevent casualties? If you get a yes, that's probably the best plan.

Otherwise, you're left with the strategy of defusing the bomb. This may be easier than you think. Demolitions experts and terrorists alike have adopted plastic explosives, resistant to shock. In US Army tests, the plastic explosive C4 has been dropped, pounded with a hammer, set on fire, nuked in a microwave, and shot with a gun, all without detonating. It takes a blasting cap to set it off. This is a small charge of another explosive that is detonated either by a fuse or by an electrical circuit.

The interviewer mentioned "ticking." That implies a clock will complete a circuit to an electric blasting cap. (Confirm.)

Any office has scissors. You should be able to identify the wires to the blasting cap and cut them.

I know—it's never that easy in the movies. The bomb is

rigged to go off if the hero cuts the wire. Or there are two wires, one red and one blue, and the hero has to cut the right one or get blown to smithereens.

There is no reason to think these plot twists apply—they're the inventions of screenwriters. So snip the wires, evacuate the building, call the police, and let the bomb-disposal squad take it from there. Assuming you succeeded in defusing the bomb, it becomes evidence to help catch the evildoer.

? A cube of ice, one meter on each side, is sitting on a wooden table in a small room where the temperature is 50° Celsius. All but one of the cube's vertical faces are one meter from the nearest wall. The other face is 30 centimeters from the wall. You are given two insulating blankets, each a meter square. Where would you place the blankets to keep the ice solid for as long as possible?

In *Walden, or, Life in the Woods,* Henry David Thoreau remarks on the exploits of Boston entrepreneur Frederic Tudor, the "Ice King." Tudor harvested tons of winter ice from Walden Pond and shipped them to sultry locales around the globe, from New Orleans to Calcutta. After a string of early failures, Tudor found that large blocks of ice could survive long sea voyages, provided they were insulated with sawdust.

To answer this question, asked at Apple, you need to know a little physics and be comfortable with metric units. For those who aren't, 50° C is 122° F. A meter is about 40 inches, and 30 centimeters is about 12 inches. Picture a big ice cube in a hot, sauna-size box.

Heat is transferred through the three means of conduction, convection, and radiation. Conduction occurs when two objects of different temperatures are in direct contact. In this case, heat could flow from the table to the ice. You might start by asking the interviewer: *Is the table at the room's 50° C temperature, or is it at ice temperature?*

Because we know the table is capable of supporting a big block of ice, it's not some plywood Ikea deal held together with pegs and wishful thinking. It's more likely a solid block of dense wood. Assuming the table is initially at the room's temperature, it could hold a lot of heat to impart to the ice by direct contact. That means you might want to put a blanket between the ice and the table. You might even want to put both blankets there. Conduction is often the most efficient means of heat transfer. (Hence the wilderness-survival hack of putting a blanket under you rather than over you; your unprotected body will lose more heat into the cold ground than into the air.)

Also, the ice would squash most of the air out of a blanket, reducing its insulation value. It might be worth having both blankets between ice and table.

But there's a complication: A one-meter cube of ice weighs a ton.

A kilogram (about 2.2 pounds) is the mass of a 10-centimeter cube of water. A meter cube of water is 1,000 kilograms, also known as a metric ton. Ice is just slightly less dense than liquid water, so you're looking at a literal ton of ice.

That's not something you could lift. Moving a ton of ice would be a big operation, requiring industrial equipment. But wait—the interviewer said the room has at most a one-meter clearance between ice and wall. You're not going to get a forklift in there.

You should therefore ask the interviewer: Do I have any way to raise the ice to put a blanket under it (because I sure can't lift a ton of ice)?

If the interviewer grants you license to magically levitate the ice (and says that the table is warmer than the ice), you should put at least one of your blankets between the ice and the table.

But let's say the interviewer rules out levitation. Then

conduction from the table is a lost cause, and we should focus on the five exposed surfaces. All are subject to the two other means of heat transfer: convection and radiation.

Convection occurs when a gas or liquid in contact with an object is able to flow, carrying heat (or cold) away from the object. Warm air around ice will cool and become denser. It will flow downward, creating a draft that will pull more air across the ice surface, helping to melt it. An ordinary blanket reduces convection by trapping air between its fibers. This is how blankets and clothing keep us warm.

The third form of heat transfer, radiation, operates even in a vacuum. All objects radiate "heat" in the form of infrared photons. These shoot out like buckshot in all directions. Even an ice block radiates heat. But the room's walls are at a higher temperature and radiate far more. A space blanket—a thin, foldable sheet of Mylar—reflects heat radiation and could virtually eliminate this kind of heating from a covered surface. So would a survival blanket consisting of Mylar bonded to a regular blanket. The latter offers insulation against all three means of heat transfer.

Ask the interviewer: What kind of insulating blanket is it?

I've mentioned the importance of paying attention to unexpected details. Here it's natural to focus on the statement that one side is only 30 centimeters from the wall. Why would the interviewer supply that detail, unless it is important?

Those who studied physics will remember that radiation falls off with the square of distance. This *inverse-square law* is one problem with fireplaces. Radiated heat diminishes steeply with distance from the fire. Pull a chair up to the fire, and your legs may get too hot while the rest of your body remains cold.

It's tempting to connect the inverse-square law to the side of the ice nearest the wall. Won't that side receive more radiation? But the question mentions the 30-centimeter business as a red herring, to test how well you understand the physics. The inverse-square law applies to point sources of radiation. A relatively small fireplace in a big, cold room can approximate that. So does the sun in the vastness of space. The farther you are from the source, the less of its heat radiation you intercept. Most of the infrared radiation spills out into empty space.

This question presents the opposite situation. The ice is inside a hollow source of radiation. The 50° C room radiates infrared photons from all its inner surfaces. That heat radiation may bounce off the walls repeatedly, being absorbed and retransmitted. But the photons will ultimately be absorbed by whatever cooler objects are in the room — in this case, the ice.

Say we put Mylar blankets on two sides of the ice. Photons that hit the blankets, from any direction, will bounce right off. They will hit a wall and be reemitted, perhaps many times. Eventually a deflected photon will strike an unprotected ice surface, doing its quantum bit to melt the ice. Of course, photons travel at the speed of light, so for practical purposes, deflected photons are *instantly* directed to an exposed ice surface.

Were it possible to cover all five exposed sides of the ice with space blankets, that would isolate the ice from heat radiation. But having just two blankets is something like having a boat with five holes in it and being able to plug just two.

It seems, then, that we can't do much about radiation, nor about conduction (barring a means of lifting the ice). That leaves convection. Covering any of the exposed surfaces would be helpful in minimizing convection.

There is a practical issue that most applicants overlook. *How are you supposed to attach a blanket to melting ice?* You can't nail, glue, or Velcro it.

One blanket can go on the top side. Gravity will keep it in place as the ice melts. That leaves one more blanket that has to go on a vertical surface. The interviewer may tell you that you can magically bond a blanket to a vertical surface. If so, it doesn't matter too much which side you choose. But if the interviewer says no magic, then here's another idea. Use duct tape to join the two blankets, producing a 1-by-2-meter rectangular blanket. Drape it over the top face, with two half-meter flaps hanging halfway down over two opposite vertical sides. This too should stay in place as the ice melts.

Use a Process of Elimination

When you have eliminated the impossible, whatever remains, however improbable, must be the truth," said Sherlock Holmes. Terms such as *deduction, logic,* and *process of elimination* are often mentioned in connection with puzzles. Clue *A* leads to surmise *B*, which leads to deduction *C*. The maze is twisty, but its branch points can be eliminated one by one.

The role of deductive logic in solving so-called logic puzzles can be overstated. As Newell and Simon noted, problems are difficult when the number of potential solutions is so exponentially vast as to defeat an exhaustive search. The good news is that most interview puzzles are not difficult in that sense. They often can be solved by a process of elimination. By that I mean you can lay out all possible solutions or approaches and search for one that meets the problem's requirements.

? Chicken McNuggets come in boxes of 6, 9, and 20. What is the largest number of McNuggets that McDonald's can't sell you?

? You have only 5- and 11-cent stamps. What is the largest amount of postage you can't make with those stamps?

The "Chicken McNuggets problem" is a staple of brainteasers as well as computer science courses. It can involve fast food, postage stamps, coins, currency, or something else. There is at least one online video of a guy going up to a McDonald's window and ordering 43 nuggets (read on to see why).

Take the version with 5- and 11-cent stamps. It's easy to see that you can't make 4 cents' worth of postage, or 7 cents, or 13 cents. What might not be apparent is that you can make *any* very large whole-cent amount you want. You can, for instance, make $2,590.97 in stamps. One way to do that is to use the 11-cent stamps to achieve the odd cents. $2,590.97 ends in 7, so count out seven 11-cent stamps. That gives 77 cents, leaving $2,590.20 to go. That figure necessarily divides by 10 cents and therefore by 5 cents. Consequently, 51,804 five-cent stamps plus 7 eleven-cent stamps will make $2,590.97. That's one example; there are many other ways to get that amount.

Given that some small amounts can't be dispensed, but all sufficiently large amounts can, it follows that there must be a highest amount that you *can't* make. This is known as the *Frobenius number*, after German mathematician Ferdinand Georg Frobenius (1848–1917).

Interviewers don't necessarily expect you to know what a Frobenius number is. When confronted with a Chicken McNuggets problem in an interview, it generally means that the numbers have been handpicked to make the problem bite-size manageable.

Chicken McNuggets were once offered in boxes of 9 and 20. The Frobenius number for (9, 20) is 151 — hard to come up with in your head. Then McDonald's added a smaller box of 6. This prompted the brainteaser asking for the largest number of McNuggets that McDonalds is *unable* to sell, given boxes of 6, 9, and 20.

Notice that 6 and 9 share the factor 3. These two sizes allow you to order any number of McNuggets divisible by 3 (from 6 upward) but not, of course, any number that doesn't divide by 3.

6: Order one 6-box
9: Order one 9-box
12: Order two 6-boxes
15: Order one 6-box and one 9-box
18: Order three 6-boxes or two 9-boxes
etc.

That means we need to worry about only those numbers that don't divide evenly by 3. We can split them into two classes: the numbers whose remainder, when divided by 3, is 1 (1, 4, 7, 10...); and the numbers whose remainder is 2 (2, 5, 8, 11...).

When 20 is divided by 3, the remainder is 2. That means one box of 20 McNuggets plus as many 6s and 9s as needed can cover *all* the large numbers with a remainder of 2. The box of 20 offsets the every-third number pattern we have with boxes of 6 and 9 alone. Of course, it also means that we have to be ordering 20-some McNuggets at a minimum.

20: Order one 20-box
23: Can't do this!
26: Order one 20-box and one 6-box
29: Order one 20-box and one 9-box
32: Order one 20-box and two 6-boxes
etc.

As you can see, it's impossible to get 23 McNuggets, but all larger remainder-2 numbers are covered.

To achieve numbers with a remainder of 1, we need two boxes of 20. That gives 40, which has a remainder of 1.

40: Order two 20-boxes
43: Can't do this!
46: Order two 20-boxes and one 6-box

49: Order two 20-boxes and one 9-box
52: Order two 20-boxes and two 6-boxes
etc.

Forty-three is the largest number we can't make this way. And since it's higher than the other limits, it's the answer to the question.

43 is the largest number that McDonald's can't sell

Divisible by 3	0	3	6	9	12	15	18	21	24	27	30	33	36	39	42	45	48
Remainder of 1	1	4	7	10	13	16	19	22	25	28	31	34	37	40	43	46	49
Remainder of 2	2	5	8	11	14	17	20	23	26	29	32	35	38	41	44	47	50

The stamp problem follows the same template. With 5-cent stamps, we can make any amount divisible evenly by 5: 5, 10, 15, 20 cents…That's all the numbers whose rightmost digit is 0 or 5.

That leaves the numbers whose remainders, when divided by 5, are 1, 2, 3, or 4. We'll use the 11-cent stamps to offset the 0 or 5 pattern.

With a single 11-cent stamp and unlimited 5s, we can make 11, 16, 21, 26…These are amounts with a remainder of 1, ending in 1 or 6. The biggest remainder-1 number that we can't make this way is 6.

Two 11-cent stamps and 5s cover all the remainder-2 amounts ending in 2 or 7, from 22 onward. The largest impossible amount is 17.

Three 11-cent stamps plus 5s buy remainder-3 amounts ending in 3 or 8. The largest impossible amount is 28.

Four 11-cent stamps plus 5s generate remainder-4 amounts ending in 4 or 9. The largest impossible amount is 39, and that's the answer: 39 cents is the largest postage amount that can't be paid with 5- and 11-cent stamps.

P.S. There is a formula for calculating the Frobenius number with two denominations (n, m). It's

$$nm - (n + m)$$

With 5 and 11, this gives

$$5 \times 11 - (5 + 11) = 55 - 16 = 39.$$

Because this formula works with two denominations only, it can't be used for the Chicken McNuggets question. Another important requirement for using this rule is that n and m must not share a common factor. If both are even, sharing the factor 2, you obviously can't make any odd-numbered amounts.

P.P.S. Marketing moves on. It did not escape the fast-food giant's attention that McNuggets were kiddie crack. A children's "Happy Meal" with 4 McNuggets was added to the menu. With all four options available (4, 6, 9, 20), the largest number it is impossible to order is 11.

It then turned out that not many customers were ordering the 9s. Some outlets dropped that option, offering 4, 6, and 20. With this set there is no Frobenius number, because all three amounts are even. All odd numbers of McNuggets are impossible.

Most of the problems we confront are not so clear-cut as the Chicken McNuggets problem. But even when dealing with ambiguity, it can be useful to lay out possibilities and try to eliminate some of them.

? I have 50 coins in my hand, and they add up to $1.00 exactly. I drop one of the coins. What is the chance it's a penny?

The interviewer doesn't say what kind of coins she's holding, yet asks for the chance that a dropped coin is a penny. That hints that the fact that 50 coins add up to $1 is sufficient to answer the question.

In the US there are 1-cent pennies, 5-cent nickels, 10-cent dimes, 25-cent quarters, 50-cent half-dollars, and 100-cent dollar coins. Only so many sets of 50 coins make $1.00 exactly. Let's hash out the possibilities, focusing on the number of pennies.

Could there be 50 pennies? No, that would add up to 50 cents, and we're told the coins are worth a dollar. There must be some higher-denomination coins.

Forty-nine pennies? No. It will be clear that you can't have 49 pennies when the sum is an even dollar. All the other coin values are divisible by 5 cents. The number of pennies must also be divisible by 5. We can rule out 48, 47, and 46, going straight to...

Forty-five pennies? Pretend there are exactly 45 pennies. We need 5 other coins (to make 50 coins total), and they must be worth 55 cents (to make a dollar). The 5 non-pennies can't all be nickels or all dimes, because the most that 5 such coins can add up to is 50 cents. There would have to be a quarter or a half-dollar.

Scratch the half-dollar. The only way of getting 55 cents with a half-dollar (and no pennies) is to pair it with a nickel. That would be 2 non-penny coins, rather than the required 5.

Two quarters would also require a nickel to make 55 cents, and we'd have just 3 coins.

It follows that there has to be exactly 1 quarter, *if* this is to work at all. Subtract the quarter's 25-cent value from 55 cents. That leaves 30 cents, and we need to make that from 4 coins that have to be nickels and/or dimes.

Easy: 2 nickels and 2 dimes are 4 coins worth 30 cents. No other combination of nickels and dimes would work.

That gives a solution: 45 pennies, 2 nickels, 2 dimes, and 1 quarter. These are 50 coins adding up to $1.

*   *   *

One problem with the deductive approach is quitting too soon. Having found one solution doesn't guarantee there aren't others. In this problem it's important to know whether there are other solutions, so let's plug on. The number of pennies must be divisible by 5, and we've just treated the case with 45 pennies. Now try 40. We would need 10 non-pennies that add up to 60 cents. Once again, a 50-cent piece (or 2 quarters) is out.

How about 1 quarter? This would require that the remaining 9 non-pennies add up to $60 - 25 = 35$ cents. But 9 nickels would be 45 cents, which is too much. A quarter is not going to work.

If there is a 40-penny combination, it's going to be heavy in nickels, since 10 nickels would be 50 cents—not too far short of the required 60 cents. Swap 2 of the 10 nickels for dimes, and we've got 60 cents. That works, yielding another possible solution: 40 pennies, 8 nickels, and 2 dimes.

Next up is 35 pennies. There would have to be 15 non-pennies adding up to 65 cents. That's a deal-breaker. Even if all 15 non-pennies were nickels, they would be 75 cents—more than 65 cents. Adding dimes or quarters would only make it worse. There is no way of getting 50 coins to total a dollar when 35 of them are pennies. This obviously applies to 30, 25, 20…and all the way down to zero pennies.

There are then exactly two ways of meeting the condition of 50 coins adding up to a dollar. This is another juncture where it's easy to lose the thread. The two sets of coins are not the answer. Remember, the interviewer asked for the *chance* that a dropped coin is a penny.

There is no way of telling which combination of coins the interviewer has. We also don't know whether all coins are equally likely to be dropped. You should point this out to the interviewer. Unless you get guidance otherwise, the reasonable approach is to regard both sets of coins as equally likely, and to assume that every coin is equally likely to be the one dropped. With one assortment,

45 out of 50 coins (90 percent) are pennies. With the other, 40 out of 50 (80 percent) are. Average the two figures to get 85 percent. That is the expected answer.

? You are given three consecutive numbers, all larger than 6. The smallest and largest are primes. Prove the middle number is evenly divisible by 6.

A prime number is a whole number, greater than 1, that is not the product of two smaller whole numbers. The primes are 2, 3, 5, 7, 11, 13, 17, and so on. Since antiquity, primes have had a mystic reputation. There are an infinite number of primes and they obey no simple pattern, though many generalizations can be proven.

In order to be prime, a number must not be divisible by any other prime. Because 2 is a prime, all primes (other than 2 itself) are odd numbers.

The question says that the smallest and largest of three consecutive numbers are primes, so they must be odd. That means the middle number has to be even (and is not a prime).

We're asked to prove this middle number is divisible by 6. Six is 2 × 3. We already know the middle number is divisible by 2, so we need to establish that it is divisible by 3.

Well, every third whole number is divisible by 3. One of the three consecutive numbers *has* to divide by 3. And it can't be either of the primes (which are larger than 6), so it's got to be the middle number again. The middle number is divisible by both 2 and 3, and therefore by 6.

Example: 17, 18, 19. The first and last are primes, and 18 divides by 6.

? You get into an elevator with five other people in a 20-story building. You hate to touch elevator buttons. (Germs!)

What's the chance that someone else presses the button to your floor?

This question, asked at Bloomberg, has the power to cause applicants to forget everything they know about elevators. They say something like "Assume each of the 5 people are equally likely to be going to any of the 20 floors..." Why should anyone assume that? It's not how elevators work.

Spider-Man aside, most people enter tall buildings at the ground floor. They take the elevator to a desired higher floor, and later return to the ground floor to exit the building.

Another important fact: Elevator landings have an up button and a down button. You press the one that applies and wait for an elevator going in your direction. You don't normally get in an elevator that's going the opposite direction.

Most elevator trips in a tall building begin or end on the ground floor (or a parking floor, but you can probably get away with ignoring that). Break it down to two likely cases:

1) You're on the ground floor going up, to a random upper floor.
2) You're on a random upper floor going down, to the ground floor.
   There is also a less likely case:
3) You're going from one upper floor to another.

You may ask the interviewer which case applies. Otherwise, a defensible approach is to ignore Case 3 and focus on the first two.

In Case 1, anyone entering an up elevator on the ground floor has 19 possible destination floors, from 2 through 20. (I'll assume there's a 13th floor.) The chance that any fellow rider is going to your floor is about 1/19. Conversely, the chance that any given person is *not* going to your floor is 18/19.

The probability that none of the five people is going to your floor is 18/19 multiplied by itself 5 times: $(18/19)^5$. You can estimate this without a calculator. 18/19 is close to 19/20, which is 95 percent. Each time you multiply 95 percent by itself, the product decreases by about 5 percent, so the 5th power is about $5 \times 5 = 25$ percent short of 100 percent, or 75 percent. That represents the chance that you will have to press the button for yourself. Subtract that from 100 percent to get the chance that at least one other person is going to your floor, about 25 percent. (The actual value of $[18/19]^5$ is about 76.31 percent, making the chance 23.69 percent.)

Case 2 is easier. You're taking a down elevator to the ground floor, and most of the five people who get in with you are probably going to the ground floor as well. On a downward trip, the chance that one of the five will press your button (if it hasn't already been pressed) verges on 100 percent.

Cases 1 and 2 are about equally common, as they'd each be a leg of a typical round trip in the building. The overall chance is the average of 25 percent and 100 percent, or 63 percent. Or it would be a little less than that, allowing for Case 3.

This is a good answer. But it depends on a couple of questionable assumptions. One is that each upper floor is an equally likely destination. This wouldn't be true in general. A penthouse floor might have a popular restaurant and get a steady stream of diners; another might be a mechanical floor and receive virtually no visitors. You are more likely to be going to a popular floor, and so are the five people who get in with you. This increases the chance that someone is going to your floor, perhaps dramatically.

Another questionable assumption is that everyone is traveling alone. Coworkers go out for lunch or carpool home; teams come in to pitch projects; family members accompany each other to a professional's office. Because groups share the same destination, this diminishes the chance that someone will be going to your floor.

It can't reduce it too much, though. Take the extreme case where all five of the other people are a dysfunctional family who came for counseling on the 15th floor. You are not necessarily going to that floor. The chance the family shares your floor is 1/19 (if going up) and nearly 100 percent (if going down). The average of 1/19 and 100 percent is a little short of 53 percent.

To sum up, the chance of not having to push the button mainly depends on whether you're going up or down. Should you average all up and down trips, it's somewhere in the neighborhood of 60 percent.

Work Backward

Here is a Wall Street interview question that leaves people with graduate degrees at a loss for words. It's a story problem with no fancy math, just arithmetic.

? Three-fourths of the passengers on a bus get off at one stop, and 10 more get on. The same happens at the next bus stop, and the one after that (three stops in all). What is the minimum number of passengers who could have been on the bus initially?

You may see one essential insight already. There can't be fractional passengers. So when the interviewer says that three-quarters of the passengers get off, he's also telling you that quantity is a whole number. This is vital to solving the problem, but it goes only so far.

You might try a process of elimination, checking every possible number of passengers. But that would be tedious (interview etiquette: try not to bore the interviewer to death). The story-problem format suggests a methodical solution; maybe an equation?

Go to the whiteboard and make a table. The table's rows start at the story's beginning and move downward to the end.

	Passengers on the bus
Original passengers, before anything happens	X
After 1st bus stop	$X / 4 + 10$
After 2nd stop	$(X / 4 + 10) / 4 + 10$
After 3rd stop	$((X / 4 + 10) / 4 + 10) / 4 + 10$

Here X is the original number of passengers, the unknown we want to find. In outline the same thing happens at each bus stop. A useful way of describing it is that *the number of passengers is divided by 4, then added to 10.* This is clearer than "three-fourths of the passengers get off" because it keeps the focus on the passengers remaining on the bus.

Now you've got a nice little table that will impress the interviewer more than just standing there speechless. What next?

The interviewer is *not* telling you how many riders remained on the bus after the third stop, and asking you to solve for X. Nor are you being asked to solve four equations in one unknown. These aren't even equations.

So what are they? Well, they're expressions that are required to be whole numbers (again, because there's no such thing as fractional people). The interviewer is asking for the minimum number that makes this true. There are many values of X that would work, an infinite number in fact, but we're looking for the smallest one.

If a certain quantity divided by 4 is a whole number, then that quantity must itself be whole. In order for each successive expression in the table to be whole, all the expressions above it must be. That means the most stringent constraint—and the only one we need to worry about—is the last one, describing the passengers after the third stop. The goal is to find the smallest X for which this is true:

$((X / 4 + 10) / 4 + 10) / 4 + 10$ *is a whole number*

This is not so easy to wrap your head around.

Erase the whiteboard and start over. This time listen to Pappus of Alexandria and work backward. Z will be the number of people left on the bus at the story's end, after the third bus stop. The new table will list the steps in reverse order. And since we're moving backward in time, the net effect of each bus stop is to subtract 10 passengers and then multiply the result by 4. If we have Z passengers after the third bus stop, we had $4(Z - 10)$, or $4Z - 40$, before the stop. The new table looks like this.

	Passengers on the bus
Passengers left at the end of the story (after 3rd bus stop)	Z
Before 3rd stop	$4(Z - 10) =$ $4Z - 40$
Before 2nd stop	$4(4Z - 40 - 10) =$ $16Z - 200$
Original number of passengers (before 1st stop)	$4(16Z - 200 - 10) =$ $64Z - 840$

The table's bottom line says that the original number of passengers (what we called X) is $64Z - 840$.

This is a lot easier to manage than what we ended up with in the first table. As before, the constraint is that this expression must be a whole number. And because you can't have negative people any more than fractional ones, $64Z - 840$ must also be a positive number.

Divide 840 by 64 and you get 13.125. Round up to get the smallest whole value of Z that works, 14.

Plug that in, and we get the original number of passengers (X):

$$64 \times 14 - 840 = 56$$

Try it. The bus starts with 56 passengers. At the first stop three-quarters (42 out of 56) get off, leaving 14. Then 10 people get on, and the bus pulls away with 24 passengers.

At the second stop, three-quarters (18 of 24) get off, leaving 6. Ten get on, making 16.

At the third stop, three-quarters (12 of 16) get off, and 10 get on. The bus ends up with 14 people.

Some puzzles are like certain garden mazes. There is an entrance and a goal. It's natural to start at the entrance and explore the many paths branching off it (most of which are ultimately dead ends). But if you can start at the goal and backtrack, you may find it much easier to locate the entrance.

? You're driving a super-fast sports car at a track. On the first lap you average 60 miles per hour. How fast do you have to drive on the second lap to average 120 mph for both laps?

This question has been asked at Nvidia, Morgan Stanley, and elsewhere. A common wrong answer is: "Let's see, 60 plus X, divided by 2, is 120. I need to drive 180 mph on the second lap, to average 120."

Try working backward. You've just finished that second lap and have averaged 120 mph for both laps. What can you conclude from that?

The driven distance (two laps) divided by the time taken

(unknown) must come to 120 mph. We haven't been told how many yards or miles a lap is, so call it d miles. Call the times taken for the first and seconds laps t_1 and t_2, both expressed in hours. Then

$$2d/(t_1 + t_2) = 120$$

Divide both sides by 2:

$$d/(t_1 + t_2) = 60$$

Hmmm... That's funny because we averaged 60 mph on the first lap, meaning

$$d/t_1 = 60$$

The two equations look similar. The only way that d/t_1 and $d/(t_1 + t_2)$ can each equal 60 is for t_1 to equal $t_1 + t_2$. That in turn means that

$$t_2 = 0$$

The car would have to travel at infinite speed, completing the second lap in no time at all, in order to average 120 mph for the two laps. Since a car can't really do a lap in zero time, it's impossible for the car to average 120 mph.

Many still find the situation puzzling. Here's a comparable situation that's easier to understand. I'm on a strict one-week diet. I declared yesterday "Cheat Day" and ate seven donuts. How many more donuts can I eat during the week, so that I average no more than one donut per day?

Obviously my seven-donut binge has already raised my weekly donut consumption to one per day. I can't have *any* more donuts without exceeding that. With the race car, the time I spent on the first lap already precludes averaging 120 mph.

? You roll a die and win the number that comes up in dollars. You don't have to accept the money; you can instead choose to roll a second time, with the same payment rule. If you don't like the second roll, you can roll a third time, but that's it (and you must then accept the result of the third roll). How do you get the best return from this game? What is the best return you can expect?

To state the obvious: If you roll a 6, you should accept the money (because it's worth $6, and you can't possibly do better). If you roll a 1, you should go again, if allowed (because it's worth $1, and you can't do worse).

A complete strategy has to cover all the in-between cases. Should you, say, be willing to settle for a 4 on the second roll?

The best way to flesh out a strategy is to work backward. Imagine you've just rolled for the third time. There is no decision to make; you have to accept the result of this roll. Therefore your expected winnings on a third roll must be the average of all six equally likely outcomes. That's ($1 + $2 + $3 + $4 + $5 + $6)/6, or $21/6, or $7/2, or $3.50.

Now rewind a step and imagine yourself on the second roll. You see the result and have a choice. If the die shows 4, 5, or 6, you should accept it. It's a sure thing—better than the risky $3.50 you can expect by going for a third roll. But if you rolled 1, 2, or 3, it's to your advantage to go for a third roll.

Using this optimal second-roll strategy, the expected gain is the average of the six payoffs or expectations: ($3.50 + $3.50 + $3.50 + $4 + $5 + $6)/6. The narrated math is easier when you hold off dividing terms by 6 until the very end. A whiteboard may help too. We have

$$(\$3.50 + \$3.50 + \$3.50 + \$4 + \$5 + \$6)/6$$
$$= (\$10.50 + \$15)/6$$
$$= \$25.50/6$$
$$= (\$24 + \$1.50)/6$$
$$= \$4.25$$

This is the value you should attach to the second roll.

Now rewind another step to the first roll. You should accept a 5 or 6 because they're better than the $4.25 you would expect by advancing to the second roll. You should reject 1, 2, 3, or 4, and opt for a second roll.

To recap, the overall strategy is to always stop at 5 or 6, and to accept 4 on the second roll. Otherwise roll as long as you're permitted.

The question asks for the game's expected return. This is what a strategic player can expect at the outset, before the first roll. Once again, it's the average of the six first-roll payoffs or expectations.

$$(\$4.25 + \$4.25 + \$4.25 + \$4.25 + \$5 + \$6)/6$$
$$= (\$17 + \$11)/6$$
$$= \$28/6$$
$$= \$24/6 + \$4/6$$
$$= \$4.67$$

Beware of Trick Questions

A *bar-raiser* is a skilled interviewer, brought in to supply an independent opinion of a promising candidate. He or she poses particularly tough questions, often outside the candidate's field. It's said that Microsoft invented the bar-raiser, but Jeff Bezos adopted it at Amazon, where it's become part of the corporate culture. Here's one of the more notorious bar-raiser questions asked at Amazon:

? An 80-meter cable is strung between the tops of two 50-meter poles. What is the distance between the poles, to one decimal place, if the center of the cable is 10 meters above the ground?

Well-educated applicants may know that the curve assumed by a chain or heavy cable suspended from its ends is a *catenary*. Thomas Jefferson coined that term, from the Latin for "chain." The simplest types of suspension bridges are catenaries, and St. Louis's Gateway Arch is an upside-down example. Mathematically, a catenary is a graph of the hyperbolic cosine function. Ready to do some trigonometry in your head?

Better to ask, *what's wrong with this picture?* You may have made a quick sketch, or just imagined one. But this is a case where

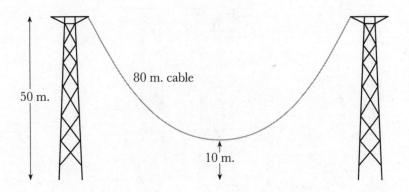

80 m. cable

50 m.

10 m.

you need to pay attention to unexpected words. *To one decimal place?!?* That's asking the near-impossible, unless it's a special, easy case. It is.

Forget the diagram you've imagined and draw an accurate one.

The cable is 80 meters long. That means that half the cable is 40 meters. Even if the two poles were touching, and the cable was crimped into a hairpin fold at its exact middle, the lowest part of the cable would be 10 meters above the ground—as stated. Therefore, the two poles are touching. To one decimal place, there are 0.0 meters between them.

This is a trick question. I'll use that term to describe relatively easy problems that dupe solvers into a time-consuming calculation or line of reasoning. The most important thing to know about trick questions is that they exist. Should a question seem to require unreasonable calculation or effort, that should raise your suspicion level. Don't invest too much time until you've checked for a simple solution—or a simple demonstration that no solution is possible.

Fortunately, trick questions are rare in hiring interviews. But trick questions grade into a more benign sort of problem in which there is a relatively quick solution and a slower, more plodding one.

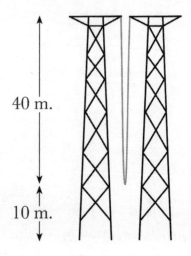

40 m.

10 m.

In such cases, the interviewer will be more impressed by those who discover the quicker solution.

? How far is Russia from the US?

Thomas Edison's notorious questionnaire asked job applicants the distances from New York to Buffalo, San Francisco, and Liverpool. This contemporary riddle is usually intended as a trick question. Big Diomede Island, part of Russia, is about 2.5 miles from Little Diomede Island, part of the US. On a clear day, each island is readily visible from the other. In 1987 American athlete Lynne Cox swam between the two islands. Others have managed to walk the distance when the Bering Strait froze over for winter (this is becoming less common as the Arctic warms).

Two and a half miles is the usual answer. But the Diomede Islands hold little sway outside trivia games, so it's possible to treat this as a standard estimation question. Russia and the US are on opposite sides of the North Pole, well within the northern hemisphere. Most of the US is south of 45 degrees north latitude, whereas most of Russia is north of it. It's not too far wrong to say that the two nations are 90 degrees apart on the globe. That's one-fourth of a great circle, and with luck you recall the Earth's circumference is about 25,000 miles. That comes to something over 6,000 miles as a typical distance between the US and Russia.

Moscow is in fact 4,860 miles from Washington, DC, and 6,070 miles from Los Angeles.

? Imagine a big cube made of $10 \times 10 \times 10$ little cubes. How many of the little cubes are not on the outside of the big cube?

Slice off the outer cube layers like unwanted heels of bread. That leaves an $8 \times 8 \times 8$ cube. It has 512 little cubes, and that's the answer.

? You're playing a game of Russian roulette. Three bullets are placed in consecutive chambers of a six-chamber revolver. The barrel is spun just once. The first player puts the gun to his head and pulls the trigger. If he survives, he hands the gun to the second player, who does the same. The gun is handed back and forth between the two players until it fires. Would you rather go first or second?

Russian roulette questions have become disconcertingly popular in hiring interviews. They can be taken as a hint that the job requires the ability to think clearly under pressure. In this case, with three bullets in six chambers, the first person has a 1 in 2 chance of being killed, right off the bat. Is it not already clear that you don't want to go first? Half the time the game ends before the second player takes the gun. You definitely want to go second.

Sometimes the interviewer asks for the exact chance of survival. This is also simple, once you realize that what happens is determined by the single spin ("the barrel is spun just once"). Call the loaded chambers 1 through 3 and the empty ones 4 through 6. They are numbered in order of firing.

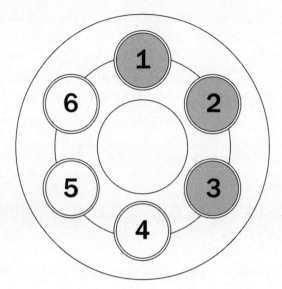

When the barrel lands on loaded Chambers 1, 2, or 3, the first player dies on the first turn, and the game is over.

When the barrel lands on empty Chamber 4, the first player survives. He hands the gun to the second player, who gets empty Chamber 5 and also survives. Then the first player goes again, getting empty Chamber 6. Having gone through all three empty chambers, the gun shifts to loaded Chamber 1. The second player, now knowing his fate, puts the gun to his head. This is the longest possible game, and it ends with the second player's death.

When the barrel lands on Chamber 5, the first player survives; the second player survives with Chamber 6; then the first player gets fatal Chamber 1.

When the barrel lands on 6, the first player survives, but the second player gets Chamber 1 and dies.

Four barrel positions out of six lead to the first player's death. Two ensure the second player's death. The strategic player goes second and has a 2 in 3 chance of survival.

Guesstimate and Refine

One thing you won't have in an interview is the luxury of silence. You are expected to soliloquize your train of thought in the course of solving a problem. There is pressure to keep making progress, and this should affect the strategy for approaching these questions.

? A frog is at the bottom of a 30-foot well. Each day he finds the energy to leap three feet upward. He then clings there, exhausted, for the rest of the day. Overnight he sleeps and slips two feet downward. How many days does it take him to escape from the well?

Asked at Bloomberg, this is a simple question stated in simple terms. But should you start out aiming for the exact answer, you may stumble or draw a blank. A wiser strategy is to begin with a quick, approximate estimate: "The frog's net progress is one foot a day. The well is 30 feet high, so it should take about 30 days to get out."

This quick estimate is not a number pulled out of the air. It uses the numbers in the problem and some straightforward math. It's just that 30 is not necessarily the exact answer. There's more work to do. But giving a quick estimate puts some points on the scoreboard right away, boosting your confidence. In interviews as in sports, that's not to be underestimated.

The next step is to refine the estimate as needed to arrive at the exact answer. Here the back-and-forth progress means the frog will reach a given level, then fall back, and pass the level several times before it's fully clear of it. Yet once the frog reaches the 30-foot level, it can hop out of the well. That means that the frog will actually get out in *less* than 30 days.

Now for the exact and final answer. Start the clock at 0 days, with the frog at height 0, measured from the bottom. Immediately it jumps up to 3 feet. That night it falls back to the 1-foot level. With each succeeding day, the frog begins the process a foot higher.

The frog therefore begins day 27 at the 27-foot mark. It jumps three feet more, and it's out. The frog takes 27 days to escape.

Timed math questions have become popular lately (with some interviewers...just about everyone else hates them).

? Apples cost 27 cents. How many can you buy for $10? You have one minute to give the exact answer.

You learned to multiply and divide in school. That method is fine for when your phone is out of charge. It's not ideal for the verbalized mental math of a job interview. It's too easy to forget a digit and end up with an answer that's way off. The guesstimate-and-refine technique lets you break the reasoning down into a succession of steps, zeroing in on the answer. You might say something like this:

"Twenty-seven cents is close to 25, a quarter of a dollar. That's four apples to a dollar, and ten dollars buys about 40 apples. The exact answer will be less than that..."

It's easiest to multiply round numbers, those with just one significant (non-zero) digit. Here we want to test an answer smaller than 40. Let's say 38. We need to multiply 38 apples by 27 cents to see whether it fits the $10 budget. Both 38 and 27 have two significant digits. But 38 can be expressed as 40 − 2, and 27 as 25 + 2. The product is going to be close to $10 (40 × 25 cents), and this can be refined by adding or subtracting additional terms. The narration might continue.

"Try 38: 38 times 25 cents is 2 times 25 short of $10, or $9.50. Thirty-eight by 2 cents is 76 cents. Add that to $9.50 and it's $10.26. Too much...

"The answer must be 37. It will be 27 cents less than $10.26, so I get 1 cent in change."

Don't worry too much about the stated time limit. The above narration (which is a little more chatty than necessary) takes about 40 seconds. Even if a merciless interviewer cuts you off before you get the final answer, you ought to get partial credit for establishing that the answer is somewhere around 38 or 37.

Mental math is best learned by practice. Here's one of the more difficult calculation questions asked in interviews:

? Calculate 15 percent of 155. You have ten seconds.

Fifteen has two significant digits, and 155 has three. That means six multiplications, three additions, and three carries using the not-so-elementary method you learned in school.

Suppose the problem was "calculate 10 percent of 200." It's 20. Done!

The answer ought to be in the ballpark of 20. We're taking more-than-10-percent of less-than-200. It's often possible to convert not-so-round numbers into numbers with one significant digit. With 15 you just double it to get 30. Figure 30 percent of 155, and remember that you doubled one factor, so the result will have to be divided by 2.

We're still left with 155. Double that and you get 310, which has one fewer significant figure. So pretend you're calculating 30 percent of 310, and remember you've doubled the expression twice. It's not too hard to see that 30 percent of 310 is 93. It's two digit-by-digit multiplications with no carry.

But we've doubled the factors twice, so the 93 will have to be divided into 4. That can use another trick. It's easiest to break the 93 into chunks that are divisible by 4. That is, 93 is 80 plus 12 plus 1. Divide each term by 4 to get 20 plus 3 plus 1/4, or 23.25.

For clarity, I've explained all this more fully than you'll be able to in the allotted 10 seconds. You might say something along these lines:

"Fifteen percent of 155 is 30 percent of 310 divided by four. That's 4 into 93, which is 20 plus 3 plus 1/4, or 23.25."

As long as your mouth can keep up with your mind, this runs about 10 seconds. Good luck.

? What is the angle between a clock's hour hand and minute hand at 3:15?

Like mental calculation, analog clocks are verging on obsolescence — except in job interviews. This one is asked by Scott Cutler, CEO of StockX, who describes it as a test of "how somebody thinks about a very new problem in a difficult situation, and how they respond to that under pressure."

To answer questions like this, you need to know how angles are measured. A full circle, like the circuit of an hour hand in 12 hours' time, is 360 degrees. The angle between any two adjacent hour numbers is 360/12, or 30 degrees.

At 3:15 the minute and hour hands almost coincide. The minute hand is on 3 (exactly), and the hour hand is on 3 (approximately). The latter is not quite on 3, however, for it has traveled one-fourth of the way from 3 to 4. That's one-fourth of the 30 degrees separating neighboring hour numbers, or 7.5 degrees. That's the angle between the hour and minute hands.

? How many times a day do the hour and minute hands of a clock form right angles?

The minute hand is 12 times faster than the hour hand, so concentrate on it. There will be right angles whenever the minute hand is offset 90 degrees from the hour hand, clockwise or counterclockwise. That's about two right angles an hour, or about 48 in a 24-hour day.

Now refine that. The real issue is the speed of the minute hand relative to the hour hand. The minute hand moves 360 degrees in an hour, while the hour hand creeps only 30. Therefore the minute hand advances 330 degrees ahead of the hour hand each hour. That is 11/12 of a full cycle in an hour. In 24 hours, therefore, the minute hand will advance $24 \times 11/12$, or $2 \times 11 = 22$ full cycles relative to the hour hand. Each of those cycles will have two right angles, so that comes to 44 right angles.

Before signing off on 44, do a quick check of edge cases. The first right angle occurs a little after 12:15 a.m., and the last a little before 11:45 p.m. As long as the "day" starts on the hour, the 44 answer is correct.

Set Up Equations

Some questions are best solved with an equation. It's not always apparent which questions.

? You flip a coin until either the sequence heads-heads-tails or heads-tails-tails occurs. Is one more likely to appear first? If so, which? What is the probability it will occur first?

Anyone who's studied probability knows that all permutations of heads and tails are equally likely for a fair coin. The chances of tossing HHT and HTT are identical. Therefore, each is equally likely to be first. Except…

By this point the attentive reader will understand that first reactions can be wrong, and you should pay attention to unexpected words. The interviewer is asking which sequence is more likely *and* what the probability is. That's a strong hint that one sequence is more likely.

How can that be? Were I to toss a fair coin exactly three times, the chance of HHT is identical to that of HTT (it's 1 in 8 in each case). But that's not quite what this question asks, and the details matter. I am to toss a coin until either triplet occurs. It's as if I'm sliding an imaginary moving window across the sequence of tosses, looking for the first instance of HHT or HTT.

T⟨HTT⟩HHTHTTT...

In this example the triplet HTT occurs first, starting with the second toss.

This requires a different type of analysis. Both HHT and HTT start with heads. It's possible the first several tosses will be tails. But nothing decisive can happen until I toss the first heads. Without losing anything important, I can ignore any tails that occur at the beginning of my sequence and focus on *the first toss of heads.*

There are then two equally likely succeeding tosses, heads and tails, and likewise for every toss after that. The chart shows the tree of possibilities through the "grandchildren" generation. Each of the solid arrows represents one potential outcome of a coin toss, having a 1 in 2 probability. At the right are the four possible triplets of tosses starting with the first heads: HHH, HHT, HTH, and HTT.

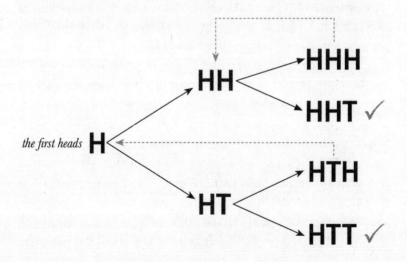

Two are the triplets we're looking for (shown with check marks). Two others are indecisive (HHH and HTH). If I got either, I'd have to keep tossing until either HHT or HTT appeared.

Take the case where I toss HHH. Should the next toss be tails, I'd have H*HHT*. That would give me an instance of HHT. But if the next toss is heads, that would simply extend the run of heads: HHHH. I'd have to toss again. Eventually the heads streak must end. The only way it can end is by tossing tails—say, HHH*HHT*. That also produces HHT. Consequently, once I get HHH, it's a foregone conclusion that HHT will turn up, and it must happen before HTT can appear (for one tails must occur before two consecutive tails can).

Another way of explaining that is to say that when I get HHH, I drop the leftmost H and toss again, inserting the new H or T in the rightmost position. This is equivalent to going back to the previous step where the tosses were HH (shown by the dashed arrow pointing backward to HH). Once I get HH, HHT must occur before HTT.

Now suppose I get HTH. I will need to toss again, at least twice. With the next toss I essentially drop the first H and append the new toss on the right: TH?. Either way, the triplet starts with T, so scratch that. Only by tossing another time can I drop the T and get a sequence that might be of interest: H??.

This is the same as starting over and going back to square one—to the first H. The chart indicates this with the dashed arrow pointing back to the first H.

Now set up equations. Let P be the probability that HHT occurs before HTT. There are two ways for this to happen. One is to toss HH, which guarantees HHT will be first. The chance of this is 1 in 2, or 1/2.

The other is to get HTH and "start over" with the same odds as before. The chance of this is 1 in 4, or 1/4. If this happens, the chance of getting HHT before HTT is the same as it originally was, *P*.

$$P = 1/2 + (1/4 \times P)$$

Simplify by subtracting $1/4 \times P$ from both sides.

$$3/4 \times P = 1/2$$
$$P = 4/3 \times 1/2 = 4/6 = 2/3$$

The answer to the question is that HHT is more likely to appear before HTT, with a 2 in 3 probability.

Looking back at the flow chart, this makes sense. On each run-through of the chart, HHT is a 2:1 favorite to be realized before HTT. There are diminishing chances of having to start over a second time, a third time, and so on. But ultimately I must get either HHT or HTT, with the former being twice as likely.

? You have two dice and will roll them repeatedly. What is the chance of rolling a 3 before rolling a 7?

In case it's not clear, the question is asking for the chance that the *first* 3 (meaning the total of both dice, not a 3 on one die) comes before the first 7 (also a total, obviously). Those who have played dice games much know that 7 is the most common total. Three is a much less common roll. Consequently the chance of rolling a 3 before a 7 will be well under 50 percent.

Draw a flow chart. We'll call rolling a 3 before a 7 "winning" and give it a value of 1. If your first roll is a 3, you win, and the game is over. If the first roll is 7, you lose, and the game is over. Any other total is indecisive. Do that, and you have to roll again with the same rules.

A fair die has six equally likely rolls. We're using two dice, and

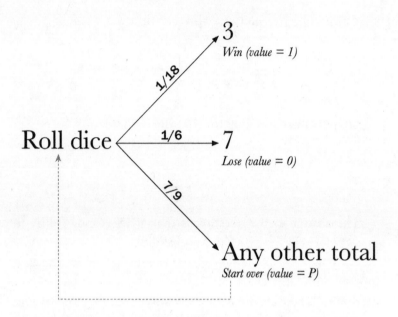

their rolls are completely independent of each other. That means there are 6 × 6 = 36 possible two-dice outcomes, all equally likely. By "outcome" I mean something like "die A lands 3, and die B lands 5."

We're interested only in the totals of the two dice's pips. There is, for instance, only one way to get a 2. It's for both dice to land on 1 ("snake eyes").

There are two ways to get a 3: 1/2 and 2/1.

But there are six ways to roll a 7: 1/6, 2/5, 3/4, 4/3, 5/2, and 6/1.

Because each of the 36 possible outcomes is equally likely, the chance of any given total is in proportion to the number of ways of rolling it. This means the chance of rolling 3 is 2/36, or 1/18. The chance of a 7 is 6/36, or 1/6.

We also need to know the chance of rolling anything other than a 3 or 7. That occurs in 36 minus (2 + 6), or 28 outcomes. Divide that by 36 to get the probability of a neither-3-nor-7 roll. It's 28/36, or 7/9.

Call P the probability of winning (rolling a 3 before a 7). It must equal the sum of the three possible outcomes, weighted by their probability. Here 1 corresponds to a certain win, and 0 is a certain loss. In the indecisive case, the chance of winning remains at P.

$$P = (1/18 \times 1) + (1/6 \times 0) + (7/9 \times P)$$
$$P = 1/18 + 7/9 \times P$$

Subtract $7/9 \times P$ from both sides:

$$2/9 \times P = 1/18$$
$$P = 9/36 = 1/4$$

That's the answer. The chance of rolling a 3 before a 7 is 1 in 4.

This question bears a resemblance to the one about the heads and tails sequences, and especially to the one about the three doors and the gold (page 155). This is one reason why it helps to have some familiarity with puzzles. A lot of interview brainteasers are repackaged versions of others.

? You've got a bowl of noodle soup, and you randomly attach the ends of the noodles together until there are no more free ends. How many loops will you have?

This Goldman Sachs question mentions no numbers at all. But you should be prepared to write a few on the whiteboard while solving it.

Start with the simplest possible version of the problem. There's just 1 noodle in the bowl. It has two ends. Attach them together magically, and you're done. You have turned spaghetti into SpaghettiO, leaving no loose ends. The answer is 1 loop.

With 2 noodles, it's possible to create 1 or 2 loops. The first joining might attach 2 different noodles, creating a double-length noodle. In the next step, its 2 ends would necessarily be joined to each other, creating a single big loop.

Alternately, the first joining might attach ends of the same noodle, creating a loop. Then the second joining would have to attach the ends of the remaining noodle, creating a second loop.

Jump to the general case of n noodles. The ultimate number of loops can be anywhere from 1 to n. One loop is possible only if every noodle end is connected to an end of a different noodle. That's highly unlikely, for it requires that every noodle just happen to connect to a different noodle. Similarly, n loops is unlikely, because that would require every end to join the other end of the same noodle. You'd expect the number of loops to be somewhere between 1 and n.

How many noodles are in a bowl of soup? Fifty? I'll use that; chances are the interviewer won't know any better. With 50 noodles, there are 100 ends. Choose any of the 100 ends and connect it to another end, randomly chosen from the 99 remaining. There are two possible outcomes:

1. The 2 ends just happen to belong to the same noodle, creating a loop. The chance of this is only 1 in 99. The net result of this action would be to decrease the number of linear noodles by 1; decrease the number of free ends by 2; and increase the number of loops by 1.
2. The 2 ends are from different noodles, creating a double-length noodle. The chance of this is 99 in 100. The net result is to decrease the number of linear noodles by 1; decrease the number of free ends by 2; and leave the number of loops unchanged (still zero, that is).

Case 1 creates a loop; Case 2 doesn't. But either way, the numbers of linear noodles and free ends decrease (by 1 and 2 respectively).

Because we start with 50 linear noodles and each joining decreases that by 1, there will be 50 joinings — no more, no less. Each offers a chance to produce 1 loop, though it need not do so.

The chance of creating a loop increases with each subsequent joining. On the second joining, there are 49 linear noodles and 98 ends. The chance of making a loop at this stage is 1 in 97. For the third joining there are 48 linear noodles, 96 ends, and a 1 in 95 chance of a loop. The decrease in noodles and increase in loop probability continues until the last joining, in which there will be 1 remaining noodle (probably a very long one) and its 2 free ends. This last joining must produce a loop.

Because a joining can produce 1 loop at most, the expected number of loops is simply the sum of all the 50 probabilities. It is:

$$1/99 + 1/97 + 1/95 + 1/93 \ldots + 1/5 + 1/3 + 1$$

That's for 50 noodles. In the general case of n noodles, the chance of creating a loop on the first joining operation is $1/(2n - 1)$. The expected number of loops is (I'll reverse the order of terms):

$$1 + 1/3 + 1/5 + 1/7 + 1/9 \ldots + 1/(2n - 1)$$

This is an exact and general answer. It's not a bad place to stop. But those with a strong math background can take it further. They can prove that the answer to the question is *close to 3 loops.*

To do that, you need to know a little about infinite series. Some series add up to (or "converge on") a finite sum. The usual classroom example is when you start with 1 and keep halving it:

$$1 + 1/2 + 1/4 + 1/8 + 1/16 + \ldots = 2$$

No matter how many terms you add, the sum always falls short of 2. The first 5 terms add up to 1.9375. Additional terms

edge ever closer to 2, yet even an infinity of them will never sur-
pass it.

Other series do not converge on a limit. The *harmonic series* is
a well-known example. It consists of 1 divided by each of the natural numbers in turn.

$$1 + 1/2 + 1/3 + 1/4 + 1/5 + 1/6 + 1/7 \ldots = ?$$

The name refers to musical overtones. On a string instrument, the wavelengths of overtones are in these terms' proportions
to a vibrating string's length.

Looking at the harmonic series, you might expect that it too
would add up to some limit. Instead the sum keeps getting larger
and larger as you add more terms. It grows quite slowly, however.
The sum of its first 100 terms is only 5.187+.

There is a family resemblance between the harmonic series
and our noodle-question series, which is the reciprocals of the odd
numbers only. You can say that the harmonic series consists of the
noodle series of odd-number reciprocals *plus* the series of even-
number reciprocals:

$$1 + 1/3 + 1/5 + 1/7 + 1/9 \ldots$$

$$+ 1/2 + 1/4 + 1/6 + 1/8 + 1/10 \ldots$$

$$1 + 1/2 + 1/3 + 1/4 + 1/5 + 1/6 + 1/7 + 1/8 + 1/9 + 1/10 \ldots$$

This tells us that the noodle series must also be a slow-growing
series. And because each term in the noodle series is a little bigger
than the corresponding term in the even-number-reciprocals
series, we can say that the sum of the noodle series is in general a
little more than half the value of the harmonic series.

As noted, the first 100 terms of the harmonic series is a little more than 5. Halve that and round up to get 3. That's a rough esti-mate of the first 50 terms of the noodle series. It's how many loops to expect, starting with a bowl of 50 noodles.

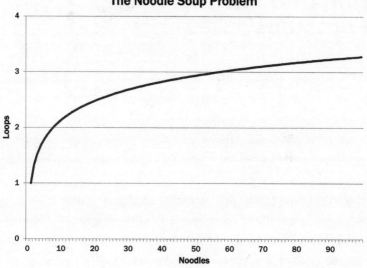

The Noodle Soup Problem

Here's a chart of the exact values, created from a spreadsheet. It takes 8 noodles to create 2 loops, on average. About 57 noodles are required to make 3 loops likely. With any realistic bowl of soup, the procedure will probably yield about 3 loops.

Don't Follow the Wrong Footsteps

Washington University physicist Alexander Calandra (1911–2006) was once asked to referee a grading dispute. A colleague thought a student's exam answer deserved a flunking score. The student thought he merited a perfect score.

The question asked how to determine the height of a tall building with a barometer. The intended answer was to use the barometer to measure the difference in air pressure between the roof and ground floor of the building. This tiny difference would, in theory, allow an estimation of the building's height. (Emphasis on the "in theory." The air pressure at the top of a 100-foot building is only about 0.36 percent less than at the ground. Good luck detecting that with a household barometer.)

The student's answer was, go to the top of the building, tie a long rope to the barometer, and lower it to the ground. Then pull up the rope and measure it. The student was trolling the teacher, of course, but Calandra had to admit that this answer had merit. However, the student's answer didn't demonstrate any knowledge of physics, and it was a physics exam. Calandra therefore asked the student to supply another answer, demonstrating knowledge of physics.

The student said he would drop the barometer off the top of the building and time its fall with a stopwatch, using the formula $d = 1/2gt^2$.

The student was well aware of the standard answer. He told Calandra he was just sick of instructors telling him how to think. He mentioned that he had still other answers: tying the barometer to a string and using it as a pendulum to measure the force of gravity at the top and bottom of the building; measuring the barometer's height and the length of the shadow it cast, then using that to compute the building's height from the length of *its* shadow; and asking the building's superintendent for the exact height, offering a brand-new barometer as payment.

Calandra ruled in favor of the student. This tale, published in 1968, drew wide attention. It spoke to the view that the "Sputnik-panicked classrooms of America," as Calandra put it, were emphasizing rote memorization over critical and creative thinking.

It also illustrates a concept known as *functional fixedness*. As defined by psychologist Karl Duncker in 1945, functional fixedness is a "mental block against using an object in a new way."

Barometers are made to measure air pressure. The mind resists the notion that they might be useful in other ways. It's been claimed that toddlers don't have functional fixedness. By about kindergarten age, however, children start to understand the grown-up world's rules. Rather than forging their own path, they may "follow the wrong footsteps" (in the words of Temple University psychologists Evangelia G. Chrysikou and Robert W. Weisberg). They fall into mental ruts.

Some interview questions test the candidate's ability to overcome functional fixedness.

? Describe how a milk carton is like a plane seat.

It's easy to come up with absurd answers. But there are many pertinent responses and, as with other oddball questions, it's a good idea to seize the opportunity to pitch your work-related skills. This question lends itself to a business, engineering, or design approach. Here's one possible response:

"Both milk cartons and plane seats are optimized solutions to the problem of packaging something perishable in a minimum of space. A milk carton is square because that allows it to be packed on a supermarket shelf more efficiently than a round bottle. And as we all know, airline seats are designed to pack the most passengers in the smallest space. In that respect, they're more efficient than the more comfortable seats they replaced.

"Milk cartons and airline seats are also engineered for lightness. Both have to be transported long distances, and the transportation cost is tied to weight. A plastic (rather than glass) milk carton and a jetliner seat's aluminum frame and foam cushions minimize weight.

"Both require a controlled climate. Milk spoils or freezes. Passengers complain when they're too hot or cold. In each case the climate-control system is heavy, placing another constraint on weight.

"Both put human lives at stake and must be engineered for safety. A milk carton needs to make it apparent when the opening has been tampered with. A seat needs to protect passengers in turbulence and hard landings and to facilitate emergency evacuations.

"Consumers of both milk and airfares are extremely price-sensitive. Milk is a common purchase that often serves as a supermarket's loss leader. They advertise a low price for milk, knowing it will draw in shoppers who will buy other things. The milk is put in the back of the store so that customers must navigate an aisle of higher-margin products. In much the same way, people choose airlines on the basis of a low fare on a travel site. In the process of buying that cheap ticket, however, they are made to run a gauntlet of higher-margin upgrades. With both milk and airfares, there is an element of bait and switch. The customer fixates on a low price, but the marketing persuades him or her to pay more for other things."

A classic functional fixedness test asks, "How many uses can you find for a brick?" A psychologist would count the number of uses offered. In this question, asked at Apple, the interviewer also hopes to hear a profusion of original, reasonably practical answers.

? If you were a pizza-delivery person, how could you benefit from a pair of scissors?

Some good responses are:

- Cut the pizza into slices (if the pizzeria people forgot to slice it, or a picky customer insists on thinner slices). Note that Italian street vendors often use scissors to cut pizza, as do upscale chefs who don't want to disrupt artfully arranged ingredients.
- Cut out discount coupons for customers.
- Snip open packets of sauce/grated cheese/pepper for customers who find it difficult to open them with their fingers.
- Use a blade of the scissors as a flat-bladed screwdriver (to secure the pizza delivery van's license plate).
- Use the scissors for self-defense against a carjacker or pizza thief.
- Use the scissors for the ribbon-cutting ceremony when you open your own pizzeria.

Don't forget: Pizza-delivery people have lives outside work. They use scissors for the same purposes anyone else does—to cut paper, string, or fabric.

? You have a broken calculator. The only number key that works is the 0. All the operator keys work. How can you get the number 24?

Add, subtract, or multiply zeros and you get zero. The only way to get a different result is to live dangerously and divide zero by zero. You'll get an error message like NOT A NUMBER. You won't get 24.

The 24 is misdirection. It leads you to think there's something unique about 24 and that the solution will produce 24 but not any old number.

But say you could produce 1. Then you could get any whole number you want.

$$1 + 1 + 1 + 1 + 1 + 1 + 1 + 1 + 1 + 1 + 1 + 1 + 1 + 1 + 1 + 1 + 1 + 1 + 1 + 1 + 1 + 1 = 24$$

Well, it's easy to get 1 from 0, so long as the calculator has scientific keys.

Punch in 0 and hit the e^x key. That gives 1. Hit +, then 0 and e^x again. That's 2. Keep going until you reach 24.

You don't have to use e^x. The 10^x, 2^x, x!, cos, and cosh keys also work.

? How would you find a needle in a haystack? You can spend only $3.

In a cartoon, a big red horseshoe magnet easily pulls a needle from a haystack. Not in real life. And sure, you can envision a massive electromagnet that could be cranked up to stupendous needle-pulling power. But the interviewer has already set a budget. What do you think you could buy for $3? Maybe a toy horseshoe magnet.

This question, asked at Google, turns on the ability to transcend the obvious. Just about everyone thinks of a magnet. It's better to recall Allen Newell and Herbert Simon's advice on searching for a needle in a haystack: "[I]dentify a small part of it in which we are quite sure to find a needle." How do you do that? Easy—you use a metal detector.

That reduces the problem to one of securing a metal detector for $3. Unlike super-powerful magnets, metal detectors are rather reasonably priced. They range from about $20 for handheld "pinpointers" to several hundred dollars for professional-quality models suited to serious haystack-searching.

You can rent metal detectors online, at prices as low as $5 a day for a handheld model. You could surely persuade *some* rental place to let you have one for $3 for a couple of hours. Promise them you'll promote their business on social media ("How I found a needle in a haystack").

George Crabtree, a senior scientist at Argonne National Laboratory, offered this alternate answer: "Take the haystack to an airport security checkpoint and shovel it (1,800 cubic feet) onto the scanner/metal detector. A line of hay measuring 2 feet wide, 2 feet high, [and] 450 feet long moving on the conveyor belt at 6 inches a second would take 15 minutes to pass through. Find needle. Submit to interrogation."

? You race two balls on different tracks. Ball A is on a straight track sloping downward. Ball B is on a track that is identical except that it has a dip in the middle. Assuming there is no friction, which ball will arrive at the end of its track first?

There are two popular responses. One is that Ball A finishes first "because a straight line is the shortest distance between two points." The other is that it's a tie "because energy is conserved."

Both answers cite the authority of maxims well-known to

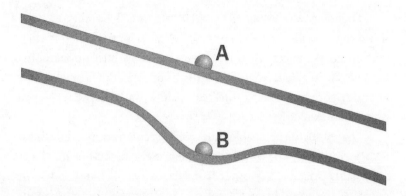

STEM grads. Both answers are wrong. Ball B, with the dip, wins the race. This is sometimes performed as a classroom demonstration, and there are YouTube videos showing that the ball with the dip wins.

A straight line *is* the shortest distance. Energy *is* conserved. The mistake is to think that the first sound bite that comes to mind settles the matter at hand.

In the top part of the track, the two balls begin accelerating under gravity. They travel apace on parallel tracks. Then Ball B hits the dip. As its track turns more steeply downward, the ball accelerates faster. B is soon going faster than A. (No mystery there; B has converted more of its potential energy into kinetic energy.)

Then the dip bottoms out. In this part of the trip, B's track is less downhill than A's, and B accelerates less than A. (If the dip is pronounced enough, B could actually be traveling uphill and slowing down.)

Then B is out of the dip. It has surrendered all the extra speed it got from the dip. At this point, and for the rest of the track, B will be traveling at the same speed as A will in the corresponding part of its track. B will finish with the same kinetic energy as A. *But it will finish first.*

That's because B traveled faster than A while it was in the dip. It never traveled slower than A.

Consider this analogy. Two hikers go for a walk. In the middle of the trail, one breaks into a run for five minutes. Then she walks the rest of the way. She will finish the trail before her friend who walks all the way. It's really that simple.

Ignore the MacGuffin

A "MacGuffin" is a plot device that seems all-important but is ultimately irrelevant. The good guys and the bad guys want the MacGuffin and go to great lengths to get it. Yet it doesn't matter. Famous MacGuffins are the Holy Grail, the Maltese Falcon, "Rosebud," and the Lost Ark. Director Alfred Hitchcock told François Truffaut that the best MacGuffin is "the emptiest, the most nonexistent, and the most absurd."

Some puzzles employ a similar gimmick. The problem creates the impression that a certain unknown (the "MacGuffin") is important. Yet the puzzle frustrates any attempt to deduce that unknown. This stops solvers in their tracks. But in reality the MacGuffin is a bit of misdirection. There is another, backdoor way of arriving at the answer.

? Jack is looking at Ann, and Ann is looking at George. Jack is married, but George is not. Is a married person looking at an unmarried person?

Ann's marital status is this interview question's MacGuffin. It seems that no answer is possible until we determine whether Ann is married. But notice that the question asks for a yes-or-no answer rather than, say, a probability. The interviewer wouldn't phrase the question that way unless a definitive answer is possible. And when you think about it, the answer can't be "no." Jack, Ann, and George could be three people in the crowd at Times Square on New Year's Eve, looking at zillions of other people, married and single. Then married Jack would certainly be looking at an unmarried person. The answer must be "yes."

Here's a more rigorous way of getting the answer. Jack, who is definitely married, is looking at Ann. If she's single, then a married person (Jack) is looking at a single person (Ann), and the answer is yes. If on the other hand Ann is married, then we know she's looking at George, who is unmarried, and that gives the same answer, yes. We therefore know the answer even though we'll never know the one thing (Ann's marital status) that seems to be essential.

? Three people rent a hotel room, paying $300 for one night ($100 each). The manager discovers that the desk clerk has charged too much: The room was supposed to be $250. He tells the clerk to return the extra $50. The clerk decides to pocket $20 for himself and returns just $30, telling the guests the room was $270. The three guests don't know this and are glad to get the room for only $90 each. They paid $270, and the clerk took $20, for a total of $290. What happened to the missing $10?

This is a vintage brainteaser that dates at least to the 1930s. It's known as the "missing dollar" riddle, as Depression-era versions used amounts one-tenth of those above. The puzzle has survived time and rising prices because it continues to mystify.

The short answer is: There is no missing $10. The guests paid $270 (net) for the hotel room, of which $250 went to the hotel and $20 to the clerk. End of story.

A politician may repeat a lie so many times that constituents believe it. That's basically what's happening here. Once you talk about a "missing $10," it takes on a life of its own. The misdirection lies mainly in the statement, "They paid $270, and the clerk pocketed $20, for a total of $290." The interviewer is adding two unrelated quantities. One is a deduction from the guests' funds, and the other is a credit to the clerk's. There is no reason to add these numbers together, and no reason to think the sum is meaningful. It's like adding the number of the hotel room to the bar tab and asking why it's different from the street address.

In accounting, cash flows must be categorized by who's paying whom. The riddle's situation is modestly confusing, for there are three distinct parties (we can count the three guests as one party, since their interests are aligned). The cash flows look like this:

$$\text{Guests: } -\$300 + \$30 = -\$270$$
$$\text{Hotel: } \$300 - \$50 = \$250$$
$$\text{Clerk: } \$20 = \$20$$

The net cash flows (−$270, $250, $20) add up to zero, which is as it should be when money is being passed around within a fixed group. No money magically appears or disappears.

The brainteaser manufactures a mystery by adding the guests' $270 and the clerk's $20. If you insist on doing that, you need to take the perspective of the hotel, as it's on the other end of both transactions. For the hotel, the $270 net payment is a positive cash flow, while the pocketed $20 is a negative cash flow.

$$\$270 + -\$20 = \$250$$

That adds up to a $250 net gain for the hotel, which is of course correct. The hotel should have received $270 for the rental but lost $20 to the clerk's petty embezzlement.

This puzzle demonstrates how easy it is to take the word of an authority figure or expert. Those who accept a misbegotten premise can waste a lot of time and effort. With this question the interviewer hopes to identify applicants with the too-rare ability to think for themselves.

? You have a medical condition that requires you to take two very expensive pills a day. One day you pick up the bottle of Prescription A and tap a pill into your hand. Then you pick up Bottle B and accidentally tap two pills into your palm. You are now holding one A pill and two B pills. That's a problem, because the two kinds of pills are absolutely indistinguishable. You need to take one A and one B. Should you skip either pill, you will die. But if you take two Bs on the same day, that's an overdose and you will die. Still, you don't want to throw out these costly pills and start over. How could you make sure you get one A and one B without wasting any pills?

It's natural to think that the solution involves figuring out which pill is which. But that's an unknown that must remain an unknown. Instead there's a strategy that makes the pills' identities irrelevant.

Look at what you do know. You've got an unequal mix of one A and two Bs. Take the bottles and pour out the opposite mix, two As and one B. Add to the original mix of one A and two Bs. This gives six pills, known to be an equal mix of three As and three Bs. It's the right blend; it's just that it's three days' worth.

Get a mortar and pestle and pulverize all six pills. Make sure the pill powder is well mixed. Carefully divide the pill dust into three equal shares (using measuring spoons or scales). These will be your doses for the coming three days.

An alternate answer is to cut each of the six pills in thirds and take a one-third-slice of each pill each day. But have you ever tried to cut a pill in *thirds*? You might as well go the pulverize route.

? You meet three strangers. One always tells the truth, one always lies, and the third speaks truths and falsehoods at random—but you don't know who is who. You have to identify the strangers by asking three yes-or-no questions. Each question must be put to one person only. What three questions would you ask?

A group of classic logic puzzles is set in a nation of truth-tellers and liars. Everyone in the nation falls consistently into one of the two categories. You meet someone and have to pose a question such that the answer will tell you what you need to know, regardless of whether that person is a truth-teller or a liar. There is a clever principle that helps solve these puzzles (read on).

But the three-strangers puzzle is much tougher. It is closely related to one that logician George Boolos (1940–1996) rated "the hardest logic puzzle ever." Boolos credited it to fellow logician, puzzle creator, and author Raymond Smullyan.

Start with the generic truth-tellers and liars puzzle. You come to a fork in the road and need to know which branch to take. There is a knowledgeable local standing there, but you don't know whether she's a truth-teller or a liar. The standard trick is to go meta: you ask a question about a question.

"If I were to ask you whether the left branch leads to the airport, would you say *Yes*?"

Should the local be a truth-teller, her answer can be taken at face value. A *Yes* response means, "Yes, I'd tell you this is the way to the airport because it *is* the way to the airport, and I'm a truthful person." Similarly, a *No* means "No, I wouldn't tell you this is the way because it isn't, and I can tell no lie."

But suppose the person is a liar. Had you asked right out, "Is this the way to the airport?" she'd say the opposite of whatever's true. But since you asked the indirect question, she's forced to lie about the lie she would have told. That double negative equals a positive. The liar is forced to say *Yes* if it's the right road and *No* if it's not. That's the same set of responses the truth-teller would give. Thus it doesn't matter which sort of person the informant is; the question guarantees the right answer.

This gimmick assumes an unrealistically scrupulous liar. She's concerned with lying for lying's sake as opposed to deceiving people by telling whatever mixture of truths and lies best suits her purposes. But that's how these puzzles work, and it applies to the one that now concerns us.

Call the three strangers True, False, and Random. Random is a more realistic liar in that you can't depend on him to lie. The standard incantation "If I asked you such-and-such..." has no power. Because Random can say anything, heedless of truth or tricky wording, he is the ultimate unreliable narrator. That means it would be helpful to identify Random *so you can ignore what he says.*

Label the three strangers #1, #2, and #3. Go up to #1 and ask:

"If I were to ask you whether #2 is Random, would you say *Yes*?"

The answer is not going to reveal the identity of #2. It is going to identify a person who is definitely *not* Random.

Suppose that #1 is True or False. As established above, the indirect question causes either to give an answer that can be taken at face value. A *Yes* would mean #2 is Random; *No* would mean he's not.

But we don't know that #1 is True or False. He could be Random.

Now put on your thinking cap. Either #1 is Random...or else #2 must be Random (if you get a *Yes* from #1)...or else #2 must NOT be Random (if you get a *No* from #1).

These logical fragments allow us to identify someone who is not Random. Take the case where #1's answer is *Yes*. Then Random must be either #2 or #1. Person #3 can be cleared of all suspicion of being Random.

Otherwise #1's answer is *No.* Then #2 is not Random — or else #1 is. That rules out #2 as Random.

Either way, we know a person (#2 or #3) who is not Random and must be either True or False. We can pose the second question to this individual. The second question also uses the gimmick.

"If I were to ask you whether you are True, would you say *Yes*?"

The answer will be *Yes* if this person is True and *No* if he's False. Simple as that. You've identified your first person.

You have one more question, but that's all you need. You might as well stick with this person. If he's True, you can ask a direct question. But for the sake of generality, let's keep to the formula. Ask:

"If I were to ask you whether *this* person [pointing to #1] is Random, would you say *Yes*?"

Yes means #1 is Random, and *No* means he isn't. Nor is #1 the person you've already identified, so you can deduce his identity with ease. That leaves the third stranger, who must be whatever identity is still unassigned.

There is an even more challenging version of this puzzle, the version that Boolos rated the hardest logic puzzle ever. It's the same except that the strangers understand your language yet will answer in their own language. You do not understand their language. All you know is that the words for *yes* and *no* are *ja* and *da* — but not necessarily in that order.

This twist was originally suggested by artificial intelligence pioneer John McCarthy. Incredibly, you don't need to know what *ja* and *da* mean to identify the three speakers.

Say you pose the question, "If I asked you, 'Will the sun rise tomorrow?', would you say *Ja*?" As long as this is directed to True or False, the answer will be *Ja.* That doesn't mean that *Ja* is "yes." Since everyone knows the sun will rise tomorrow, True will say *Ja*, provided that's his word for *Yes*. But if *Ja* means *No*, then True would also have to say *Ja* to this indirect question. In effect he'd be saying "No, I wouldn't answer *No* to your question, because the answer is *Yes*."

False would also say *Ja* because of the gimmick. (I'll spare you the details. Feel free to work them out if you have any doubt.)

In this case a *Ja* answer is foreordained, since there's no doubt that the sun will rise tomorrow. But the indirect question is designed so that the speaker will say *Ja* if the inner question is true and *Da* if it's false. The key point is that the word mentioned in the question (*Ja*) elicits the same word in response if the inner question is true and the other word (*Da*) if it's false.

The solution to the *Ja-Da* version of the puzzle is almost identical to the original's. The difference is that, in your three indirect questions, you substitute *Ja* for *Yes*. First, ask #1:

"If I were to ask you whether #2 is Random, would you say *Ja*?"

Take *Ja* as if it were a *Yes* and *Da* as a *No*. The procedure is the same from there, with the same substitutions. This will allow you to deduce all three identities—without ever learning what *Ja* and *Da* mean.

List, Count, Divide

Calculating the odds is key to any business. Wall Street employers have a long tradition of asking puzzles involving probability. They know the subject is a counterintuitive one that often confuses well-educated people. It is easy to be overconfident of hunches, estimates, and models (the root cause of all the financial industry's meltdowns). Interviewers ask probability questions to make sure that candidates have a healthy respect for the land mines.

Most of these questions don't require a deep understanding of probability or statistics. One simple, three-step technique works for a surprisingly large share of such questions:

1) List a set of equally probable outcomes or scenarios
2) Count the relevant outcomes
3) Divide two of the tallies to get the answer

Some will recognize this method as the essence of Bayes's theorem. Named for Thomas Bayes, a country preacher and mathematician in 18th-century England, Bayes's theorem describes how to use indirect or circumstantial evidence to adjust probabilities. It is the foundation of big data and is a mental model that should be familiar to anyone in the financial or technology industry. Here's an interview question (asked at Madison Tyler Holdings) where the three-step method is useful.

? There are five coins on a table, all showing heads. One of them is a trick coin with heads on both sides. You pick up a coin and toss it five times. Each time it lands heads. What is the probability that you have the trick coin?

Given that the chosen coin landed heads five times in a row, and given that you know there *is* a trick coin, there is good reason to suspect the tossed coin as gimmicked. The question is *how sure* you should be of this.

With a regular coin, tossing five heads in a row is unlikely. The chance is only $1/2 \times 1/2 \times 1/2 \times 1/2 \times 1/2$, or $1/32$. With the trick coin, five heads is a sure thing. That doesn't prove your coin is the trick one, but it is circumstantial ("Bayesian") evidence for it.

Using the list, count, divide method, the first step is to identify a set of equally likely outcomes. At the outset there are five coins, each equally likely to be chosen. Each coin has two sides, equally likely to land up. The complication is that, for the trick coin, both sides have a bas-relief portrait of a dead president.

Don't let that throw you. The trick coin's two sides are distinguishable in principle. You might imagine writing "A" and "B" on the trick coin's sides with a laundry marker. Then we can say that every coin toss — of whatever coin — has two distinct and equally likely outcomes. After five tosses, there will be 32 potential permutations of the chosen coin's two sides.

In all that gives $5 \times 32 = 160$ scenarios of picking a coin and then tossing it five times. A typical scenario might be choosing Coin 4 and tossing it to get THHTH. That would of course prove that Coin 4 is not the trick coin. Another scenario is to choose the trick coin and toss it to get AAABA, which of course counts as HHHHH.

The only cases that concern us are those yielding HHHHH. There is one such outcome for each of the four fair coins, plus all 32 of the trick coin's outcomes. That's 36 HHHHH outcomes in all.

The final step is to divide. Thirty-two of the 36 HHHHH outcomes are due to the trick coin. Since all are equally likely, the chance of having the trick coin is 32/36 or 8/9 or about 89 percent. That is the answer.

Probability questions don't always involve coins, dice, or cards. Try the list, count, divide strategy with this example.

? Ten people are sitting at a diner's counter. What's the chance that they are seated in order of increasing age?

Calculate the number of possible ways that 10 people might be seated at a counter. Any of the 10 might be seated on the first stool. Once that person is identified, there are nine remaining people who might occupy the second stool. There will likewise be eight possibilities for the next stool; seven for the stool after that; and so on. In all there are $10 \times 9 \times 8 \times 7 \times 6 \times 5 \times 4 \times 3 \times 2 \times 1$ possible orderings. This expression is called "ten factorial" and written as *10!*. So long as you mention the magic word *factorial*, the interviewer probably won't ask you to figure it out in your head. A phone's scientific calculator can tell you it comes to 3,628,800.

As far as we know, all 3,628,800 seating orders are equally likely. But only one arrangement has everyone in ascending order of age. Therefore the chance of 10 people just happening to sit down in age-increasing order is 1 in 10!, or 1/3,628,800. This is the usual answer.

Sometimes it is worth asking how realistic the so-called right answer is. We are assuming there are no ties by age. Of any two people, one is older, if only by days or minutes or seconds. But should we adopt the convention of rounding ages down to the last birthday, then having people of the same age is certainly possible.

Say there are two 26-year-olds, Olivia and Lucas. We might say that Olivia can be seated ahead of Lucas, or vice versa, and it still counts as "seated in order of increasing age." Then there would be two arrangements that count as age-sorted, and the chances would be 2 in 3,628,800. A three-way age tie would increase the chances by six (since there are $3 \times 2 \times 1 = 6$ ways of arranging three people the same age). But unless the group is a school class on a field trip, the odds would still be steeply against an age-ordered seating.

That raises another point. People often eat as part of a group, and groupings often involve people about the same age. Unaccompanied singletons may also tend to sit next to someone their own age. Self-sorting by age could greatly increase the chance of an age-ascending order. The 1/3,628,800 answer, then, is best regarded as a floor. Though it is unlikely that 10 people would just happen to rank themselves by age, the real-world probability must be substantially greater than the idealized case.

? You call a coworker at home. A boy named "Billy" answers. The colleague has two children: What is the probability that both children are boys?

Martin Gardner published this puzzle in a 1959 issue of *Scientific American* magazine. It has generated controversy ever since and is encountered in job interviews at Goldman Sachs and elsewhere.

Given the question's Eisenhower administration pedigree, you are to assume that everybody's got a binary gender. You may also pretend that boys and girls are equally common, and that there is no correlation between the gender(s) of siblings.

The commonsense answer is 1 in 2. We know nothing about

Billy's sibling, so the chance of a boy is the same as it ever was, 50-50. That's so obvious that you should suspect there's something more to it than that.

Using B for *Boy* and G for *Girl,* there are four possibilities for the genders of two children: BB, BG, GB, and GG. Each possibility is equally likely…until Billy answers the phone. Then we can cross GG off the list. That leaves three still-viable cases: BB, BG, GB. Just one of the three, BB, entails two boys. The chance that Billy has a brother is therefore 1 in 3.

Or is it? In listing the four possibilities, we are making a distinction between BG and GB, implying that the order matters. Those who've been exposed to probability theory know that we do this in tallying outcomes of coin tosses or dice throws. We might similarly list the children's genders in order of their age, or in alphabetical order by first name. So let's agree to list Billy's gender first. Then we can rule out GB as surely as GG. We are left with BB and BG. Just one has a boy as the other child, so the chance of two boys is 1 in 2.

Which answer is correct? It depends on how you came by the information you have. Gardner offered a pair of riddles:

1) Mr. Smith has two children. At least one of them is a boy. What is the probability that both children are boys?
2) Mr. Jones has two children. The older child is a girl. What is the probability that both children are girls?

Gardner argued that the two questions have different answers: 1 in 3 for Mr. Smith and 1 in 2 for Mr. Jones. Some *Scientific American* readers objected, and Gardner conceded that "the problem was ambiguously stated and could not be answered without additional data."

Ultimately the probabilities depend on the narrator's agenda.

Why is the poser of the riddle telling us what he has? Is any information being withheld?

Proud parents-to-be throw gender-reveal parties with exploding glitter-filled piñatas. It's hard to imagine a parent saying, *At least one of my children is a boy.* That is the cryptic wording of a logic puzzle. The Mr. Smith narrator seems more intent on mystifying than informing.

One possible reading is that the narrator learned the genders of the Smith children and then—intending to pose a conundrum—announced, "At least one child is a boy." This leaves the possibilities BB, BG, and GB, and the chance of the other child being a boy is 1 in 3.

By comparison, the Mr. Jones narrator is more conversational. You can imagine a father saying, *My oldest child is a girl...* If this reading is correct, then the fact that the older child is a girl is incidental. It has no bearing on the other, younger child, whose chance of being a girl is the usual 1 in 2.

In both of Gardner's riddles, it's necessary to fill in some narrative gaps. You need to decide what information was acquired at random and what may have been cherry-picked. This is true of many probability paradoxes and puzzles.

The wording of the "Billy" question is particularly treacherous. You're asked to pretend that this is your experience: *you* called up an imaginary colleague and spoke to Billy. Despite that, you know only what the interviewer has chosen to tell you.

You're led to believe that speaking to Billy was an accident. You called when you did and just happened to speak with a random child. The only thing you know is that there's a kid you spoke to and one you didn't; the former is a boy. That leaves BB and BG as the only viable possibilities. Thus 1 in 2 is the better, easier-to-justify answer.

Yet a complete response should acknowledge this ambiguity. The bit about Billy may simply be a way of dramatizing the information that *At least one child is a boy.* In that case, 1 in 3 is defensible.

The two-child problem has come to the attention of behavioral economists. They've found that minor changes in wording can shift opinions of the odds. This finding should be regarded as a warning, pertinent whenever quants and other experts make predictions about the financial markets—or anything else. The objective, analytical side of probability cannot be separated from the intuitive, often unconscious process of assessing what is relevant. It's easy to cook up "rigorous" models founded on fallible instincts.

? Before getting on a plane to Seattle, you call three friends in the city to ask about the weather. All three say it's raining. However, these friends are unreliable; they tell the truth only two-thirds of the time. What is the chance it really is raining in Seattle?

Our social networks swarm with unreliable narrators. This interview question, posed at Facebook, asks who you can trust and how confident you should be.

It's worth laying out some assumptions. One is that the Seattle weather is not *Rashomon.* Either it's raining or it's not, and everyone can agree on which it is. Another is that you called the three friends in such quick succession that the weather didn't change while you were talking, and these friends live so close to one another that they are reporting on the same local weather.

A common wrong answer to this question is that the chance of rain is 2 in 3. That would be an acceptable answer, were there just one friend (who tells the truth two-thirds of the time). It fails to take into account the fact that there are *three* independent witnesses. This clearly increases the chance that it's raining.

Another wrong response is to say the chance of rain is 3 out of

3 (100 percent!). That's the tally of your quick phone poll, but we all know that polls can be misleading.

Look at it this way. All three friends say the same thing. Therefore, all three are telling the truth, or all three are lying. Those are the only possibilities.

The chance of the three friends telling the truth (about the weather or anything else) is $2/3 \times 2/3 \times 2/3$. That comes to 8/27, or about 29.6 percent.

The chance of all three lying is $1/3 \times 1/3 \times 1/3$, or 1/27, or about 3.7 percent.

This means that our evidence—of all three friends saying the same thing—is much more likely if they're all telling the truth (that is, it is indeed raining). Specifically, it's 8 times more likely. The odds are therefore 8 to 1 in favor of rain. The chance that it's raining is $8/(8 + 1)$, or 8/9, or about 88.89 percent. This is a good answer.

There's a better one. I've glossed over an important feature of the problem, which is how often it normally rains in Seattle. This ought to be taken into account in evaluating the friends' testimony.

Seattle has an undeserved reputation as a place where it rains 24/7. But statistics say that Seattle has 150 days of measurable rain a year. Of course, it doesn't usually rain all day in Seattle or anywhere else. The finest-grained statistics I found are for hours with measurable rain. Seattle has 822 hours a year with measurable rainfall. That translates into a 9.38 percent chance of measurable rain in a given hour. So even without any eyewitness testimony, the background chance that it's raining in Seattle right now would be somewhere around 9 percent.

Add to that the evidence of three friends. Their testimony is consistent with two scenarios: that it's raining and the friends are telling the truth, or that it's not raining and the friends are lying. I've worked out the joint probabilities.

	Seattle climate statistics	Eyewitness evidence	Joint probability
Scenario 1: It's raining and all three friends are telling the truth	9 percent chance of rain	8/27 chance that all three friends are telling the truth	2.67 percent
Scenario 2: It's not raining and all three friends are lying	91 percent chance of no rain	1/27 chance that all three friends are lying	3.37 percent
Takeaway	Background chance of rain is 9 percent (ignoring witnesses)	89 percent probability that all three friends are telling the truth (ignoring rain data)	44 percent it's raining (taking into account rain data and friends' testimony and reliability)

The no-rain scenario is now more probable than the rain one (3.37 percent v. 2.67 percent). We know one of the two scenarios must apply. That means the chance of rain, given the three friends' testimony, is 2.67/(2.67 + 3.37) percent, or only about 44 percent.

You won't be expected to trot out Seattle climate statistics in the interview. But it is relevant to point out that you should make a Bayesian calculation, adjusted for how much it rains in Seattle.

It's human nature to rely more on what we heard at the water-cooler or saw on Facebook than on overall statistics that might supply context. Psychologists know this as *base-rate neglect*. Critical thinking is in order even when a source is reasonably reliable. Companies use focus groups, marketing tests, and the expertise of consultants to predict the success of new ventures. These ways of forecasting may have impressive track records. But you also need to consider how many comparable products come on the market every year, and how many of those flop. The chance of a breakout success is small. When shooting for the moon, there is cause to discount the optimism of normally reliable forecasts.

Look for a Parallel to the Job

Problem-solving is the art of drawing analogies. Many interview questions can be answered by drawing a connection to the body of knowledge required for the job. This gimmick is so prevalent that it merits its own rule: *Look for a parallel to the job.*

? Arnie and Britney each live on desert islands. The two islands are connected only by a ferry service. The ferryman, Fred, has a boat with a box that can be locked with a padlock. Arnie and Britney each have a padlock and a key. Arnie wants to send Britney a valuable diamond. But Fred can't be trusted. The diamond must be locked securely in the box, and Fred can't be given the key (he's able to duplicate keys). How should Arnie send the diamond to Britney without Fred swiping it?

A logic puzzle about ferrying a wolf, a goat, and cabbages across a river is recorded from 8th-century England. Hundreds of variations exist, and some have been used in hiring interviews.

There are two ways to solve this particular puzzle. One is to apply techniques we've already covered: work backward, take a detour, use a process of elimination, and don't follow the wrong footsteps. The other is to look for a job-related analogy that will give away the solution. (Hint: This question is asked at Oracle and other tech companies.)

Let's start by working backward. A correct solution surely must end with Arnie locking the diamond in the box and sending it to Britney. Fred is not able to open the box en route, presumably because he doesn't have the key. When the boat arrives, Britney does have the key and is able to open the box.

The issue is not so much the diamond as the key. How does Arnie send his key to Britney? He can't do that without either handing the key to unscrupulous Fred or putting it in the lockbox along with the diamond. In the first case, Fred uses the key to open the lockbox and pockets the diamond. In the second, nobody can open the lockbox, ever.

All crossing-the-river/ocean questions require a conflict move. You must make a "useless" detour or send something the "wrong" way. For instance: Maybe Britney sends her key to Arnie? But this has the same problem: Fred could swipe it—or, worse, duplicate Britney's key, so that the theft wasn't apparent. Neither islander can send his/her key to the other, unless it's locked in a box that person can't open.

The upshot is that (a) nobody can send the diamond directly and (b) nobody can send a key directly. Both conclusions are correct. But what else can Arnie and Britney send? We've ruled out everything except *locks*.

Right. We think of a strongbox as a place to store valuables, such as a diamond. A lock is supposed to be on the outside. But this is a functional fixedness puzzle, for the solution requires putting the lock *inside* the box.

It works like this: The next time Fred's boat docks at her island, Britney puts her open padlock in the box, along with a note saying, ARNIE, I'VE FIGURED IT OUT. SEND ME THE DIAMOND AND USE THIS LOCK.

The box is left unlocked. Snoopy Fred reads the note and sees the lock. But he can't do anything about it, at least not without it being obvious.

When the boat arrives at Arnie's island, Arnie reads the note. He puts the diamond in the box and secures it with Britney's lock.

When the boat returns to her island, Britney opens her lock with her key (which has never left her possession) and gets the diamond.

Anyone with a background in software engineering should recognize an analogy. The problem's story parallels the problem of sending money or private information across the internet. It's Cyber Monday, and Arnie wants to send a payment to Britney's online store. Fred is the big, bad internet, full of hackers and scammers. For those who recognize this parallel, it's a major nudge. The e-commerce protocol is a blueprint to the solution.

The online economy is founded on *public-key cryptography*. RSA (the security protocol invented by Ron Rivest, Adi Shamir, and Leonard Adleman in 1978) is built on the premise that everyone can have a personal "lock" and "key" for their digital strongbox. These locks and keys are made of code rather than tempered steel. A lock may be published, incorporated into websites, sent across the internet, and hacked. But everyone keeps their key to themselves (on the private "island" of a phone or computer). If I want to buy a graphic novel from a dealer in Tokyo, I (in effect) use the dealer's lock to enclose my payment information. Of course, I'm not aware of the mechanics; it's all handled by software. But no one other than the dealer can unlock my payment, for no one else has the dealer's key.

Everyone applying for a job in a technology field should be familiar with RSA. If you make the connection to RSA, the solution is straightforward. It's necessary to think outside the box— send the lock, not the key—which is how RSA works.

There are people who study for the test and quickly forget what they learned. There are others who remember their education but can apply it only in narrowly defined contexts. Questions like this test the ability to make productive connections.

? How many dogs in the world have the same number of hairs?

The answer depends on the number of dogs in the world and the number of hairs on an average dog. No job candidate is expected to know either quantity (not even when interviewing at PetSmart). But these are things that anyone can estimate.

The world population of humans is approaching eight billion. The dog population is at least loosely related. Most dogs are pets. (The wild dogs of Africa and India are endangered.) A quick guess is that the number of dogs is comparable to the number of humans.

Look at how much space in the grocery story is devoted to dog food, as opposed to people food. Somebody's eating all that human food, and the dogs are eating all that dog food. But there's a lot more human food. This is reason to think there are more humans than dogs (even allowing that humans eat more).

The US is an affluent nation that loves its dogs. In much of the developing world it is not realistic to feed and care for an animal that doesn't earn its keep and (in most cultures) isn't eaten. That is further reason to think that the number of dogs in the world must be less than the human population. As usual we want a round number, so let's put the global dog population at about 1 billion.

How many hairs are on a dog? Imagine that Cruella De Vil has an ottoman. It's a one-foot cube upholstered in dog fur. The ottoman is about the size of a dog, but it has six sides, making six square feet of fur.

You might guess that dog hairs are spaced about 1/100 inch apart, in a neat grid. Then there would be about $100 \times 100 = 10,000$ per square inch.

There are $12 \times 12 = 144$ square inches per square foot. We immediately want to simplify 144, with its three significant figures. One option is to round it down to 100. But we're going to multiply 144 by the ottoman's 6 square feet, and that gives something like 1,000 square inches. That would mean the ottoman has 10,000 times 1,000, or 10 million hairs. With the ottoman as a surreal surrogate for a dog, a typical canine would also have about 10 million hairs.

It's not hard to see that, with a billion dogs and 10 million hairs per average dog, there must be many dogs with the same number of hairs. This is a consequence of the *pigeonhole principle*.

As articulated by German mathematician Peter Gustav Lejeune Dirichlet in 1834, the principle says that when you have more things ("pigeons") than containers or categories for those things ("pigeonholes"), some of the things must share the same container or category. When a hotel has 115 guests and 100 rooms, some are going to have to double up.

Not surprisingly, Dirichlet was not the first to appreciate this. "It is necessary that two men have the same number of hairs, écus, or other things as each other," wrote Jean Leurechon (1591–1670), a French Jesuit priest and mathematician, in 1622. (An écu was a gold coin.) By the early 1700s, Leurechon's claim had become an English brainteaser: Do two people in London have the same number of hairs on their heads? The answer, of course, is yes.

Other logic puzzles use the same idea. "A sock drawer contains red and blue socks. The lights are out, and you can't see them. How many socks do you need to take to be sure of getting two of the same color?" Many kick themselves when they hear the answer (three). There are only two colors of socks, red and blue. Take three and at least two have to be the same color.

Note that you don't know which color that is. Nor do you know whether two socks match or all three do. You just know that with three socks of two possible colors, it's impossible for there *not* to be a match.

Dogs Categorized by Hair Count

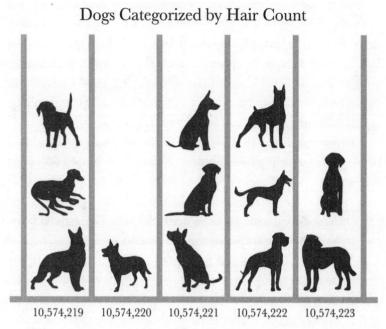

| 10,574,219 | 10,574,220 | 10,574,221 | 10,574,222 | 10,574,223 |

We would now like to apply the pigeonhole principle to dogs. The diagram shows the basic idea. We want to classify dogs by their hair count. Though the average dog may have about 10 million hairs, dogs vary greatly in size and hairiness.

A dog's skin area is proportional to the square of its height. A Great Dane is about twice as tall as an average dog, so that means it would have about four times the skin area and hair, all else being equal.

There must be a gamut of hair counts, running from virtually zero (for a Xoloitzcuintli or "Mexican hairless") to something like 40 million (for a really big dog). Each of those 40 million possible hair counts is a pigeonhole. With about a billion dogs in the world, there are about 25 times more dogs than pigeonholes. Therefore, some have to share their number of hairs with other dogs.

Were the dogs equally apportioned among hair counts, then each dog would have the same number of hairs as about 25 other dogs. But it's far more likely that there is a bell-shaped curve of hair counts. Few dogs occupy the extremes; most dogs cluster somewhere in the middle. In that case, a typical dog—neither too big nor too small, too hairy nor too hairless—might share a hair count with many more than 25 other dogs.

Answering a question like this often means tossing out a lot of ideas. Interviewers value closure. You should button up your answer with a summary.

- There are unquestionably dogs walking this Earth with the exact same number of hairs as other dogs.
- This isn't an unusual distinction. It's true of nearly all the world's dogs.
- A typical dog will have the same number of hairs as 25 other dogs at least, and probably a lot more than that.

The pigeonhole principle is relevant in coding—and that's one reason why this question has become popular in interviews for software engineers. It applies to lossless data compression, in which a big, unruly mess of data (a Spotify song, a Netflix movie) is condensed into an abbreviated format that can be recovered with full fidelity. There the pigeonhole principle is so important that it should be familiar to software engineers.

? An astronaut in Earth's orbit throws a baseball. What happens to the baseball? Can the astronaut throw the baseball so that it hits the Earth?

In 2008 American astronaut Garrett Reisman threw a ceremonial first pitch for the New York Yankees while aboard the

International Space Station. Reisman lobbed the ball lightly in the direction of the camera. He claimed it was a 17,500-mile-per-hour pitch, for the space station circles the Earth at about that speed.

That's a fundamental insight for this interview question. Even before it's thrown, the baseball will be traveling at close to 17,500 mph. A pitch won't change that very much. Major-league fastballs have been clocked at 100 miles per hour (not that a typical astronaut could manage that in a spacesuit). The pitch velocity will be added to the orbital velocity, but it won't be anything more than a rounding error. No matter which direction an astronaut throws a baseball, it will remain in orbit—and a hardly changed orbit at that.

To take things further, you need a passing acquaintance with several laws of Newton and Kepler. Newton's first law of motion says that objects keep moving in a straight line unless they're acted upon by a force. A spacewalking astronaut should therefore expect to see a thrown baseball receding into the void, in whatever direction it was thrown. No surprise there.

Kepler's first law says that planetary orbits are ellipses, with the Sun at one focus of the ellipse. The same law applies to baseballs in space, though "Sun" must be replaced with "Earth," or more exactly "the center of the Earth." The baseball starts in a circular orbit (a circle is a limiting case of an ellipse). The pitch changes that orbit into a slightly more elliptical one.

Say the astronaut throws the baseball in the direction of her orbital motion. This will propel the ball into a bigger, more elliptical orbit that takes it farther away from Earth. Meanwhile the astronaut continues in a circular orbit, or almost so (the slight recoil from the pitch can hardly budge her orbit).

Kepler's third law says that the squares of planets' orbital periods are proportional to the cubes of their mean distances from the Sun. We don't need all of Kepler's math. The upshot is, the bigger the orbit, the longer it takes to make a complete circuit.

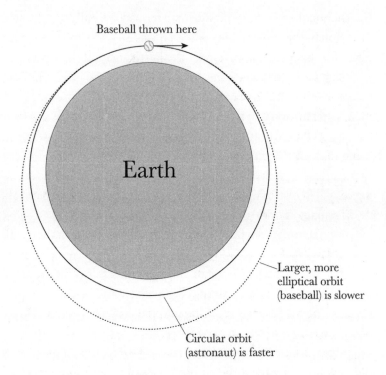

Baseball thrown here

Larger, more
elliptical orbit
(baseball) is slower

Circular orbit
(astronaut) is faster

The pitched baseball's bigger orbit will therefore have a longer period than the astronaut's smaller orbit. This means the baseball will lag behind the astronaut. From the astronaut's perspective, the ball will first recede into the distance. But her orbit will soon overtake the baseball's, and the baseball will then be "overhead," away from the center of the Earth. This won't take long. The International Space Station completes a circuit of the Earth in about 92 minutes.

Assuming the baseball were close enough to be visible, it would then sink into the horizon behind the astronaut. She would keep overtaking the baseball like this with each circuit of the Earth.

Were the baseball thrown in other directions, it would also

assume an elliptical orbit. Should the astronaut throw the baseball in the direction opposite her motion, the ball's orbit would be smaller and faster. The baseball would periodically overtake her, and at each pass it would be "underneath" her, toward the Earth.

Space agencies track space junk—orbiting debris that might damage a spacecraft. The baseball would be another such hazard. Its orbit would coincide with that of the astronaut and her space station at the top of the diagram above, the point where the baseball was originally thrown. There's no danger unless the baseball and the astronaut return to this point in their orbit at the same time. But eventually this must happen, at a moment of karma in which the baseball smacks into the astronaut at the same speed with which she originally threw it.

Can the astronaut throw a baseball to hit the Earth? The instinct is to lob it straight down, toward the center of the Earth, as hard as you possibly can. But this would hardly deflect its forward motion. The optimal strategy is for the astronaut to pitch the baseball in the *opposite* direction from her own orbital motion.

Suppose she had superpowers and could pitch a baseball at 17,500 mph. A backward pitch would nullify the baseball's orbital motion, leaving it motionless relative to the Earth. Gravity would do the rest. It would fall straight down (a "dead drop").

At the space station's altitude of about 250 miles, the Earth's gravity is not too much less than it is on the planet's surface. The baseball would begin falling at nearly the familiar rate, quickly picking up speed. As it entered the lower atmosphere, its cowhide, twine, and cork would blaze red-hot, then white-hot. It would burn up like a meteor, transmuting itself to gas and motes of dust.

Even if the astronaut could finesse the ballistics, the baseball wouldn't splash into the ocean or bonk someone on the head. It would just be molecules raining down.

As it turns out, an astronaut doesn't need superpowers to

accomplish that result. Suppose she throws the baseball backward, against her orbital motion, as fast as she possibly can manage. This will reduce the ball's speed a little, transforming the circular orbit into a slightly more elliptical one that makes a closer approach to Earth.

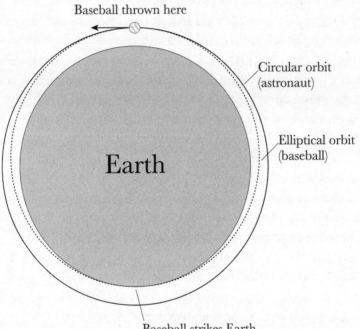

Baseball thrown here

Circular orbit (astronaut)

Elliptical orbit (baseball)

Earth

Baseball strikes Earth

Were the new orbit's perigee (lowest point) right at the Earth's surface, then the baseball would skim the Earth. Maybe it would hit a tree or a cow or a big-box store. But propelling a baseball into an Earth-skimming orbit is way beyond the abilities of any astronaut.

However, there is air resistance even at the 250-mile height of the International Space Station. Thin wisps of atmosphere cause the space station to lose about 15 miles of altitude a year. It has to be periodically boosted upward with rocket power; otherwise it would have long since reentered the thick part of the atmosphere and burned up.

This means that the orbit of a space station—or a baseball at rest with respect to it—is not strictly an ellipse but a spiral. With each circuit, it ends up a little closer to the Earth. The baseball is destined to reenter the atmosphere even without any action by the astronaut. However, the astronaut could shift the baseball into a slightly lower orbit, causing it to encounter more air resistance and spiral downward faster.

This isn't just theory. In 2008 American astronaut Heidemarie Stefanyshyn-Piper lost a tool bag during a spacewalk. She didn't throw it; she nudged it accidentally and was unable to retrieve it safely before it drifted off. The tool bag, tracked by the world's space agencies as hazardous junk, took eight months to fall to Earth and vaporize upon reentry.

An astronaut in low-Earth orbit who pitched a baseball with all her might against her orbital motion could accelerate the projectile's normal orbital decay, perhaps substantially. The baseball would reach the Earth's surface as atoms in a matter of months. So in that limited sense, an astronaut *can* throw a baseball to Earth.

As asked at SpaceX, this frivolous-sounding question has serious implications. Engineers applying for a job should recognize that the baseball poses analogies to the ever-growing problem of space junk. The quickest, most permanent solution for space junk is a dead drop. That, however, requires more energy than any other plausible maneuver. Aging satellites rarely have fuel to spare. It takes fuel to keep a satellite in service, and space agencies want to extend scientific missions as long as possible.

A more practical strategy is the one described above: slow the object enough to send it into a spiraling, atmosphere-grazing orbit, where it will eventually burn up.

The opposite approach is to boost an orbiting object to escape velocity. This would send the object beyond the Earth's gravitational pull, but doing so takes a lot of energy. More often, objects are boosted into a "graveyard orbit"—one high enough where the object is unlikely to do any damage (for the foreseeable future, anyway).

? When a hot dog expands, it splits. Which direction does it split in, and why?

Long used in interviews at Oxford, this question has been adopted by SpaceX. Start with the easy part. Do grilled hot dogs (sausages, chorizo, bratwurst, kielbasa) split lengthwise or into circular sections?

Maybe you don't grill. But you eat, right? Imagine you've gained weight and are wearing really tight jeans. Your thighs are bursting through the fabric, Incredible Hulk–style. Are the jeans going to rip the long way or the short way?

Or picture a long balloon, the kind used to make balloon animals. When it bursts, does it burst into long shreds or short rubber bands?

Most of us have enough experience with grilling, tight pants, or balloons to know the answer. Any cylindrical volume under pressure, enclosed by a tight surface layer, splits that surface layer lengthwise. This is a law of our universe, and of the Marvel Universe. (See Incredible Hulk movies and comics.)

The harder part of the question is to explain why. I'll give an intuitive answer suitable for Oxford and then a more rigorous one for SpaceX engineers.

A hot dog's juicy interior expands as it cooks. This puts pressure on its skin. It becomes a balloon of mystery meat. One feature of a "balloon"—meaning a thin skin enclosing an incompressible fluid—is that the pressure inside is uniform. This is known as Pascal's law.

However, the way this internal pressure stresses the skin

depends on the balloon's shape. A spherical balloon has complete symmetry, so the pressure is applied equally to every bit of surface. The more the shape departs from a sphere, the more the stress on the skin will be directional.

As the hot-dog filling tries to expand outward, it is more constrained in the narrow direction than in the long direction. The skin is particularly stressed around the small circumference, and that's where it is most likely to burst. A burst there propagates in the long direction because that best relieves the stress. The hot dog "unzips" lengthwise.

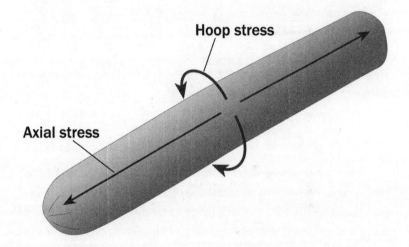

Now here's a more detailed answer. Some terminology is in order. The word *stress* applies not just to a person undergoing a job interview but also, in physics, to a force divided by an area. In this case we're talking about the nearly uniform internal pressure of an expanding sausage applied to the cross-section area of its skin or casing.

A mass-produced hot dog is close to being a meat cylinder. It has two kinds of stress. *Hoop stress* runs around the sausage at its small diameter (like the hoops on a barrel). It's caused by the tendency of the hot dog to plump up as it cooks, stretching the skin crosswise. *Axial stress* runs across the hot dog's length. It's due to the hot dog lengthening, stretching the skin the long way.

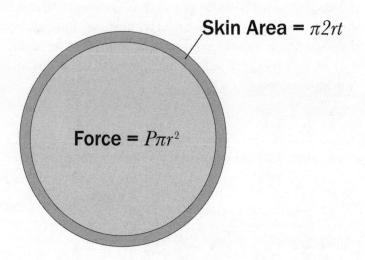

$$\text{Skin Area} = \pi 2rt$$

$$\text{Force} = P\pi r^2$$

Next we're going to do some calculus with a sharp kitchen knife. The plan is to chop the hot dog into many identical prosciutto-thin slices. We will think of the hot dog as being made up of a large (even infinite) number of these very thin (or infinitesimal) slices. These slices are representative of the stress on the skin. By analyzing one, we can understand what's going on with the whole frankfurter.

So imagine slicing the hot dog from one end to the other, perpendicular to its length, into a succession of thin circular disks. Each slice represents axial stress. (Yes, this is counterintuitive. You might expect a circular cross-section to represent hoop stress. But each slice transmits axial stress to its immediate neighbors, all along the length of the hot dog. For those who know calculus, the thin circular slices are differentials of axial stress.)

The force on each circular slice is the uniform internal pressure (P) multiplied by the circle's cross-sectional area. The area of a circle is $\pi r2$, where r is the radius.

$$\text{Force} = P\pi r^2$$

This force is applied over the thin, circular band of skin or casing. Its cross-sectional area is essentially the thickness (t) of the skin multiplied by the hot dog's circumference ($\pi 2r$), or $\pi 2rt$. The axial stress on the skin is the force divided by the area. This comes to $Pr/2t$.

$$\text{Axial Stress} = \text{Force}/\text{Area} = P\pi r^2 / \pi 2rt = Pr/2t$$

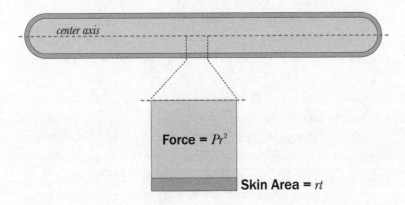

Now for the hoop stress. This requires some fancy slicing. We want to cut the hot dog into long and narrow slices about the center axis (dashed line). Each slice transmits hoop stress to its neighbors, all around the small circumference. But since the slices are so long and uniform, we don't need a whole one. For simplicity we can take just a square section of one slice and work from that. The sides of this square section will be the hot dog's radius, r.

As before, there is a force equaling the internal pressure times the square slice's area, r².

$$Force = Pr^2$$

This force is now being applied to the thin strip of skin at bottom. It's r long and t thick, with an area of rt. Hoop stress comes to Pr/t.

$$Hoop\ Stress = Force/Area = Pr^2/rt = Pr/t$$

The expressions for the axial stress and the hoop stress look the same except that the axial stress has a 2 in the denominator. That means the hoop stress is twice the magnitude of the axial stress. When a hot dog's skin bursts, it's likely because of hoop stress, and that creates a longways split.

Some have trouble with the fact that hoop stress causes a split lengthwise rather than in its own direction. Think of it this way: When wearing tight pants, the belt is in the direction of hoop stress. But if the pants split, the split seams will be up-and-down, not horizontal like the belt.

Reality is complicated. A hot-dog casing will have random flaws, and these also affect the splitting. But the twofold difference between hoop and axial stress favors lengthwise splits.

What do hot dogs have to do with SpaceX rockets? Everything. Rockets are titanium-skin tubes made to enclose fantastically high pressures. When they fail, they rupture like hot dogs, for the same reasons. Ditto for frozen water pipes, overloaded pressure boilers, submarine hulls, and aircraft fuselages. A SpaceX engineer candidate who truly understands the science should be able to connect the dots.

Introduce a New Feature

Problems are expressed in words, numbers, and ideas. You try to rearrange these concepts into new configurations, like a Rubik's cube. That doesn't always work. It may be necessary to invent a new feature (George Pólya called it an *auxiliary element*). This could be a new concept, a strategy, a numerical expression, or an added shape in a diagram. The new feature provides an original way of thinking about the problem and what's important in it. It functions like a scaffolding on a building. It's not in the blueprint; it's something you add on to build the structure (solve the problem).

? You have 10 red, 11 blue, and 12 green chameleons. When two chameleons of different colors meet, both change into the other color — a red and a blue chameleon would turn green. When two chameleons of the same color meet, nothing happens. Can all the chameleons ever be the same color?

This is a pretty weird setup, so you should begin by talking through an example. Say that 10 red chameleons meet 10 greens.

They fist-bump and instantly turn into 20 blues. Add them to the original 11 blues, and you have 31 blues. But there would be 2 greens left over. Should those 2 greens meet 2 blues, they'd turn red. Then there would be 4 reds, 29 blues, and no greens. If the goal is to make all the chameleons the same color, we lost ground with that last change. It's Whac-A-Lizard.

The difficulty rests with the fact that there are leftover chameleons that can't be paired off by color. Work backward by imagining a situation in which we succeeded in getting all the chameleons the same color. How did that happen?

There must have been equal numbers of 2 colors. Say we had 3 reds, 3 blues, and all the rest were greens. The 3 reds could have met the 3 blues, producing 6 greens and therefore an all-green set.

The question specifies different numbers of each color (10, 11, and 12). That means we can't get to all-one-color in a single step. You may have a hunch that the numbers of colors have been chosen to make it impossible for all the chameleons to end up the same color. The trick is to prove it.

It's not easy to do that because there are so many possible meetings and color changes. Say we want to establish that it's impossible to arrive at equal numbers of reds and blues. When a red and a blue chameleon meet, this happens:

The number of red chameleons decreases by 1
The number of blue chameleons decreases by 1
The number of green chameleons increases by 2

In general, at any meeting of different-colored lizards, 2 colors decrease by 1 and the other color increases by 2.

This puzzle talks of reds, blues, and greens. You can play around with those colors for some time without getting anywhere. So I'm going to invent a new concept, the *red-versus-blue surplus*.

This is simply the number of reds minus the number of blues (R − B, for short).

Notice that if R − B ever equals 0, then the number of reds must equal the number of blues, and we will be able to produce an all-green set. The goal is to make R − B zero.

Look what happens to R − B when two lizards meet. The four possible outcomes of a meeting are:

- If the two lizards that meet are the same color, then nothing happens and R − B is unchanged
- If a red meets a blue, there is 1 less red and 1 less blue; R − B, however, remains unchanged
- If a green meets a red, there is 1 less red and 2 new blues; R − B decreases by 3
- If a green meets a blue, there is 1 less blue and 2 new reds; R − B increases by 3

In some interactions R − B is unchanged. When it does change, it can increase or decrease only by a multiple of 3. That's what we need to know.

The question says we start with 10 reds and 11 blues. That means that R − B is initially −1. R − B can therefore take on values like 2, 5, 8, 11…(or −4, −7, −10, −13…), but there's no way that R − B can ever be 0. That in turn means it's impossible for all the chameleons to be green, for that would require R − B to be 0 − 0 = 0. We can just as easily invent a *red-versus-green surplus* and a *blue-versus-green surplus*. By similar reasoning, it's impossible to have the chameleons all blue or all red. The answer is that the chameleons can't all end up the same color.

? A king learns that an enemy has poisoned exactly one of the 100 bottles of wine intended for a celebration. The only way he can test a bottle is by giving a few drops of wine to a monkey.

If the wine is poisoned, the monkey will die within 24 hours. The celebration is tomorrow night. What's the smallest number of monkeys the king needs to identify the poisoned bottle?

What do health agencies do when there's an outbreak of food poisoning? They ask the sick to list what they ate or drank. It's then a process of elimination to identify what food the poisoning victims had in common.

Monkeys can't talk or write. The solution—which isn't monkey-friendly—is to mix a unique cocktail for each monkey, containing samples from different sets of wine bottles. Properly done, this would allow us to deduce the poisoned bottle from which monkeys survive.

The solution amounts to specifying an individualized recipe for each monkey, telling which bottles are sampled. This recipe is going to be fairly complicated since there are 100 wine bottles and an unknown number of monkeys. There must be a way of referring to the wine bottles. For instance, we could number them 1 through 100.

But there's a better scheme: to use binary numbers. This will be almost as natural for software engineers, and it has a handy feature. Each digit is a 1 or a 0, which can be identified with a monkey getting, or not getting, a sample from a particular bottle. This is the new feature we've introduced—a binary code that both identifies bottles and tells how to distribute samples.

Convert the numbers 1 through 100 into base 2. Fill in leading zeros so that each base-2 number has seven digits. Bottle #1 is 0000001, bottle #2 is 0000010, and so on. That means that bottle #100 is 1100100. (The base-2 number signifies $1 \times 64 + 1 \times 32 + 0 \times 16 + 0 \times 8 + 1 \times 4 + 0 \times 2 + 0 \times 1 = 100$.)

The seven digits can also correspond to seven monkeys, for that's all that are needed. Call the monkeys Ava, Brooklyn, Cheetah, Delilah, Ethan, Francisco, and Curious George. Each is identified with one of the seven digit-positions in the binary code. A 1 means that monkey gets a sample of the bottle identified by the binary code, and a 0 means it doesn't.

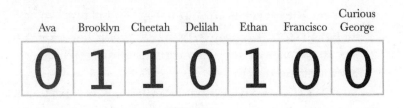

Ava	Brooklyn	Cheetah	Delilah	Ethan	Francisco	Curious George
0	1	1	0	1	0	0

Example: Bottle #52 is 0110100 in binary form. Its digits tell us that Brooklyn, Cheetah, and Ethan are to get a few drops of bottle #52 in their cocktail, while the other monkeys don't receive anything from this bottle.

Twenty-four hours later, check whether the monkeys are alive. The fatal bottle's number will be spelled out in simian corpses. Should Brooklyn, Cheetah, and Ethan die, we could see that they were the only monkeys to sample bottle #52 (0110100). And if they're the only monkeys that died, that must be the poisoned bottle.

What about bottle #53 (0110101)? The three dead monkeys also sampled that bottle. But so did Curious George, who is fine. The fact that Curious George survived proves that bottle #53 is OK. There were other bottles that the three dead monkeys sampled, but—by design—there are living monkeys offering proof that these bottles weren't the fatal one.

This scheme requires seven monkeys because seven binary digits span numbers up to 127 in decimal notation. Up to six monkeys may die (if the fatal bottle is #63 or 0111111), but it will usually be less.

Curious George might have a hangover. He will have had to sample from 50 different bottles—all the odd-numbered ones.

This system requires that the poison be far more toxic than alcohol itself, so that a drop or two will suffice to test a bottle.

? Seven people sit in a circle, each wearing a colored hat. Each can see the hats that the other six are wearing, but not his or her own. The hat colors are drawn from a list of seven colors, but not all colors necessarily occur. It could be that all seven hats are green — or any other permutation of seven colors. Everyone is aware of this.

On a given signal, all seven persons are required to yell out a guess about his or her own hat color. Provided at least one of the guesses is correct, everyone will be allowed to take off their hats and go home. If no guess is right, everyone will be executed.

The seven are allowed to confer on a strategy before receiving their hats. What should they do?

This question, asked at Jane Capital, is insanely tough. Be prepared to employ everything in the problem-solver's tool belt.

Use an analogy. Those with experience of brainteasers will recognize this as a *colored-hat problem*. Such puzzles obey stylized rules. One is that every person is "perfectly logical," able to deduce consequences instantly and always looking many moves ahead. In a typical puzzle, one person is able to figure out his hat color from the fact that someone else has been unable to deduce his. This is the classic gimmick.

Your first reaction is wrong / Don't follow the wrong footsteps. Experienced puzzle-solvers will therefore expect a solution similar to the standard colored-hat gimmick. But in the usual sort of colored-hat puzzles, the hat-wearers take turns guessing their hat color. This puzzle is different: the guesses must be simultaneous. A guesser doesn't learn anything from the others until he's irretrievably committed to his own guess. A fundamentally new approach is required.

Pay attention to unexpected words. Several phrases ought to stand out: "not all colors necessarily occur"; "at least one of the guesses"; "confer on a strategy."

In a typical colored-hat puzzle, the people are able to draw some conclusion about their own hat color from the hats they see. But that appears to have been ruled out here: no matter what colors you see, your own hat could be any color (from the "list of seven," anyway). The interviewer expends a whole sentence nailing down the point that all seven hats could be green, or any other combination.

It certainly sounds like the intended solution is a team effort. The people are to agree on a strategy so that *at least one* of the guesses is correct. It's not required that everyone be right.

Try a simpler version of the problem. Imagine that there were just two people and two hat colors (black and white). You look at the other guy and see he's wearing a black hat. Now what? His hat color has no bearing on your own.

But you're allowed to collaborate on a strategy. The two-person case makes it easier to lay out possible strategies. One is no strategy at all:

- Each person independently guesses a random color

Even this isn't so bad as you might think. Each guess has a 1 in 2 chance of being right. The penalty is only for the case in which both are wrong. The chance of that is 1 in 4. That means the pair have a 75 percent chance of survival.

The goal is to improve those odds. Here are some simple cooperative strategies.

- Each person guesses black, no matter what.
- Each person guesses white, no matter what.
- One person is assigned to guess black and the other to guess white.

Hash these out and you'll see that none is any better (or worse) than a random guess. None can guarantee that at least one person will guess right.

Albert Einstein supposedly said that everything should be made as simple as possible, but no simpler. When the simple strategies aren't working, try something a little more complicated.

Strategies can be conditional, depending on the color of the other person's hat. For instance:

- Each person guesses whatever color he sees the other person wearing.
- Each person guesses whatever color the other person *isn't* wearing.
- One guesses the color he sees, and the other guesses the color he doesn't see.

Bingo. That last one works. If the colors are the same, then the person who guesses the color he sees is certain to be right about his own hat color. If the colors are different, then the person who guesses the color he doesn't see must be right.

The guessers are acting as a team, and there is no *I* in *team.* They are not trying to maximize the chance of their own guess being right; rather, they are trying to ensure that at least one guess will be right (because that's what the puzzle demands).

We have now solved a simpler version of the problem. The next step is to scale the idea up to the case of seven people and seven hat colors. Often the scaling-up is straightforward. Unfortunately, this is not one of those cases. (I told you it's a difficult problem.)

The MacGuffin doesn't matter. The two-person solution divides a universe of possibilities into two all-inclusive, mutually exclusive cases (the colors are the same; the colors are different). Each hat-wearer is assigned to one of the two cases and is instructed to guess *as if* that case applied. We don't need to know which case is right.

That's a MacGuffin. The important thing is that one of the guesses has to be right.

Here's another simpler version of the problem, this time with seven people. The goal is to guess the day of the week that Genghis Khan was born. At least one person out of seven must guess correctly, or else.

But Genghis Khan's mom and dad were nomads, and his date of birth — sometime in the year 1162 AD — is lost to the sands of Mongolia. Nobody, not even historians, knows the right answer. Doesn't matter! Just make sure that each of the seven persons calls out a different day of the week. Somebody has to be right.

We likewise want to find a way to split the interview question's universe of colored-hat possibilities into seven cases, one of which must apply. It's evident that this strategy can't be too simple. Each hat-wearer may see any combination of colors, and this potentially affects his guess, maybe in a complicated way. Strategies like "guess the color you see the most of" or "guess a color you don't see" wouldn't work.

Add a new feature. Let's assign numbers to the colors, 1 through 7. One advantage of numbers is that you can add them. The color-numbers of the seven hats must add up to a sum. Anyone who learned that sum would be able to compute their own hat color. Say you're told the sum is 29. You see six hats and know their colors have the identifying numbers 2, 5, 3, 5, 5, and 3. This adds up to 23. The one hat you can't see, your own, must have the value 6, in order for all the hats to add up to 29. Your hat is whatever color corresponds to 6.

Nobody knows the sum of the hat color-numbers because nobody can see all seven hats. That need not be a problem, given that only one person has to be right. A tentative strategy is to assign possible sums to each hat-wearer and have them deduce their hat color from that sum. Then someone would have the right sum and would give the right answer.

The hitch is that there are more possible sums than people. The sum of seven color codes, ranging from 1 through 7, could be anywhere from 7 to 49. That's 43 possible sums versus just seven hat-wearers.

There's an easy remedy. Divide the sum by seven and take the remainder. This remainder must be in the range of 0 to 6. That's seven possibilities in all, one for each hat-wearer. The remainder is sufficient to deduce a hat color.

Example: I'm assigned the remainder 5. It doesn't matter whether that's the actual remainder. My job is to pretend it is and act accordingly. I see six colored hats and total their number values to get a sum of 31. Divide 31 by 7 and it goes 4 times, leaving a remainder of 3.

That's 2 less than 5, so my unseen hat must be the color that corresponds to 2. I guess that color.

The other people follow similar strategies, but with different assigned remainders. Provided all seven people follow these directions without error, the success rate will be 100 percent. Six of seven guesses will always be wrong, and one will always be right.

Afterword: The Edison Fallacy

Thomas Edison was wrong: There is no magic question(naire) that tells whether someone will be a capable employee. Too many of today's employers make a similar error. Psychologists have assembled evidence that all widely used assessment techniques are fallible, and none is nearly as predictive of job performance as just about everybody takes for granted. No matter what types of questions are asked, the interview process risks becoming an exercise in confirmation bias.

There are nonetheless ways to conduct better interviews, even when assessment techniques (and those using them) are imperfect. This afterword looks at strategies for doing that.

The first thing for an employer to recognize is that most of the winnowing of applicants takes place before the interview. It's often the bots and apps—résumé-scanning software, targeted social-media ads, AI-based phone interviews, psychometric games—that determine who gets invited to a formal interview. This is where false negatives and hiring bias are most likely to occur, and where they can most readily be minimized. Those who hire need to take these preliminaries as seriously as they do the later stages of hiring. They should consider ways to implement the "blind audition" philosophy into their screening.

Interviews are not just about identifying a most qualified applicant. An interview is also an essential opportunity for employers and candidates to meet and establish a comfort level with one another before making a big mutual commitment. The candidate is evaluating the company as well as vice versa. Should a company make an offer, it does so in the hope that the candidate will be able to make a quick decision—in its favor, of course. This decision will be based in large measure on how comfortable the candidate was with the interview experience.

Oddball questions, by definition, do not appear to have anything to do with the job. Interviewers who use them owe applicants a quick explanation about the purpose of such questions. If you can't readily explain why you're using a question, that's a sign you shouldn't be asking it.

There is a certain tolerance for culture-fit questions ("What's your superpower?") in group interviews for entry-level jobs. The same questions can be seen as insulting in one-on-one interviews with experienced applicants. A company is not a frat house looking for a certain "type" and trying to keep everyone else out. What matters is the ability and willingness to do the job. Anything not connected with that is a distraction.

Companies that use logic puzzles in interviews are announcing the importance of creative problem-solving and the ability to learn new skills on the job. To the extent that these qualifications apply, there is likely to be correlation between candidates who do well on the puzzle and those who do well on the job.

The best use of puzzles (or any kind of interview questions) is to challenge the snap judgments that interviewers make about candidates. Psychologists recommend structured interviews— those where the same set of questions is posed to each candidate. This checks the unconscious tendency to choose questions that confirm what an interviewer already believes about a candidate. Given that questions get exposed online or in books, it may not be practical to repeat the same questions indefinitely. But interviewers can and should pose the same questions to each of the candidates for a given job opening.

Experienced interviewers realize that brainteasers are not just about a right answer. "The point of the question is to generate a half hour of conversation," said former Microsoft interviewer Joel Spolsky. "You tell how smart the person is based on the conversation you have."

There are ways to manage the inherent subjectivity in this. A scoring key provides uniform guidelines for rating answers. Here's a sample key, one that Jeremiah Honer and colleagues used to rate answers to the question, "How many gas stations are in the United States?"

1 point:
> Unable to grasp the problem
> Gives an estimate with no rationale

3 points:
> Develops/discusses some rationale for estimation.
Examples:
> - Number of cars
> - Number of people, and how many people have cars
> - Number of licensed drivers
> - How often each car is filled up
> - Amount of gas used in a time period
> - Average distance traveled
> - Average gas mileage

5 points:
> Develops a specific rationale, linking numerous variables.
> Example: estimating the number of cars by relating it to the US population, accounting for family size and how many cars there are per person

These benchmarks allowed interviewers to grade responses on a scale of 1 to 5, and there was consistency between different interviewers' ratings. An interview question can't be fair unless a given response receives nearly the same ratings from different interviewers.

There has been an arms race among some employers in asking difficult brainteasers. The question is presented as a sword in the stone, for a unicorn candidate who may never arrive. But some questions are just too hard to be practical as interview assessments. The ones about lying and truth-telling strangers and the seven people with colored hats may fall into that category. It might take a good 20 minutes to have a shot at cracking a really difficult puzzle. Realistically, no one can or should devote that much interview time to a single question.

Smart employers understand that job interviews are a noisy indicator. It is best to hedge your bets: Ask many questions, none requiring too much time, rather than one super-difficult one. Ask different types of questions, rather than just one type. Above all, don't place too much weight on the response to any one question.

Edison framed himself as a great demythologizer of genius. "To invent, you need a good imagination and a pile of junk," he was quoted as saying. The innovator is not so much a creator as a tinkerer who keeps putting old ideas together in new ways—until something clicks. "I never had an idea in my life," Edison said. "My so-called inventions already existed in the environment—I took them out. I've created nothing. Nobody does."

To no small degree, this was humblebragging. But Edison recognized that even his signature inventions weren't completely new. Edison was a great improver, and improving ideas is hard work. This thesis also runs through the partly apocryphal body of aphorisms attributed to Edison: "Opportunity is missed by most people because it is dressed in overalls and looks like work."

"Genius is one percent inspiration, ninety-nine percent perspiration." "Many of life's failures are people who did not realize how close they were to success when they gave up."

These themes have in turn been reprised by generations of innovators. "Creativity is just connecting things," runs one of Steve Jobs's best-known maxims. "Failure is an option here," said Elon Musk. "If things are not failing, you are not innovating enough."

Creative problem-solving does involve trial and error. But this statement can be misunderstood. Good problem-solvers don't really try things at random. They have a constantly updated gut sense of what to try next. Their strategy changes as their understanding of the problem evolves.

At their best, puzzles and games distill the luck, frustration, and triumph of life into manageable form. One of the most important things employers can learn about applicants is how they handle the inevitable setbacks. Creative problem-solvers are comfortable with uncertainty. They are quick to recognize dead ends and move on. They persist. All this — a matter of grit no less than genius — is crucial to meeting the challenges of our disruptive century.

Acknowledgments

I've now written three books on unconventional interview questions (the first two being *How Would You Move Mount Fuji?*, 2003, and *Are You Smart Enough to Work at Google?*, 2013). Readers of the previous books have kept me informed of new questions and techniques. Thanks to everyone who's contributed, including those who requested their names not be used.

Special recognition goes to Paul M. Dennis, who documented the legacy of the Edison questionnaire (for good or ill) in shaping thinking about hiring. Edward Cussler pointed me to the tradition of Oxbridge questions as a precedent to brainteaser interview questions, and I drew from Sinclair McKay's published research on the use of crossword and logic puzzles at Bletchley Park. Frida Polli was an enthusiastic guide to new thinking on gender and ethnic bias in hiring and how psychometric games might supply a remedy.

Thanks also to Luis Abreu, Rakesh Agrawal, Adam David Barr, Joe Barrera, Tracy Behar, Kiran Bondalapati, John Brockman, Max Brockman, Curtis Fonger, Alicia Godfrey, Randy Gold, Ryan Harbage, Astrid De Kerangal, Larry Hussar, Philip Johnson-Laird, Rohan Mathew, Gene McKenna, Alex Paikin, Eric Polin,

Acknowledgments

Michael Pryor, Michelle Robinovitz, Christina Rodriguez, Brett Rudy Sr., Arthur Saint-Aubin, Chris Sells, Joel Shurkin, Alyson Shontell, Jerry Slocum, Jerome Smith, Norman Spears, Joel Spolsky, Noah Suojanen, Karen Wickre, the staff of the UCLA Research Library, Rod Van Mechelen, and Roxanne Williams.

Sources

Abreu, Luis (2015). "700 Billion: My experience interviewing at Apple" (blog post). Feb. 24, 2015. lmjabreu.com/post/700-billion/

Agry, David (2019). "As an interviewer, what question has ruined a perfectly solid interview of a candidate for you?" *Quora* answer, September 10, 2019.

Allport, Gordon W. (1961). *Pattern and Growth in Personality*. New York: Holt, Rinehart and Winston, 1961.

Allport, Gordon W., and Henry S. Odbert (1936). "Trait names: A psycholexical study." *Psychological Monographs* 47: 211.

Alvarez, Simon (2019). "Elon Musk's Tesla, SpaceX top list of most attractive employers for engineering students." *Teslarati*, June 7, 2019.

Ambady, Nalini, and Robert Rosenthal (1993). "Half a Minute: Predicting Teacher Evaluations from Thin Slices of Nonverbal Behavior and Physical Attractiveness." *Journal of Personality and Social Psychology* 64, 431–441.

Anderson, Chris (2012). "Elon Musk's Mission to Mars." *Wired*, October 21, 2012.

Anderson, Chris (2013). "The mind behind Tesla, SpaceX, SolarCity." bit.ly/3cDhAUi

Ankeny, Jason (2017). "NRF Foundation unveils retail education, credentialing program." *Retail Dive*, Jan. 15, 2017.

Baritompa, Bill, Rainer Löwen, Burkard Polster, and Marty Ross (2018). "Mathematical Table Turning Revisited." June 28, 2018. arXiv:math /0511490v1 [math.HO]

Baron-Cohen, Simon, Sally Wheelwright, Jacqueline Hill, Yogini Raste, and Ian Plumb (2001). "The 'Reading the Mind in the Eyes' Test Revised Version: A Study with Normal Adults, and Adults with Asperger Syndrome or High-functioning Autism." *Journal of Child Psychology and Psychiatry* 42, 241–251. 10.1111/1469-7610.00715

Bartling, Björn, and Alexander W. Cappelen, Mathias Ekström, Erik Ø. Sørensen, and Bertil Tungodden (2018). "Fairness in Winner-Take-All-Markets." NHH Department of Economics Discussion Paper No. 08/2018.

Berg, W. Keith, and Dana L. Byrd (2002). "The Tower of London Spatial Problem-Solving Task: Enhancing Clinical and Research Implementation." *Journal of Clinical and Experimental Neuropsychology* 24, 586–604.

Berg, Joyce, John Dickhaut, and Kevin McCabe (1995). "Trust, Reciprocity, and Social History." *Games and Economic Behavior* 10, 122–142.

Bertrand, Marianne, and Sendhil Mullainathan (2004). "Are Emily and Greg More Employable than Lakisha and Jamal? A Field Experiment on Labor Market Discrimination." *The American Economic Review* 94, 991–1013.

Bock, R. Darrell, and Donald Kolakowski (1973). "Further Evidence of Sex-Linked Major-Gene Influence on Human Spatial Visualizing Ability." *American Journal of Human Genetics* 25, 1–14.

Boolos, George (1996). "The Hardest Logic Puzzle Ever." *The Harvard Review of Philosophy,* Spring 1996, 62–65.

Bortkiewicz, Ladislaus Josephovich (1898). *Das Gesetz der kleinen Zahlen* ["The law of small numbers"]. Leipzig, Germany: B.G. Teubner.

Bradley, Robert L. Jr. (2011). *Edison to Enron: Markets and Political Strategies.* New York: Wiley.

Braythwayt, R. S. (2012). "A Woman's Story." bit.ly/3cMWCm0

Brigham, Carl C. (1923). *A Study of American Intelligence.* Princeton: Princeton University Press, 1923.

Brigham, Carl C. (1930). "Intelligence Tests of Immigrant Groups." *The Psychological Review* 37, 158–165.

Bruce, Laura (2003). "Penny Facts." *Bankrate,* June 17, 2003.

Sources

Buckley, M. Ronald, Amy Christine Norris, and Danielle S. Wiese (2000). "A brief history of the selection interview: May the next 100 years be more fruitful." *Journal of Management History* 6, 113–126.

Calandra, Alexander (1968). "Angels on a Pin." *Saturday Review,* December 21, 1968, 60.

Carr, Austin (2018). "Moneyball for business: How AI is changing talent management." *Fast Company,* August 16, 2018.

Chen, Desiree (2005). "How Would I…Find a Needle in a Haystack?" *Chicago Tribune,* March 27, 2005.

Chrysikou, Evangelia G., and Robert W. Weisberg (2005). "Following the Wrong Footsteps: Fixation Effects of Pictorial Examples in a Design Problem-Solving Task." *Journal of Experimental Psychology: Learning, Memory, and Cognition* 31, 1134–1148.

Connley, Courtney (2019). "Amazon HR exec: This interview misstep can kill your chances of getting hired." CNBC, Jan. 18, 2019.

Constine, Josh (2017). "Pymetrics attacks discrimination in hiring with AI and recruiting games." *TechCrunch,* September 20, 2017.

Coren, Stanley (2012). "How Many Dogs Are There in the World?" *Psychology Today,* September 19, 2012. bit.ly/3cIZbp5

Csapó, Beno, and Joachim Funke (2017). *The Nature of Problem Solving: Using Research to Inspire 21st Century Learning.* Paris: OECD Publishing.

Dennis, Paul M. (1984). "The Edison Questionnaire." *Journal of the History of the Behavioral Sciences* 20, 23–37.

Deutschman, Alan (2004). "Inside the Mind of Jeff Bezos." *Fast Company,* August 1, 2004.

D'Onfro, Jillian (2019). "Chris Urmson, CEO of Hot Self-Driving Startup Aurora, on Hiring and Humility." *Forbes,* September 11, 2019.

Duncker, Karl (1945). "On problem solving." *Psychological Monographs* 58, 5.

Durant, Elizabeth (2003). "70th reunion for Edison discovery." *MIT News,* June 4, 2003.

Fast Company staff (2016). "Apple's Angela Ahrendts on What It Takes to Make Change Inside a Successful Business." *Fast Company,* February 2016.

Feloni, Richard (2016). "Facebook's most asked interview question is tough to answer but a brilliant way to find the perfect fit." *Business Insider,* February 23, 2016.

Fimbel, Eric, Stéphane Lauzon, and Constant Rainville (2009). "Performance of Humans vs. Exploration Algorithms on the Tower of London Test." *PLoS ONE* 4 (9): e763.

Forbes, B. C. (1921). "Why Do So Many Men Never Amount to Anything?" *American Magazine* 91, 86.

Friedersdorf, Conor (2013). "President Obama Would Choose to Fight the Horse-Sized Duck." *The Atlantic,* January 11, 2013.

Gaddis, S. Michael (2017). "How Black Are Lakisha and Jamal? Racial Perceptions from Names Used in Correspondence Audit Studies." *Sociological Science* 4, 469–489.

García-Gallego, Aurora, Nikolaos Georgantzis, and Maria J. Ruis-Martos (2019). "The Heaven Dictator Game: Costless Taking or Giving." *Journal of Behavioral and Experimental Economics* 82, 1–10.

Gardner, Martin (1959). *Mathematical Puzzles & Diversions.* New York: Simon & Schuster.

Gardner, Martin (1961). *The 2nd Scientific American Book of Mathematical Puzzles & Diversions.* New York: Simon & Schuster.

Gardner, Martin (1986). *Knotted Doughnuts and Other Mathematical Entertainments.* New York: W.H. Freeman.

Gardner, Martin (1989). *Penrose Tiles to Trapdoor Ciphers.* New York: W.H. Freeman.

Gershgorn, Dave (2018). "Companies are on the hook if their hiring algorithms are biased." *Quartz,* October 22, 2018.

Gillett, Rachel, Áine Cain, and Marissa Perino. "Here's what Elon Musk, Richard Branson, and 53 other successful people ask job candidates during interviews." *Business Insider,* August 22, 2019.

Goldberg, Emma (2020). " 'Techlash' Hits College Campuses." *New York Times,* January 11, 2020.

Goldin, Claudia, and Cecelia Rouse (1997). "Orchestrating Impartiality: The Impact of 'Blind' Auditions on Female Musicians." Cambridge, Mass.: National Bureau of Economic Research. Working paper 5903, January 1997.

Hastings, Michael (2013). "How Obama Won the Internet." *BuzzFeed News,* January 8, 2013.

Heilwell, Rebecca (2019). "Artificial intelligence will help determine if you get your next job." *Vox,* December 12, 2019.

Highhouse, Scott (2008). "Stubborn Reliance on Intuition and Subjectivity in Employee Selection." *Industrial and Organizational Psychology* 1, 333–342.

Hjelle, Larry A., and Daniel J. Ziegler (1992). *Personality Theories: Basic Assumptions, Research, and Applications,* 3rd edition. New York: McGraw-Hill.

Hoffman, Elizabeth, Kevin A. McCabe, Keith Shachat, and Vernon Smith (1994). "Preferences, Property Rights, and Anonymity in Bargaining Games." *Games and Economic Behavior* 7, 346–380.

Hogan, Robert, Joyce Hogan, and Brent W. Roberts (1996). "Personality measurement and employment decisions: Questions and answers." *American Psychologist* 51, 469–477.

Honer, Jeremiah, Chris W. Wright, and Chris J. Sablinski (2007). "Puzzle Interviews: What Are They and What Do They Measure?" *Applied Human Resource Management Research* 11, 79–96.

Huffcutt, Allen I., and Winfred Arthur Jr. (1994). "Hunter and Hunter (1984) Revisited: Interview Validity for Entry-Level Jobs." *Journal of Applied Psychology* 79, 184–190.

Hunter, Darryl L. Jr. (2017). "Using Work Experience to Predict Job Performance: Do More Years Matter?" Master's Thesis, San Francisco State University, May 2017.

Hunter, John E., and Ronda F. Hunter (1984). "Validity and Utility of Alternative Predictors of Job Performance." *Psychological Bulletin* 96, 72–98.

Ip, Chris (2018). "To find a job, play these games." *Engadget,* May 4, 2018.

Isaacson, Walter (2011). *Steve Jobs.* New York: Simon & Schuster.

Jackson, Abby (2017). "Elon Musk puts potential SpaceX hires through a grueling interviewing process one former employee calls a 'gauntlet.'" *Business Insider,* December 4, 2017.

Jackson-Wright, Quinisha (2019). "To Promote Inclusivity, Stay Away from Personality Assessments." *New York Times,* August 23, 2019.

Kahneman, Daniel, Jack L. Knetsch, and Richard Thaler (1986). "Fairness as a Constraint on Profit-Seeking Entitlements in the Market." *The American Economic Review* 76, 728–741.

Kidd, David Comer, and Emanuele Castano (2013). "Reading Literary Fiction Improves Theory of Mind." *Science* 342, 377–380.

Klein, Christopher (2012). "The Man Who Shipped New England Ice Around the World." *History Channel*, August 29, 2012.

Konop, Joe (2014). "10 Job Interview Questions You Should Ask." *Next Avenue*, June 18, 2014. bit.ly/2S5SMfX

Kraitchik, Maurice (1943). *Mathematical Recreations*. London: George Allen & Unwin.

Lambert, Fred (2018). "Tesla says it received 'nearly 500,000 applicants' last year as it grows to over 37,000 employees." *Electrek*, March 21, 2018.

Lebowitz, Shana (2016). "Here's the tricky interview question Larry Ellison asked to hire extremely smart employees." *Business Insider*, February 10, 2016.

Lejuez, C. W., Jennifer P. Read, Christopher W. Kahler, Jerry B. Richards, et al. (2002). "Evaluation of a behavioral measure of risk taking: The Balloon Analogue Risk Task (BART)." *Journal of Experimental Psychology: Applied* 8, 75–84.

Lievens, Filip, Scott Highhouse, and Wilfried De Corte (2005). "The importance of traits and abilities in supervisors' hirability decisions as a function of method of assessment." *Journal of Occupational and Organizational Psychology* 78, 453–470.

Literary Digest, uncredited (1921). "Mr. Edison's Brain-Meter." *Literary Digest* 69, 28.

Live Science Staff (2010). "Ocean's Depth and Volume Revealed." *Live Science*, May 19, 2010. bit.ly/2Y3ei8Q

Mac, Ryan (2012). "Reid Hoffman and Peter Thiel in Conversation: Finding the Best Candidates for the Job." *Forbes*, May 1, 2012.

Madhok, Diksha (2019). "Indian employers are stubbornly obsessed with elite students—and it's hurting them." *Quartz India*, November 20, 2019.

Mansour, Iris (2013). "Why your Halloween costume matters if you want to work for Warby Parker." *Quartz*, October 31, 2013.

Matousek, Mark (2020). "Elon Musk says you still don't need a college degree to work at Tesla. Here's what he looks for in job applicants instead." *Business Insider*, January 8, 2020.

Matson, John (2009). "Tool kit dropped from space station is orbital junk no more." *Scientific American* blog, August 3, 2009. bit.ly/2zoHm01

McKay, Sinclair (2017). *Bletchley Park Brainteasers*. London: Headline, 2017.

McLaren, Samantha (2019). "The Go-To Interview Questions of Companies Like Warby Parker, Airbnb and More." *LinkedIn Talent Blog,* February 26, 2019.

Meisenzahl, Mary (2019). "The most incredible perks Silicon Valley workers can take advantage of, from free rental cars to travel stipends." *Business Insider,* September 15, 2019.

Minsky, Marvin (1960). "Steps Toward Artificial Intelligence." bit.ly/2VC4Mrm

Minsky, Marvin (1986). *The Society of Mind*. New York: Simon & Schuster.

Mishel, Lawrence, and Jessica Schieder (2017). "CEO pay remains high relative to the pay of typical workers and high-wage earners." Washington, DC: Economic Policy Institute, July 20, 2017. epi.org/130354

Mischel, Walter, and Ebbe B. Ebbesen. "Attention in Delay of Gratification." *Journal of Personality and Social Psychology* 16, 329–337.

Mohan, Pavithra (2019). "9 CEOs share their favorite interview questions." *Fast Company,* July 25, 2019.

Moren, Dan, and Jason Snell (2019). "Apple Earnings Call: Live Update." *MacWorld,* January 21, 2009.

Morris, Edmund (2019). *Edison*. New York: Random House.

Munger, Charles (1994). "A Lesson on Elementary, Worldly Wisdom as It Relates to Investment Management and Business" (speech given at USC Business School). bit.ly/3aDeu17

The Naked Scientists (2007). "When to add the milk." *The Naked Scientists* (podcast), November 11, 2007. bit.ly/2KxJZz4

Nalebuff, Barry (1989). "Puzzles: The Other Person's Envelope Is Always Greener." *Journal of Economic Perspectives* 3, 171–181.

National Commission on Testing and Public Policy. (1990). "From gatekeeper to gateway: Transforming testing in America." Chestnut Hill, Mass.: National Commission on Testing and Public Policy, Boston College.

Nayeri, Farah (2019). "When an Orchestra Was No Place for a Woman." *New York Times,* December 23, 2019.

Neisser, Ulric (2002). *Wolfgang Köhler 1887–1967*. Washington, DC: National Academy Press. Biographical Memoirs, volume 81.

Newell, Allen, and Herbert A. Simon (1972). *Human Problem Solving.* Englewood Cliffs, N.J.: Prentice-Hall.

Novak, Matt (2015). "Take the Intelligence Test That Thomas Edison Gave to Job Seekers." *Gizmodo,* March 12, 2015.

Paquette, Danielle (2019). "Employers are offering to help pay off workers' student loans." *Washington Post,* January 15, 2019.

Paunonen, Sampo V., and Douglas N. Jackson (2000). "What Is Beyond the Big Five? Plenty!" *Journal of Personality* 68, 821–835.

Phillips, H. I. (1926). "Is a Prune a Social Climber? A Nut? Or a Kind of Fruit?" *American Magazine* 102, 56.

Polli, Frida (2019). "Seven very simple principles for designing more ethical AI." *Fast Company,* August 6, 2019.

Pólya, G. (1945). *How to Solve It: A New Aspect of Mathematical Method.* Princeton: Princeton University Press.

Poundstone, William (2003). *How Would You Move Mount Fuji? Microsoft's Cult of the Puzzle: How the World's Smartest Companies Select the Most Creative Thinkers.* Boston: Little, Brown.

Poundstone, William (2010). *Priceless: The Myth of Fair Value (and How to Take Advantage of It).* New York: Hill and Wang.

Poundstone, William (2012). *Are You Smart Enough to Work at Google?* New York: Little, Brown.

Povey, Thomas (2015). *Professor Povey's Perplexing Problems.* London: OneWorld.

Prickett, Tricia J., Neha Gada-Jain, and Frank J. Bernieri. "The Importance of First Impressions in a Job Interview." Presented at annual meeting of the Midwestern Psychological Association, Chicago, May 2000.

Rondeau, René (1997–2019). "Lost in History: Thomas A. Edison, Junior." bit.ly/2VZ8Ocj

Rossen, Jake (2017). "How Thomas Edison Jr. Shamed the Family Name." *Mental Floss,* April 21, 2017.

Roth, Daniel (2017). "LinkedIn Top Companies 2017: Where the world wants to work now." LinkedIn, May 18, 2017.

Ryan, Kevin J. (2018). "Tesla and LinkedIn Think Résumés Are Overrated. They Use These Neuroscience-Based Games Instead." *Inc.,* June 6, 2018.

Sackett, Paul R. and Philip T. Walmsley. "Which Personality Attributes Are Most Important in the Workplace?" *Perspectives on Psychological Science* 9, 538–551.

Salkeld, Lauren (2017). "Slicing pizza? 14 surprising uses for kitchen scissors." *Today,* April 3, 2017.

Seltzer, George (1989). *Music Matters: The Performer and the American Federation of Musicians.* Metuchen, N.J.: Scarecrow Press.

Shallice, Tim (1982). "Specific impairments of planning." *Philosophical Transactions of the Royal Society of London B* 298: 199–209.

Smith, Jacquelyn (2015). "The unusual interview question the president of Overstock asks every job candidate." *Business Insider,* September 8, 2015.

Sonnleitner, Philipp, Ulrich Keller, Romain Martin, and Martin Brunner (2013). "Students' complex problem-solving abilities: Their structure and relations to reasoning ability and educational success." *Intelligence* 41, 289–305.

Spolsky, Joel (2000). "The Guerrilla Guide to Hiring." bit.ly/2xZtUzn

Stephen, Michael, David Brown, and Robin Erickson (2017). "Talent acquisition: Enter the cognitive recruiter." In *Deloitte Human Capital Trends,* 2017. bit.ly/2S4XCtO

Stross, Randall E. (2007). *The Wizard of Menlo Park: How Thomas Alva Edison Invented the Modern World.* New York: Crown.

Swenson, Ola (1981). "Are we all less risky and more skillful than our fellow drivers?" *Acta Psychologica* 47, 143–148.

TeamBlind (2018a). "About LeetCode and the Recruitment Process in Silicon Valley." *Medium,* May 21, 2018. bit.ly/2KyXej2

TeamBlind (2018b). "Is FAANG really that special?" *Medium,* May 23, 2018. bit.ly/3cJCUHz

Thiel, Peter, and Blake Masters (2014). *Zero to One: Notes on Startups, or How to Build the Future.* New York: Random House.

Thompson, Clive (2019). "The Secret History of Women in Coding." *New York Times,* February 13, 2019.

Tiku, Nitasha (2019). "Three Years of Misery Inside Google, the Happiest Company in Tech." *Wired,* August 13, 2019.

Truffaut, François (1984). *Hitchcock.* New York: Simon & Schuster.

Tukey, John (1958). "The Teaching of Concrete Mathematics." *The American Mathematical Monthly* 65, 1–9.

Tupes, Ernest C., and Raymond E. Christal (1961). "Recurrent personality factors based on trait ratings." *USAF ASD Technical Report,* 61–97.

Umoh, Ruth (2018). "Elon Musk asks this tricky interview question that most people can't answer." CNBC, October 9, 2018. cnb.cx/2yDXZ7I

Useem, Jerry (2019). "At Work, Expertise Is Falling Out of Favor." *The Atlantic*, July 2019.

Vakhania, Nicholas (2009). "On a Probability Problem of Lewis Carroll." *Bulletin of the Georgian National Academy of Sciences* 3, 8–11.

Vance, Ashlee (2015). *Elon Musk: Tesla, SpaceX, and the Quest for a Fantastic Future*. New York: Ecco.

Ward, Geoff, and Alan Allport (1997). "Planning and Problem Solving Using the Five-disc Tower of London Task." *The Quarterly Journal of Experimental Psychology* 50A, 49–78.

Weber, Lauren, and Elizabeth Dwoskin (2014). "Are Workplace Personality Tests Fair?" *The Wall Street Journal*, September 29, 2014.

Weinberg, Gabriel, and Lauren McCann (2019). *Super Thinking: The Big Book of Mental Models*. New York: Penguin.

Winterhalter, Benjamin (2014). "ISTJ? ENFP? Careers hinge on a dubious personality test." *Boston Globe*, August 31, 2014.

Notes

3   **Cherry tree story:** *Forbes* 1921, 85.

3   **"exceedingly simple":** *Forbes* 1921, 86.

3   **"Yet every large concern":** *Forbes* 1921, 86.

4   **Poll found Edison greatest living American:** The poll was conducted by the *New York Times.* See Bradley 2011, 34.

4   **"These Men Are Ignoramuses":** *Boston Herald,* May 15, 1921.

5   **"thereby become one of us":** *New York Times,* May 15, 1921, 14.

5   **"he could not say off-hand":** *New York Times,* May 15, 1921, 14.

5   **"make up new lists of questions":** *Literary Digest,* 1921.

5   **Some employers took Edison's advice:** See Dennis 1984, 30.

5   **"I am sure Mr. Edison":** *New York Times,* May 22, 1921.

6   **Dennis noted Edison's questionnaire's role:** Dennis 1984.

6   **500,000 applicants for 2,500 positions:** Lambert 2018.

7   **"If you're trying to hire competitively":** Carr 2018.

7   **Likened to matchmaking:** Frida Polli interview, March 10, 2020.

7   **"I was a 38-year-old single mom,"** biography: Pymetrics website, www.pymetrics.com/about/; Polli interview, March 10, 2020.

7   **"Moneyball for HR":** Carr 2018.

9   **"Fluid, learning-intensive environments":** Useem 2019.

10   **out-of-syllabus questions:** Madhok 2019.

13   **Trust game:** Berg, Dickhout, McCabe 1995.

19   **"If 4 is more than 2":** Brigham 1923, 4.

20   **"The army mental tests had proven":** Brigham 1921.

21   **"The Pierce Arrow car":** The answers are Buffalo, poet, and tobacco.

22   **"with its entire hypothetical superstructure":** Brigham 1930, 164.

22   **"This review has summarized":** Brigham 1930, 1964.

22   **"feeble-minded" immigrants in steerage:** See Wikipedia entry for Henry H. Goddard, en.wikipedia.org/wiki/Henry_H._Goddard

26   **"Just like with the rest":** Heilweil 2019.

26   **"a force for equal employment opportunity":** Hogan, Hogan, and Roberts 1996, 475.

27   **"systematically discriminate against any ethnic or national group":** Hogan, Hogan, and Roberts 1996, 473.

27   **"five relatively strong and recurrent factors":** Tupes and Christal 1961, 14.

28   **60 to 70 percent:** Weber and Dwoskin 2014.

28   **$500 million a year:** Weber and Dwoskin 2014.

28   **"Item endorsements are self-presentations":** Hogan, Hogan, and Roberts 1996, 471.

29   **"screen out the 30 percent of applicants":** Weber and Dwoskin 2014.

30   **"there's a sucker born every minute":** There is no contemporary record of P. T. Barnum ever saying or writing this. The widespread belief that Barnum said it, perpetuated by internet quotation sites, helps prove the point.

30   **"It's intuitively appealing":** Weber and Dwoskin 2014.

31   **HireVue's video platform for interviews:** See HireVue site, www.hirevue.com

31   **"We capture tens of thousands":** Carr 2018.

31   **HireVue clients:** See www.hirevue.com/customers

32   **"Anyone can talk about themselves":** Rudy, interview April 8, 2020.

33   **"might be open" ... "Absolutely!":** Abreu 2015.

33   **"My time was definitely a commodity":** Luis Abreu, personal e-mail, July 8, 2019.

34   **SpaceX policy of halting interviews:** Jackson 2017.

35   **"over-optimizing for one single thing":** TeamBlind 2018a.

35 **"the ability to think about the overall architecture":** TeamBlind 2018a.

35 **"Does anybody believe":** TeamBlind 2018a.

36 **"I'd rather interview 50 people":** Deutschman 2004.

36 **50 applicants for every open position:** Poundstone 2012, 37.

38 **"There really is no right answer":** Gillett, Cain, and Perino 2019.

38 **Ellison's "smartest person" question:** Lebowitz 2016.

38 **"fun and quirkiness"; "If we hire":** McLaren 2019.

38 **"It sort of tests for originality of thinking":** Mac 2012.

39 **"open but unsuspected secrets":** Thiel and Masters 2014.

39 **"On a scale of 1 to 10":** Poundstone 2012, 46.

40 **"an interviewee said they identified with a red panda":** Smith 2015.

42 **experiment by University of Toledo psychologists:** Prickett, Gada-Jain, and Bernieri 2000.

42 **"Where do you picture yourself 10 years from now?":** Prickett, Gada-Jain, and Bernieri 2000.

43 **"a personnel director's assessment":** Prickett, Gada-Jain, and Bernieri 2000.

43 **"All large-sample studies":** Hunter and Hunter 1984.

45 **"The notion that analysis outperforms":** Highhouse 2008, 336.

45 **"Relying on expertise":** Highhouse 2008, 339–340.

47 **Biden vowed to ban standardized tests:** *Yahoo! News,* December 16, 2019.

47 **"an effective means of establishing rapport":** Prickett, Gada-Jain, and Bernieri 2000.

50 **"at least as important":** Tukey 1958, 3.

50 **"the kind where you have to figure out":** Braythwayt 2012.

51 **"It was like working logic puzzles":** Thompson 2019.

55 **"Where else could it be?":** Umoh 2018.

55 **"one of the poles":** Umoh 2018.

55 **2007 study of puzzle questions:** Honer, Wright, and Sablynski 2007.

55 *How Would You Move Mount Fuji?:* Poundstone 2003.

56 **"Something that I learned":** Agry 2019.

60 **"I just don't think":** Seltzer 1989.

60 **Berlin, Vienna orchestras did not hire women:** Nayeri 2019.

60   **horns, cellos objections:** Nayeri 2019.

60   **"the more women":** Seltzer 1989.

60   **5 percent:** Goldin and Rouse 1997. **40 percent:** Nayeri 2019.

60   **careful 1997 study:** Goldin and Rouse 1997.

62   **"You are often skeptical of others":** This is one on-screen comment from Pymetrics' version of the trust game.

62   **"Most recruiters agree résumés are terrible":** Polli interview, March 10, 2020.

62   **"proxy variables":** Polli interview, March 10, 2020.

63   **Amazon's problem with AI and résumés:** Gershgorn 2018; Polli interview, March 10, 2020.

63   **"Jared" and lacrosse:** Gershgorn 2018.

64   **"nondirectional":** Polli interview, March 10, 2020.

64   **"If I wanted to figure out":** Ip 2018.

64   **"A lot of our clients want to feel":** Ryan 2018

64   **"We then had [Unilever's] top employees":** Lauren Cohen, Pymetrics Internal Demo Day Pitch, January 30, 2017. See youtu.be /hzSlmZZQZgQ

65   **three things not in a job description:** Polli, interview March 10, 2020.

65   **modest... *negative* correlation:** Hunter 2017.

65   **"there's no need to have a college degree":** Matousek 2020.

66   **Polli ruled out biased games such as spatial reasoning tasks:** Polli interview, March 10, 2020.

66   **spatial reasoning link to X chromosome:** Bock and Kolakowski 1973.

66   **"In the model-building process":** Ip 2018.

66   **audit-AI source code:** github.com/pymetrics/audit-ai

68   **A 2017 Deloitte report:** Michael, Brown, Erickson 2017.

70   **On-screen games... ever-changing:** See Csapó and Funke 2017.

71   **"In analysis, we start":** Pólya 1945.

71   **"Problem-solving was regarded by many":** Simon and Newell 1972.

72   **"We need not be concerned":** Newell and Simon 1972.

73   **"80 or 90 important models":** Munger 1994.

81   **Köhler biography, chimp experiments:** Neisser 2002. (There's no need to write me to say your dog or cat understands the detour

principle. Later research has demonstrated this. In detour experiments, much depends on how familiar the animal is with the environment and whether it has been exposed to detours before.)

82   **Tower of London task:** Shallice 1982 and Berg and Byrd 2002.

83   **five-disk version:** Ward and Allport 1997.

90   **marshmallow test:** Mischel and Ebbesen 1970.

102   **dictator game:** See Kahneman, Knetsch, and Thaler 1986; Poundstone 2010, 116–119.

103   **$0 to the partner:** See Hoffman, McCabe, Shachat, and Smith 1994.

103   **entrepreneurs show altruism in dictator game:** Frida Polli interview, March 10, 2020.

103   **monumental 2018 study:** Bartling, Cappelen, Ektröm, et al. 2018.

104   **heaven dictator game:** García-Gallego, Georgantzis, and Ruiz-Martos 2019.

107   **2013 study on literary fiction:** Kidd and Castano 2013.

111   **"Some candidates will instantly blurt out":** Gillett, Cain, and Perino 2019.

111   **"Ten cents is too easy":** Gillett, Cain, and Perino 2019.

113   **Test with hot tea for podcast:** *The Naked Scientists* 2007.

115   **Starbucks sold beans and coffee grinders:** See Wikipedia entry for "Starbucks," en.wikipedia.org/wiki/Starbucks

116   **YouTube videos of balloons in vacuum chamber:** See bit.ly/2Y6tuSG

117   **necktie paradox described in a 1943 book:** Kraitchik 1943.

117   **version with two envelopes:** See Nalebuff 1989; Gardner 1989, 147–148.

118   **legitimate case for switching:** Nalebuff 1989.

125   **described by Martin Gardner:** Gardner 1959, 25 and 33.

126   **history of horse-sized duck meme:** See Know Your Meme entry for "Horse-Sized Duck," bit.ly/3cKu0cY; also Friedersdorf 2013.

126   **Obama staffers ignored the question:** Hastings 2013.

126   **Bill Murray video:** youtu.be/THUGHEJjjGc. **Aaron Paul:** youtu.be/hZMuC8ILkwg. **Bruce Springsteen:** youtu.be/wWlAXm1rwW0

128   **"figuring that the neck is mostly feathers":** youtu.be/THUGHEJjjGc

128   **"It is hard to have a good idea":** Pólya 1945.

136   **mouse gets through pencil-diameter (1/4-inch) hole:** See bit.ly /357uJCh

140   **13 billion pennies a year, 130 billion in circulation:** Bruce 2003.

147   **365,000 tons:** See the "Empire State Building Fact Sheet" at bit .ly/2xQOGkW

162   **93 percent of drivers better than average:** Swenson 1981.

166   **Gardner's uneven-floor riddle:** Gardner 1986.

166   **"If one does not mind the tabletop":** Gardner 1986, 72. This was originally published in Gardner's "Mathematical Games" columns for the May and June 1973 issues of *Scientific American*.

167   **proof that square table can be balanced:** See also Baritompa, Löwen, Polster, Ross 2018 and its references.

168   **"The theorem is actually useful":** Gardner 1986, 81.

170   **2015 film *The Martian*:** It was based on a 2011 novel of the same name by Andy Weir. Ridley Scott directed from a screenplay by Drew Goddard.

172   **Amazon's "Leadership Principles":** www.amazon.jobs/en /principles

172   **Fredkin's paradox:** This widely applicable bit of wisdom was articulated by Carnegie Mellon University computer scientist Edward Fredkin. See Minsky 1986, 52.

173   **"Smart candidates understand":** Spolsky 2000.

174   **"People don't know what they want":** Isaacson 2011, 316.

175   **Skittles question:** Roxanne Williams interview, March 17, 2020. There are many variations. Sometimes the candy is jelly beans; sometimes the goal is to remove the candy in edible form.

179   **Thoreau and Frederic Tudor, "Ice King":** Klein 2012.

185   **video of ordering 43 Chicken McNuggets:** See Numberphile, "How to order 43 Chicken McNuggets," bit.ly/2VC69GN

204   **Edison questionnaire asked distances from New York to Buffalo, other cities:** Novak 2015.

210   **how somebody thinks about a very new problem":** Mohan 2019.

222   **Alexander asked to referee grading dispute:** Calandra 1968.

223   **"Sputnik-panicked classrooms":** Calandra 1968.

223   **"mental block against using an object":** Duncker 1945.

223   **"follow the wrong footsteps":** Chrysikou and Weisberg 2005.

225 **scissors for slicing pizza:** See Salkeld 2017.

227 **"[I]dentify a small part of it":** Newell and Simon 1972.

227 **"Take the haystack to an airport":** Chen 2005.

228 **YouTube videos of racing balls on tracks:** See for instance Bruce Yeany's, youtu.be/_GJujClGYJQ

230 **"the emptiest, the most nonexistent":** Truffaut 1984, 139.

231 **"missing dollar" riddle goes back to 1930s:** Similar problems appear in two 1933 books: Cecil B. Read's *Mathematical Fallacies* and R. M. Abraham's *Diversions and Pastimes*.

234 **"the hardest logic puzzle ever":** Boolos 1996, 62.

242 **"Mr. Smith has two children":** Gardner 1961, 152–153; 159.

242 **"the problem was":** Gardner 1961, 159.

245 **822 hours of rain in Seattle:** Western Regional Climate Center, bit.ly/2KwHE7l

248 **recorded from 8th-century England:** Alcuin of York (c. 735–804 AD) described a puzzle about crossing a river with a wolf, a goat, and cabbages. See Poundstone 2003, 222–223.

254 **Reisman threw first pitch for Yankees:** See video at bit.ly/3azpRqZ

259 **In 2008 astronaut lost tool bag:** Matson 2009.

259 **easier to throw baseball to infinity:** This is discussed with more detail in Povey 2015, 254–259.

272 **Einstein supposedly said:** There is no evidence that Albert Einstein said this. It may be a paraphrase of a statement in a 1933 speech at Oxford: "It can scarcely be denied that the supreme goal of all theory is to make the irreducible basic elements as simple and as few as possible without having to surrender the adequate representation of a single datum of experience." See Quote Investigator, bit.ly/3ePrDrh

277 **"The point of the question is to generate":** Poundstone 2003, 124.

277 **"How many gas stations are in the United States?":** Honer, Wright, and Sablynski 2007.

278 **"To invent, you need a good imagination":** See bit.ly/2xbDZJi

278 **"I never had an idea in my life":** Morris 2019.

278 **"Opportunity is missed by most people":** Though found on many internet quote sites, this was apparently not attributed to Edison until 1962, long after his death. See the Quote Investigator entry, bit.ly/2VDGLjG

279 **"Genius is one percent inspiration":** Versions of this statement were reported in Edison's lifetime. He was most often quoted saying the breakdown was 2 percent/98 percent. The 1 percent/99 percent version is now most often encountered. See Quote Investigator, bit.ly/352Rk36

279 **"Many of life's failures":** This is ubiquitous on quote sites, but I am not aware of a source dating to Edison's lifetime.

Index

Index

Index

Index

Index

Index

Index

Index

Index

Index

Index

Index

Index

About the Author

William Poundstone is the author of seventeen books, including *The Doomsday Calculation, Are You Smart Enough to Work at Google?, How Would You Move Mount Fuji?,* and *Fortune's Formula,* which was Amazon Editor's pick for the number one nonfiction book of the year. He has written for *The Believer, The Economist, Encyclopaedia Britannica, Esquire, Harper's Magazine, Harvard Business Review,* and the *New York Times* op-ed page and book review. Follow Poundstone on Twitter (@WPoundstone) and learn more at his website, william-poundstone.com.